HONDUR___

The Facts Speak for Themselves

The Preliminary Report of the National Commissioner for the Protection of Human Rights in Honduras

translation by

**Human Rights Watch/Americas
(formerly Americas Watch)**

Center for Justice and International Law

**Human Rights Watch
New York • Washington • Los Angeles
London • Brussels**

ISBN: 156432-134-7
LCCCN: 94-76209

Human Rights Watch/Americas, (formerly Americas Watch)
Human Rights Watch/Americas was established in 1981 to monitor human rights in Latin America and the Caribbean. Cynthia Arnson and Anne Manuel are acting executive directors; Ellen Lutz is California Director; Sebastian Brett, Robin Kirk, and Gretta Tovar Siebentritt are research associates; Steven Crandall and Vanessa Jiménez are associates. Peter D. Bell is the chair of the advisory committee and Stephen L. Kass and Marino Pinto Kaufman are vice chairs.

The Center for Justice and International Law (CEJIL)
CEJIL was established in 1991 as a consortium of nine human rights organizations from North, Central and South America and the Caribbean. CEJIL conducts international human rights litigation and provides free legal advice in the use of international human rights instruments to non-governmental organizations (NGO's) in developing countries. CEJIL is the first human rights organization to offer an integrated program of full-time litigation, free legal service and monitoring of the inter-American human rights system. In its three years of operation, CEJIL has provide cousel to several human rights NGO's and numerous victims and their families. José Miguel Vivanco is its Executive Director, Viviana Krsticevic is their director of legal defense, Lilian Obregon serves as their director of investigations and publications, and Bess Abrahams is their associate.

CONTENTS

ACKNOWLEDGMENTS

The English language version of this report is the product of a joint effort by Human Rights Watch/Americas and the Center for Justice and International Law (CEJIL).* James L. Cavallaro, Jr., former Orville Schell Fellow for Human Rights Watch, is responsible for the translation of the Spanish text, as well as an initial edit of that translation. Ben Penglase, Human Rights Watch/Americas Research Associate, and Lucien Chauvin assisted in the translation. Anne Manuel, Acting Director of Human Rights Watch/Americas, and José Miguel Vivanco, Executive Director of CEJIL, also edited the English version.

Special thanks is due to the MacArthur Foundation, without whose generous support this publication would not have been possible. Human Rights Watch/Americas and CEJIL would especially like to thank Kimberly Stanton, Research Associate for the Program on Peace and International Cooperation at the MacArthur Foundation, for her role in the realization of this project.

Editor's Note: This publication contains the principal substantive portions of the original report published in Spanish. Some sections have been omitted, and the editors have made other modifications, including deletions, to prepare it for an English-speaking audience.

LIST OF ACRONYMS

ACAFADE: Central American Association of Relatives of the Detained-Disappeared (Asociación Centroamericana de Familiares de Detenidos-Desaparecidos)

CEDOH: Honduran Documentation Center (Centro de Documentación de Honduras)

CODEH: Committee for the Defense of Human Rights in Honduras (Comité para la Defensa de los Derechos Humanos en Honduras)

CODEHFOR: Honduran Forestry Development Corporation (Corporación Hondureña de Desarrollo Forestal)

COFADEH: Committee of Relatives of the Detained-Disappeared in Honduras (Comité de Familiares de Detenidos-Desaparecidos en Honduras)

DIA: Defense Intelligence Agency

DIES: Directorate of Special Investigations (Dirección de Investigaciones Especiales)

DNI: National Investigations Directorate (Dirección Nacional de Investigaciones)

ESF: Economic Support Funds

FDN: Nicaraguan Democratic Force (Fuerza Democrática Nicaraguense)

FESE: Federation of Secondary School Students (Federación de Estudiantes de Segunda Enseñanza)

FEUH: Honduran Federation of University Students (Federación de Estudiantes Universitarios de Honduras)

FMLN: Farabundo Martí National Liberation Front (Frente Farabundo Martí de Liberación Nacional)

FRU: University Reform Front (Frente de Reforma Universitaria)

FSLN: Sandinista National Liberation Front (Frente Sandinista de Liberación Nacional)

FUR: Revolutionary University Force (Fuerza Universitaria Revolucionaria)

FUSEP: Public Security Force (Fuerza de Seguridad Pública)

FUTH: Unitary Federation of Workers of Honduras (Federación Unitaria de Trabajadores de Honduras)

JCS: Joint Chiefs of Staff

NSA: National Security Archives

NSC: National Security Council

NSPG: National Security Planning Group

OAS: Organization of American States

PANI: National Children's Foundation (Patronato Nacional de la Infancia)

SEPCAMAT: Union of Public Employees of Roads and Airport and Terminal Maintenance (Sindicato de Empleados Públicos de Caminos, Mantenimento de Aeropuertos y Terminales)

SECOPT: Department of Communication, Public Works and Transportation (Secretaría de Communicaciones, Obras Públicas y Transporte)

SITRAINA: National Agrarian Institute Employees' Union (Sindicato de Trabajadores del Instituto Nacional Agrario)

SITRASANAA: National Autonomous Service of Aqueducts and Sewers Employees' Union (Sindicato de Trabajadores del Servicio Autónomo Nacional de Acueductos y de Alcantarillado)

STENEE: Union of Workers of the National Electrical Energy Company (Sindicato de Trabajadores de la Empresa Nacional de Energía Eléctrica)

UNAH: National Autonomous University of Honduras (Universidad Nacional

Autónoma de Honduras)

UNHCR: United Nations High Commissioner for Refugees

URP: People's Revolutionary Union (Unión Revolucionaria del Pueblo)

PREFACE

The legacy of a CIA-trained death squad is one of the most painful and vexing issues facing Honduras today, although the Cold War rivalries which motivated its formation have long since disappeared. These issues present a stiff challenge to the now inaugurated government of President Carlos Roberto Reina, a respected lawyer known for his advocacy of human rights. President Reina has promised to support the process of truth seeking being led by Leo Valladares Lanza, author of this pathbreaking report, *The Facts Speak For Themselves*. Moreover, President Reina has supported the notion that those responsible for the disappearances documented here be prosecuted and punished, no matter who they are.

Prosecuting those responsible for the disappearances would be the most effective means of protecting Hondurans from future human rights violations. The task will test Honduras's civilian political institutions, however, as many of those officers involved in disappearances remain in positions of great power in today's armed forces.

The United States had a special relationship with those who committed gross human rights violations in Honduras, as the following report shows, and is thus in a position to make a serious contribution to the struggle for truth and justice in Honduras. Human Rights Watch/Americas and the Center for Justice and International Law (CEJIL) together publish this translation of the most important sections of *The Facts Speak For Themselves* in English to prompt examination of the U.S. role in Honduras's dark years; to spur a truth-telling process in the U.S. that would complement and reinforce that underway in Honduras.

In the early 1980s, Battalion 3-16, a Honduran military unit whose members were instructed by and worked with CIA officials, "disappeared" scores of leftist activists—students, teachers, unionists, and would-be guerrillas—who were never seen again, dead or alive. But with the Cold War over, Honduras is no longer in the forefront of the U.S. offensive against leftist forces in Central America. Instead of losing interest, Washington should now help Hondurans cope with the consequences.

The Facts Speak for Themselves is a preliminary report; its sequel to be produced at the end of this year. This process was set in motion by the families of the victims and human rights groups, hoping for an official investigation to account for the disappeared as did the Truth Commission of El Salvador, established under United Nations auspices. As in El Salvador, much remains untold about the American connection to deadly repression.

National Commissioner Leo Valladares wrote to U.S. Ambassador William Pryce on December 31, 1993, requesting information from several U.S. government agencies regarding the disappearances documented in this report. The list of questions submitted to the Embassy is included in the appendices to this report. On November 23, 1993, Senator Foreign Relations Committee Chairman Claiborne Pell, House Foreign Affairs Committee Chair Lee Hamilton, and seven other lawmakers wrote to President Bill Clinton urging him to "make available any relevant facts and documents as soon as possible." President Clinton wrote back to Senator Pell and Representative Hamilton on December 18, stating "my Administration is committed to open government and to assisting efforts to shed light on past instances of human rights abuses." Clinton noted that the U.S. would need time to process the request, noting that "[p]reliminary checks indicate that the Department of State's holdings of possibly responsive documents amount to well over 2,000 for the period 1981-84 alone." Yet six months later, Valladares has received none of the documents he requested.

The release of relevant documents would be an important first step. Beyond that, Human Rights Watch/Americas and CEJIL recommend that a congressional committee investigate thoroughly the relationship between the United States and Honduras during the 1980s to determine 1) whether or not U.S. officials hid what they knew about gross violations of human rights by Honduran government officials; 2) what links—formal and informal—existed between U.S. government agencies and Battalion 3-16, the secret unit responsible for most of the disappearances; and 3) what steps can be implemented to ensure that U.S. aid, whether covert or overt, is not used again to carry out crimes against civilians.

◆ ◆ ◆

The nightmare began for Honduras in August 1980. Twenty-five Honduran army officers were flown from Central America to a desert air strip in the southwestern United States, according to the sworn testimony before the Inter-American Court of Human Rights of Florencio Caballero, a military intelligence officer who participated.[1] They spent six months learning interrogation techniques from a team of CIA and FBI trainers. Caballero says the

---

[1] The Inter-American Court of Human Rights is a judicial arm of the Organization of American States, based in San José, Costa Rica.

U.S. instructors taught different methods of eliciting information from uncooperative prisoners without resorting to physical violence.

When the officers returned to Honduras, the courses continued. The American trainers were joined by instructors fresh from the "dirty wars" in Argentina and Chile in which thousands of suspected leftists were abducted and executed by security forces. These sessions, according to Caballero, focused on surveillance and techniques for following suspects and rescuing kidnap victims. This group of officers went on to become a secret division of Honduran military intelligence, which had different names at different periods, but has come to be known as Battalion 3-16.

That Battalion 3-16 engaged in a systematic program of disappearances and political murder, mostly between the years of 1981 and 1984, is beyond question. *The Facts Speak for Themselves* adds a richness of detail to the pattern of facts proven before the Inter-American Court of Human Rights during its trials of Honduras for the disappearances of Saúl Godínez Crúz and Angel Manfredo Velásquez Rodríguez.

In testimony before the court, Caballero and other witnesses described Battalion 3-16's modus operandi: weeks of surveillance followed by capture by disguised agents using vehicles with stolen license plates (in a few scuffles, Caballero told the court, his colleagues lost their wigs and moustaches). Interrogation and torture in clandestine jails were usually followed by execution and secret burial.

At one point, a judge of the Inter-American Court asked Caballero about the attitude of Battalion 3-16 officers towards Honduran judges who sought to establish the whereabouts of the disappeared. "The group made fun of what was being said outside," Caballero replied. "They said they [the judges] are stupid. Why are they asking for this one, when this one will never return?"

Because the United States has not accepted the jurisdiction of the Inter-American Court of Human Rights, the trial did not dwell on the American role in the terror. But the CIA's intimate connection with Battalion 3-16 was later confirmed by General Gustavo Alvarez Martínez, who created and commanded the death squad from 1980, when he became chief of the national police force (FUSEP), until March 1984, when he was ousted from his position as chief of the Honduran armed forces. "The CIA trained my people in intelligence," Alvarez told a Reuters reporter years later. "They gave very good training, especially in interrogation." Alvarez said the agency provided his men with lie detectors, phone-tapping devices and electronic equipment to analyze intelligence data.

According to Caballero, the CIA trainers explicitly rejected violent coercion.[2] But he said that the CIA operatives working with Battalion 3-16 were informed when suspected leftists were abducted and at times participated in interrogations. The Hondurans felt compelled to deceive their sponsors about the fate of the victims, Caballero says. When bodies were found, the Hondurans would tell the Americans they had freed their detainees, and that they were subsequently killed by guerrillas for having given information during their captivity.

Inés Consuelo Murillo, a victim of Battalion 3-16 who was eventually released following pressure from the German government, said she was interrogated by the American agent known as "Mike." (According to Caballero and other Honduran defectors, Mike was one of the CIA advisers who worked with Battalion 3-16.) During the first 40 days of her 78-day captivity, Murillo was tortured and kept naked in a filthy cell by Honduran soldiers who wanted her to confess to being a leftist guerrilla. When Mike first came to interrogate her, her cell was cleaned and she was allowed to dress and bathe for the first time. The Hondurans never tortured her in front of Mike, Murillo says. But "it was very obvious I was in bad condition," she recalled in an interview with Cox News Service.[3]

"The CIA had nothing to do with picking people up," one American official told the *New York Times*, "but they knew about it and when some people disappeared, they looked the other way."[4]

Meanwhile, U.S. officials publicly denied abuses by the Honduran military. To their great shame, State Department officers instead attacked the credibility of those who denounced the disappearances. "It is simply untrue to state that death squads have made their appearance in Honduras," U.S.

---

[2] Nonetheless, in an interview with Cox News Service in 1994, Caballero said that one of the American advisors, known to the Hondurans only as "Mike," told him privately that electrical shocks were "the most efficient way to get someone to talk when they resisted." (Anne Marie O'Connor, "Who Was 'Mike' and What Was he Doing in a Honduran Torture Cell?" Cox News Service, March 13, 1994.)

[3] *Ibid.*

[4] James LeMoyne, "C.I.A. Accused of Tolerating Killings in Honduras," *New York Times*, February 14, 1986.

Ambassador John Negroponte wrote in the *Economist* in 1982.[5] The State Department echoed Negroponte's denial, while reserving its ire for the Committee for the Defense of Human Rights in Honduras (CODEH), the group that did the most to expose Battalion 3-16. Throughout the 1980s, CODEH was repeatedly denounced by the State Department as "communist," "anti-democratic" and, ironically, as a terrorist front group.

In 1984, General Walter López Reyes, now Honduras's vice president, deposed General Alvarez in a barracks coup. Forced into exile in Miami, Alvarez quickly landed a consulting job with the Pentagon. He was paid $400 a day for writing a classified report on "low-intensity conflict."[6]

The number of disappearances declined sharply after Alvarez's ouster in 1984. In 1988, the Inter-American Court of Human Rights found Honduras responsible for the pattern of disappearances that had claimed the lives of Saúl Godínez Crúz and Angel Manfredo Velásquez Rodríguez. Ordered to pay damages to their relatives, the government complied only partially. (President Reina has promised to bring Honduras into full compliance.) Meanwhile, the officers who commanded Battalion 3-16 continue to occupy positions of power in Honduras to this day. General Luis Alonso Discua, who commanded Battalion 3-16 in 1984 (see appendix), is now the chief of the Honduran armed forces.

Now, ten years after the worst of the Honduran abuses have passed, some U.S. officials are willing to concede in private that their hands were dirtied in the Honduran repression. "The green light was kill a commie," a senior State Department official told Cox News Service recently. "Everybody was winking and nodding. This fostered an environment where everyone was freelancing and tolerating all kinds of things they shouldn't have. Was it policy? People said no, but you could get away with it."[7]

The Facts Speak for Themselves is a valiant and unusual official effort at self-examination; perhaps one of the most truly democratic steps taken by any Honduran government. The veil of secrecy surrounding CIA activities has thus

---

[5] Letter to the Editor, John D. Negroponte, *The Economist*, October 23, 1982.

[6] Charles R. Babcock and Terri Shaw, "Ousted Chief of Honduran Military Was Hired as U.S. Defense Consultant," *Washington Post*, May 10, 1987.

[7] O'Connor, "Who Was 'Mike'and What Was he Doing in a Honduran Torture Cell".

far prevented a comparable study of the U.S. government's role in Battalion 3-16's formation and activities. A congressional intelligence committee looked into the CIA's sponsorship of Battalion 3-16 in 1988, but its findings remain classified. That the U.S. officials who turned a blind eye to crimes committed by their clients have never been questioned is bad enough. Worse, the absence of any public accountability for such CIA covert operations leaves no guarantee that it won't happen again.

Anne Manuel, Human Rights Watch/Americas
José Miguel Vivanco, CEJIL
June 1994

FOREWORD

The great countries of the world are not those that have never experienced periods of darkness and barbarity, but rather those that have been able to examine such times without fear and overcome them. True democracies must be capable of examining their past; only in this way can they embrace the future. We have faith that Honduras can cross the threshold of silence by showing the gruesome extremes to which it arrived with disappearances. The nation can move beyond silence, however, not to seek vengeance, nor only to show the barbarism and the hate that some Hondurans had towards others, but to achieve national reconciliation. True peace does not come from silence nor from ignorance, but from the clear and open recognition of our limits and errors.

The National Commissioner for the Protection of Human Rights (the Commissioner) would have liked not to find what he discovered upon revising these sad pages of recent history. We would have liked to tell the country that no one was ever disappeared. We would have preferred to inform the country and the world that members of official institutions never had anything to do with a disappearance or an execution. We would have liked to say that torture has never been practiced in Honduras. However, the reality that we discovered was otherwise. Regrettably, there were disappearances. And worse still, there was both silence and responsibility on the part of civil and military authorities. These facts can be a source of pride for no one, of sadness for all.

With a mandate that is moral and patriotic even before it is legal, the Commissioner has sought to commit to writing all that he has heard, read, and seen regarding disappearances in Honduras. We know that the forces that we confront in so doing are powerful and that they have recognized no limits in their combat against those whom they consider their enemies. Yet, at the same time, we are comforted by our conviction that all Hondurans will appreciate the importance of knowing the truth. In so doing, we move closer to our ultimate goal of preventing the recurrence of gross violations of human rights in our country.

We also would like to say that not all that we uncovered during these years was evil. Difficult moments also reveal great men and women, and Honduras has them. As we mention in Chapter VI, there were Hondurans who denounced what was happening. The press, which provided truthful testimony of what was happening, deserves special mention. There were also common citizens, politicians, lawyers, priests, and even military personnel who objected to what was happening and who manifested their opposition and criticism. Along with the often misunderstood human rights activists, they constitute what in Chapter VI we have called "the moral reserve of the country."

Because of the broad scope of the research, and in recognition of the need to exhaust all relevant sources of information before rendering final conclusions, this report is still preliminary. The Commissioner still expects to receive information requested from authorities, governments, and institutions. It also hopes to obtain many more direct testimonies, and encourages those who have not yet told what happened to them to come forward. In this regard, this report seeks only to be a catalyst of a much more complete and coordinated effort of all Honduran authorities to explain the disappearances. Only after such a joint effort can we turn the page of this sad chapter of our national history.

The Commissioner has imposed on himself the obligation of presenting this report before the end of 1993. The reasons for this decision were many. Perhaps the factor that most weighed in favor of early release were the just demands of those citizens whose relatives have been disappeared. Their demands do not allow for bureaucratic delays and must be addressed promptly. Honduras's democratic institutions must prove to the nation's citizens that they function effectively and are not mere formalities. It is time to take concrete steps: until now, neither the judiciary nor other authorities has made any progress in investigating these cases.

In drafting this report we have come up against limited resources and time, a lack of access to various sources, and incomprehension from some politicians and public officials. In spite of all these difficulties we have tried to deliver to the people of Honduras the results of a patient and objective work.

Chapter I of this report gives a brief review of the legal definition of disappearances and of the mandate of the Commissioner, thus establishing the legal basis for our work.[8]

Chapter II presents a list of the disappeared. To compose it, we have used information provided by the United Nations, by domestic and international human rights groups, and by directly obtained testimonies. The list is still provisional. The exact number of persons disappeared is likely greater and will be established only when all the relatives of the victims dare to come forward and state their claims.

Chapter III presents a selection of some illustrative cases. As shown in

---

[8] *Editor's Note:* In this English language version, we have omitted the original Chapter II, a detailed chronology of human rights-related events from 1980 until 1993.

the first part of this chapter, the cases of disappearances form clear patterns, which may be categorized according to victims, perpetrators, zones of the country, and the years in which they occurred. Of the dozens of similar cases, fourteen were chosen which are indicative of the rest.

Chapter IV presents some testimonies. Here we have sought to allow the participants to speak for themselves, in their own simple and direct language.[9]

Chapter V studies the international context in which most of the violations occurred. As shown, the systematic practice of disappearances might not have been possible without the environment of the cold war and the limitless ideological confrontation to which it subjected us. The response of our country's civil and military authorities when faced with the pressures imposed by foreign interests will have to be judged by posterity.

Chapter VI discusses the conclusions reached after this investigation. Though still preliminary, the conclusions address the fundamental questions posed at the beginning of this investigation: Who was disappeared? Why were they disappeared? Who did it? How did they do it? Who helped them? How did the judiciary react? The chapter thus briefly reviews the Commissioner's findings.

The final chapter, VII, sets forth something that we consider indispensable in a report of this type. That chapter not only shows how the disappearances occurred, but also takes the critical step forward of proposing to the citizenry means to prevent this from ever happening again. The recommendations therein contemplate compensation of victims and their relatives, legal reform, the responsibility of those presumably guilty, and the affirmation of the democratic and civilian control of domestic institutions, as well as the promotion of a culture of life and peace in Honduras.

Upon making this report public we should thank the President of the Republic, Rafael Leonardo Callejas who provided his constant support and gave us the confidence to proceed with this work. President Callejas had the nobility to respect fully the work of the Commissioner, even though the report covers the period of time in which he was in office.

---

[9] *Editor's Note:* We have substituted the testimony of Florencio Caballero, former member of Battalion 3-16, for the testimony contained in the original document of René Velásquez Díaz, an attorney who represented relatives of victims of disappearances. Both testimonies are transcribed from public hearings before the Inter-American Court of Human Rights in San José, Costa Rica.

We also would like to thank President-elect, Carlos Roberto Reina.[10] In our interviews with him, we sensed a particular regard for our work. We are certain that his long and renowned work as a defender of the law, the Constitution, and the well being of all Hondurans assure that during his period as president the violations listed in this report will not re-occur.

A special mention should be made of our advisory organization, the National Reconciliation Commission, presided over by Monsignor Oscar Andrés Rodríguez and composed of Hernán Corrales Padilla, César A. Batres, Ubodoro Arriaga Iraheta, and Olban Valladares, all of whom gave constant support to this project.

This work would not have been possible without the collaboration of Alfredo Forti and Carlos Chipoco, both of them United Nations consultants. We should also point out that this report was made possible by the unselfish and highly efficient labor of the staff of the office of the National Commissioner for the Protection of Human Rights: Sonia Marlina Dubón de Flores, Radhames Lagos Valle, Jorge Alberto Valladares and Eduardo Federico Rosales Ramírez.

The cooperation of the Honduran Documentation Center (Centro de Documentación de Honduras-CEDOH), was essential, particularly that of Director Víctor Meza whose documentary assistance was of great importance. We appreciate the courage of Mrs. Gertrudis Lanza, who has suffered in her own flesh this tragedy; once more, she has shared with us her painful experience. Additionally, we would like to recognize the important battle undertaken by Dr. Ramón Custodio López, President of the Committee for the Defense of Human Rights (Comité para la Defensa de los Derechos Humanos-CODEH), as well as the valuable advice which he afforded us. We extend this same recognition to the Committee for the Relatives of the Disappeared of Honduras (Comité de Familiares de Detenidos Desaparecidos de Honduras-COFADEH) and their active leadership.

We also should mention the persons and institutions that supported and contributed valuable information and analysis to the Commissioner. Among those we mention are: Jóse Miguel Vivanco of the Center for Justice and International Law (CEJIL); the Working Group on Enforced or Involuntary Disappearances of the United Nations; Edith Márquez and Osvaldo Kreimer of the Inter-American Commission of Human Rights of the Organization of American States; the Inter-American Court of Human Rights; Juan Méndez and

---

[10] *Editor's Note*: President Callejas turned over power to President Reina in January 1994.

xiv

Anne Manuel of Human Rights Watch/Americas; Peter Kornbluh of National Security Archives; Robert Goldman, Professor of Law at American University; Lauren Gilbert of the Center for International Policy, who made an outstanding contribution; Amnesty International, London; the Washington Office on Latin America; Gare Smith, office of Senator Edward Kennedy; Kristin Brady, office of Senator Claiborne Pell; Deborah Hauger, office of Congressman Lee Hamilton; Jim McGovern, office of Congressman Joe Moakley; Janice O'Connell, office of Senator Chris Dodd; Bill Spencer, office of Congressman Joseph Kennedy; Alex Arriaga of the Human Rights Caucus; Rosemary Gutiérrez of the Center for International Policy; Joy Olson of the Central American Working Group; Interights, London.

I especially want to thank my wife, Daisy Pineda de Valladares because at every moment, as in other occasions of my life, I have been able to count on her support.

Tegucigalpa, M.D.C., December 29, 1993.

Leo Valladares Lanza
National Commissioner
for the Protection of Human Rights

I

LEGAL DEFINITION AND MANDATE
OF THE NATIONAL COMMISSIONER
FOR THE PROTECTION OF HUMAN RIGHTS

The 1980s was a decade characterized by a wave of violence throughout the nations of the Latin American subcontinent. Our country, Honduras, was no exception. The phenomenon of "disappearances" afflicted the region, more notably the countries under military dictatorships, but also in some nations with governments of legitimate origin.

The victims of this practice are not only those who are disappeared, but also their parents, spouses, children, and other relatives, who are placed in an uncertain condition of prolonged anguish, often lasting many years. For this reason, disappearances open deep wounds in the social fabric of the national community, which affect political, social, and professional circles and create fissures in the fundamental institutions of the country.

Characteristic of this practice is the systematic denial by authorities of the detention of the victims despite convincing proof establishing that they have been seized by political or military authorities. In some cases, these authorities continue to deny the detention of persons even when clear evidence indicates the specific detention sites where the detainees are held.

The practice of disappearance is cruel and inhuman, and as experience shows, constitutes not only an arbitrary privation of liberty, but also a grave danger for the personal integrity, security, and very life of the victim. Disappearance is a method employed to avoid the application of legal measures in defense of individual liberty, physical integrity, and the dignity of human life.

1. What is the disappearance of persons?

Forced or involuntary disappearance may be defined as *the detention of a person by agents of the state or by others with the acquiescence of the state, without an order from appropriate authorities and in which the detention is denied and no official information on the fate or location of the detainee exists.*

The following elements characterize a disappearance:

a)   There must be an arbitrary detention or abduction. This typifies the disappearance not only because it fails to meet the

1

minimum legal requirements for an arrest (*i.e.* a judicial warrant or an *in flagrante delicto* arrest; or, during states of emergency, an administrative order reasonably based on the causes of the state of emergency); but also because it shows that the real motive for a detention is political persecution and not the investigation or prevention of crime;

b)   The abduction of a person, though usually carried out secretly, is effectuated by government agents, whether uniformed or in civilian clothes, who are members of the police or the armed forces (or paramilitary forces operating under their control). Disappearance does not occur when common criminals kidnap a person for ransom, for example. Thus, action on behalf of the state is critical to the crime's definition;

c)   Especially grave in this type of crime is the impunity enjoyed by those responsible; these individuals can count on the tolerance or the protection of the government;

d)   The abduction and confinement of the victim is denied by the authorities. The *disappearance* of the detainee occurs when the security forces deliberately deny information to relatives regarding the whereabouts of the detainee and when they positively assert that he is not detained. Official denial is the result of a deliberate and conscious policy to avoid responsibility for the arrest itself and for the physical integrity and life of the detainee. In some occasions this deliberate denial is maintained only for a time, and later the person is made to "reappear," almost always officially detained. These situations could be described as "temporary disappearances" as opposed to "permanent disappearances;"

e)   Finally, the ultimate fate of the victims is execution and the concealment of the cadaver. Various methods have been used to eliminate the disappeared, though the most prevalent method is execution by firearm, frequently with the participation of several people. Similarly, a variety of methods are used to dispose of the remains: clandestine burials; tombs marked with "N:N:";[1] by disposal in the bottom of lakes and rivers, or at sea from planes and helicopters, etc. In each case, the objective is to prevent discovery of the remains, or if they are discovered, to prevent their positive identification. This aspect distinguishes forced disappearances from another equally tragic form of human rights violation, the extrajudicial execution.

As long as the whereabouts of the victim or the circumstances of death cannot be determined, he or she should be considered disappeared, even though death may be presumed by the passage of time or by the telling circumstances of the detention. The consequences of this distinction are important because once the government acknowledges that a homicide has occurred, at least formally, it recognizes its obligation to investigate and prosecute those responsible. But in the case of a forced disappearance, in which the government never recognizes the detention of the victim, the authorities usually contend that they are under no obligation to investigate and prosecute those responsible. International human rights law establishes that, at a minimum, the government should investigate the fate and whereabouts of the disappeared and inform his or her relatives.

The fundamental defining characteristic of forced disappearances is that each individual case forms part of a deliberate and conscious policy. Further, this policy is adopted by the government at a level of authority with the capacity not only to issue the order to disappear a person and assure its completion, but also to guarantee the impunity of those who execute the orders. Thus, isolated cases in which the whereabouts of a detainee are unknown may not rise to the level of disappearance if it can be shown that the relevant government has made efforts to investigate the case, inform the relatives, and punish the public officials responsible.

Forced disappearances constitute flagrant violations of fundamental rights and freedoms guaranteed in the Constitution of the Republic of Honduras, such as: the right to the liberty and the security of the individual, the inviolability of the dignity of the human person (Art. 59); the right to life, to individual security, to liberty (Art. 65); to respect for physical, psychological, and moral integrity, and the prohibition of torture and cruel, inhuman and degrading treatment (Art. 68); to liberty, the right not to be detained or held *incommunicado* for more than twenty-four hours without being brought before

---

[1] Editor's Note: "N:N" indicates that the identity of the person buried is unknown (no name).

appropriate authorities (Art. 71); the right to present a defense and free access
to the courts (Art. 82); the right to be free from arrest unless by virtue of a
written mandate from the appropriate authority, issued in accord with, and for
a cause previously established by law (Art. 84); the right of the detainee to be
clearly informed, at the time of arrest of (1) his or her rights, (2) the acts of
which he or she is accused, and (3) the right to communicate his or her
detention to a relative or person of the detainee's choice; the right of every
detainee or prisoner to be assigned to those places determined by law (Art. 85);
the right to be free from violence and coercion designed to force a person to
render a statement; in some cases, the inviolability of the home (Art. 99).

At the international level, the following provisions of the American
Convention on Human Rights or the "Treaty of San José [Costa Rica]," ratified
by the State of Honduras, are violated by forced disappearances: the right to
liberty and security of the person and the right to be free from arbitrary arrest
(Art. 7); the right to an impartial trial in criminal matters (Art. 8); the right to
a humane manner of detention and to be free from torture and cruel, inhuman
or degrading treatment (Art. 5) and, generally, the right to life (Art. 4), all of
these rights in conjunction with the general obligation to respect and ensure the
full enjoyment of the rights protected under the Convention (Art. 1.1).

Due to its nature, the crime of forced disappearance violates both
international and domestic legal norms. International legal doctrine considers
forced disappearance to be a specific and autonomous crime with the following
aspects:

a)   Due to its extreme gravity and cruelty, forced disappearance
       should be considered a crime against humanity, which implies
       that the crime is subject to no statute of limitations and is
       subject to universal jurisdiction for its prosecution and
       punishment;

b)   Forced disappearance should be considered a common crime
       for the purposes of extradition and political asylum. Those
       responsible should be barred from raising their political
       motives as a defense to extradition or in support of a claim for
       political asylum;

c)   While it is considered a crime against humanity in
       international law, the crime of disappearance must be codified
       in the penal codes of individual states. The crime must be
       subject to punishment that comports with its extremely grave
       nature. Similarly, the states in whose territory forced

disappearances occur should penalize criminal participation at
every level: perpetrator, accomplice, and accessory, and
should expressly prohibit the defenses of mistake, coercion,
necessity, or due obedience;

d)   States should adopt complimentary measures that tend to
prevent the practice of forced disappearances, such as
prohibiting the maintenance of secret detention sites. States
must assure that their detention facilities conform to commonly
recognized international norms codified in the United Nations'
"Standard Minimal Rules for the Treatment of Prisoners";
States also should codify their obligation to maintain a list of
all persons deprived of liberty for whatever reason, and to
notify the relatives of detainees when arrest is made;

e)   Legislation guaranteeing that the writ of *habeas corpus* may
never be suspended, even during states of emergency must be
enacted.

None of this should be construed as limiting the state's duty rapidly and
effectively to act in those cases in which there are sufficient indicia that a forced
disappearance has occurred.

In our country, in particular, it is important to undertake a revision of
the *habeas corpus* procedure, as well as a more thorough codification of the
crimes of abuse of authority, illegal detention, and torture.

Because of these characteristics which convert the crime of forced
disappearance into an autonomous figure, efforts are underway in the inter-
American system to draft an Inter-American Convention to prevent and sanction
forced disappearances. Although this convention has not been completed, various
international resolutions have condemned forced disappearances. For example,
the General Assembly of the Organization of American States (OAS) has declared
that the forced disappearance of persons constitutes a crime against humanity.
(Resolutions 666 (XIII-0/83) and 742 (XIV-0/84) of the OAS General Assembly).

The United Nations General Assembly has repeatedly spoken out on this
topic: in a resolution adopted on December 20, 1978 (A/RES.33.173), it urged
the Human Rights Commission to consider the topic and to formulate
recommendations. Later, the Human Rights Commission established a Working
Group on Forced or Involuntary Disappearances, whose mandate continues in
force. The United Nations once again addressed the topic of forced
disappearances in resolutions issued by two recent General Assemblies (G.A.
Res. 40/147, December 13, 1985, and G.A. Res. 41/45, December, 1986). In

recent years, the Working Group has carried out observations *in loco* and has published numerous reports on disappearances in various countries.

2. Why is the Commissioner writing this report?

The National Commissioner was created as a body at the service of Hondurans (and foreign nationals that find themselves in the country) to provide adequate protection for the fundamental rights of every individual.

The need to create an official institution able to assist victims of abuse, negligence, and omission by those charged with law enforcement in Honduras has been recognized for some time. The creation of such an institution was contemplated as part of the system of "state modernization" undertaken by the administration of President Callejas. This institution, it was believed, should be patterned after what is known in the international doctrine of protection of human rights as an "Ombudsman," *Defensor del Pueblo* (Defender of the People), or *Procurador de los Derechos Humanos* (Attorney General for Human Rights).

In Honduras, the title National Commissioner for the Protection of Human Rights was chosen because the President of the Republic, in accordance with the General Law of Public Administration, has the power to appoint "Commissioners" to perform specific functions. However, because this Commissioner would require public support, it was considered important that the designation of Commissioner be made by the National Reconciliation Commission, created within the framework of the peace and democratization process in Central America embodied in the Esquipulas accords.

Thus, by Decree No. 26-92 of June 8, 1992, the President created the Office of the National Commissioner for the Protection of Human Rights. That decree also authorized the National Reconciliation Commission to act as "a body of consultation and support for the National Commissioner for Human Rights" and to propose to the President a list of candidates for his choice. The decree also limited the President's power to dismiss the Commissioner; removal may only be accomplished by proposal of two thirds of the members of the National Reconciliation Commission.

In response to a request by the National Reconciliation Commission, the President of the Republic issued Executive Decree No. 51-92 on September 8, 1992, which guaranteed the Commissioner's "absolute independence in the performance of his duties." The position, however, remains administratively dependent on the presidency.

The functions of the National Commissioner of Human Rights, include the following:

1.   Oversight of acts and measures for the respect and defense of human rights;
2.   Oversight of the respect of human rights by the state and individual citizens;
3.   Power to immediately address and duly pursue any and all complaints regarding the violation of human rights;
4.   Oversight of the application of laws relating to human rights and the power to implement them, when necessary.

To accomplish these functions, the Commissioner may:

a)   Request from any authority or person information regarding alleged human rights violations;
b)   Make observations and relevant recommendations to domestic authorities concerning violations of human rights;
c)   Elaborate and propose programs of prevention and development in the area of human rights as well as in judicial, economic, educational, cultural, and other arenas; and
d)   Assume responsibility for the fulfillment, within Honduran territory, of international treaties, agreements, and accords ratified by Honduras, and to promote other instruments of a similar nature.

As a guarantee of its activity, it is established "that the investigations conducted by the Office of the National Commissioner for Human Rights in the areas within its jurisdiction, whether instigated by complaint or its own initiative, shall not be suspended, interrupted, postponed, or in any form hindered by order, mandate, or act of any authority."

II

LIST OF THE DISAPPEARED IN HONDURAS

The following is a list of Honduran citizens and foreigners reported as disappeared in Honduras from 1980 to the present. The list has been compiled from various reports that the Commissioner has received from governmental and nongovernmental human rights organizations (domestic and international) during the process of preparing this Preliminary Report.

1980

No. 1

PERSONAL DATA

NAME: ESTANISLAO MARADIAGA LINARES (39)
NATIONALITY: HONDURAN
PROFESSION: UNION LEADER

DESCRIPTION OF EVENTS

Detained May 24, 1980, from his house, located across from the airstrip in the department of Choluteca, Honduras by five FUSEP agents. Maradiaga Linares was a member of the National Autonomous Service of Aqueducts and Sewers Employees' Union. *See* Chapter III.

ALLEGED RESPONSIBILITY

Five Public Security (FUSEP) agents

SOURCES

Committee for the Defense of Human Rights in Honduras
U.N. Working Group on Enforced or Involuntary Disappearances

1981

No. 2

PERSONAL DATA

NAME: WILLIAM TOMAS SANTAMARIA CABRERA (22)
NATIONALITY: NICARAGUAN
PROFESSION: UNKNOWN

DESCRIPTION OF EVENTS

Disappeared February 25, 1981, along with his uncle, Roberto Elvis Cabrera Otero, while travelling from Nicaragua to Honduras. The two men disappeared mysteriously after passing through the border post at El Guasaule. The family received information that the two men had been kidnapped by a group of contras (Alejandro Moncada Beltrán, Leslie Amador, Oscar Baldelomar, Delgadillo Baldelomar, Guillermo Gasteazoro and Fabricio Castillo), all of whom were former Nicaraguan National Guardsmen involved in stealing cars and bringing them to Guatemala. The car driven by the Cabrerases entered Guatemala March 11, 1981, driven by Alejandro Moncada Beltrán (Nicaraguan Passport No. 5532) who was accompanied by an unknown man using Roberto Elvis Otero's passport.

ALLEGED RESPONSIBILITY

Former Nicaraguan National Guardsmen Alejandro Moncada Beltrán, Leslie Amador, Oscar Baldelomar, Delgadillo Baldelomar, Guillermo Gasteazoro and Fabricio Castillo

SOURCES

Committee for the Defense of Human Rights in Honduras

No. 3

PERSONAL DATA

NAME: ROBERTO ELVIS CABRERA OTERO
NATIONALITY: NICARAGUAN
PROFESSION: UNKNOWN

DESCRIPTION OF EVENTS

Disappeared February 25, 1981, along with his nephew, William Tomás Santamaría Cabrera, while travelling from Nicaragua to Honduras. The two men disappeared mysteriously after passing through the post at El Guasaule. The family received information that the two men had been kidnapped by a group of contras (Alejandro Moncada Beltrán, Leslie Amador, Oscar Baldelomar, Delgadillo Baldelomar, Guillermo Gasteazoro and Fabricio Castillo), all of whom were former National Guardsmen involved in stealing cars and bringing them to Guatemala. The car driven by the Cabrerases entered Guatemala March 11, 1981 driven by Alejandro Moncada Beltrán (Nicaraguan Passport No. 5532) who was accompanied by an unknown man using Roberto Elvis Otero's passport.

ALLEGED RESPONSIBILITY

Former Nicaraguan National Guardsmen Alejandro Moncada Beltrán, Leslie Amador, Oscar Baldelomar, Delgadillo Baldelomar, Guillermo Gasteazoro and Fabricio Castillo

SOURCES

Committee for the Defense of Human Rights in Honduras

No. 4

PERSONAL DATA

NAME: ANA ELSA ARCE ROMERO (22)
NATIONALITY: SALVADORAN
PROFESSION: STUDENT

DESCRIPTION OF EVENTS

Disappeared April 22, 1981, from the Miramontes neighborhood in Tegucigalpa. Sources indicate that Arce Romero was detained with 13 other persons, including her sister. These detainees were Salvadoran refugees in Honduras. Their whereabouts remain unknown.

ALLEGED RESPONSIBILITY

National Investigations Directorate (DNI) agents

SOURCES

Human Rights Commission of El Salvador (Comisión de Derechos Humanos de El Salvador
Salvadoran Committee on Human Rights (Comité Salvadoreño sobre Derechos Humanos)
Amnesty International
U.N. Working Group on Forced and Involuntary Disappearances

No. 5

PERSONAL DATA

NAME: ENOE DE JESUS ARCE ROMERO (25)
NATIONALITY: SALVADORAN
PROFESSION: STUDENT

DESCRIPTION OF EVENTS

Detained April 22, 1981, in the Miramontes neighborhood of Tegucigalpa in circumstances similar to those of 13 other persons, including his sisters. These Salvadorans were refugees in Honduras.

SOURCES

Committee for the Defense of Human Rights in Honduras
Human Rights Commission of El Salvador
Salvadoran Committee on Human Rights
Amnesty International
U.N. Working Group on Forced and Involuntary Disappearances

ALLEGED RESPONSIBILITY

DNI agents

No. 6

PERSONAL DATA

NAME: EVA SARA ARCE ROMERO (23)
NATIONALITY: SALVADORAN
PROFESSION: STUDENT

DESCRIPTION OF EVENTS

Detained April 22, 1981, in the city of Tegucigalpa. The Honduran Permanent
Mission in Geneva indicated that according to immigration files, Arce Romero
never entered the country.

ALLEGED RESPONSIBILITY

DNI agents

SOURCES

Committee of Relatives of Detained-Disappeared in Honduras
U.N. Working Group on Forced and Involuntary Disappearances

No. 7

PERSONAL DATA

NAME: MAURICIO BARRILLAS (33)
NATIONALITY: SALVADORAN
PROFESSION: BUSINESS ADMINISTRATOR

DESCRIPTION OF EVENTS

Detained April 22, 1981, in Tegucigalpa's Miramontes neighborhood. Sources indicate that Barrillas was detained along with 13 other people, among them his wife, NORA TRINIDAD GOMEZ VALENCIA, and his three children, NORA PATRICIA (11), MAURICIO GERARDO (5) and JOSE DANIEL (2). The detainees were Salvadoran refugees in Honduras.

ALLEGED RESPONSIBILITY

DNI

SOURCES

Committee for the Defense of Human Rights in Honduras
Salvadoran-American Human Rights Committee
Amnesty International
U.N. Working Group on Enforced or Involuntary Disappearances

No. 8

PERSONAL DATA

NAME: ANA ELISA CORDOBA RAMIREZ (23)
NATIONALITY: SALVADORAN
PROFESSION: PEASANT

DESCRIPTION OF EVENTS

Detained April 22, 1981, in Tegucigalpa's Miramontes neighborhood. Sources report that Cordoba Ramírez was detained along with 13 other people. Her whereabouts remain unknown.

ALLEGED RESPONSIBILITY

DNI

SOURCES

Committee for the Defense of Human Rights in Honduras (Reported by CODEH as Ana Isabel Córdova)
Salvadoran-American Human Rights Committee
Amnesty International.
U.N. Working Group on Enforced or Involuntary Disappearances.

No. 9

PERSONAL DATA

NAME: CLAUDIA MARIA DOMINGUEZ AMADOR
NATIONALITY: SALVADORAN
PROFESSION: PEASANT

DESCRIPTION OF EVENTS

Detained April 22, 1981, in Tegucigalpa's Miramontes neighborhood along with 13 other people.

ALLEGED RESPONSIBILITY

DNI

SOURCES

Committee for the Defense of Human Rights in Honduras
Salvadoran-American Human Rights Committee

Amnesty International.
U.N. Working Group on Enforced or Involuntary Disappearances.

No. 10

PERSONAL DATA

NAME: SALVADOR FABIAN (29)
NATIONALITY: SALVADORAN
PROFESSION: PEASANT

DESCRIPTION OF EVENTS

Detained April 22, 1981, in Tegucigalpa's Miramontes neighborhood.

ALLEGED RESPONSIBILITY

DNI

SOURCES

U.N. Working Group on Enforced or Involuntary Disappearances
Committee for the Defense of Human Rights in Honduras
Salvadoran-American Human Rights Committee
Amnesty International

No. 11

PERSONAL DATA

NAME: FRANCISCO GARCIA (27)
NATIONALITY: SALVADORAN
PROFESSION: UNKNOWN

DESCRIPTION OF EVENTS

A Salvadoran refugee in Honduras, García was detained April 22, 1981, in

Tegucigalpa's Miramontes along with 13 other people.

ALLEGED RESPONSIBILITY

Honduran Armed Forces.

SOURCES

Committee for the Defense of Human Rights in Honduras
Amnesty International
U.N. Working Group on Enforced or Involuntary Disappearances

No. 12

PERSONAL DATA

NAME: NORA TRINIDAD GOMEZ DE BARRILLAS
NATIONALITY: SALVADORAN (THREE CHILDREN)
PROFESSION: ARCHBISHOP OSCAR ROMERO'S FORMER SECRETARY

DESCRIPTION OF EVENTS

Detained April 22, 1981, in Tegucigalpa's Miramonte neighborhood along with
13 other people, including her husband Mauricio Barrillas and her three
children, Nora Patricia (11), Mauricio Gerardo (5), and José Daniel (2).

ALLEGED RESPONSIBILITY

DNI

SOURCES

Committee for the Defense of Human Rights in Honduras
Salvadoran-American Human Rights Committee
Amnesty International
U.N. Working Group on Enforced or Involuntary Disappearances

No. 13

PERSONAL DATA

NAME: MARTA ALICIA NAVARRO
NATIONALITY: SALVADORAN
PROFESSION: STUDENT

DESCRIPTION OF EVENTS

Detained April 22, 1981, in Tegucigalpa's Miramontes neighborhood along with 13 other people, including two of her sisters, Ursula María and Concepción (3), and her mother, by members of the security forces. All of the people arrested were Salvadoran refugees in Honduras. The children were later turned over to Salvadoran authorities by the Inspector of Immigration and a female police officer.

ALLEGED RESPONSIBILITY

Security Forces

SOURCES

Committee for the Defense of Human Rights in Honduras
Amnesty International
U.N. Working Group on Enforced or Involuntary Disappearances

No. 14

PERSONAL DATA

NAME: CONCEPCION NAVARRO (55)
NATIONALITY: SALVADORAN
PROFESSION: UNKNOWN

DESCRIPTION OF EVENTS

Disappeared April 22, 1981, in Tegucigalpa. Her daughter, Marta Alicia

Navarro, also disappeared.

SOURCES

Committee for the Defense of Human Rights in Honduras

No. 15

PERSONAL DATA

NAME: ANA MARIA SIERRA (23)
NATIONALITY: SALVADORAN
PROFESSION: STUDENT

DESCRIPTION OF EVENTS

Detained April 22, 1981, in Tegucigalpa.

ALLEGED RESPONSIBILITY

DNI

SOURCES

Committee of Relatives of the Detained and Disappeared in Honduras
U.N. Working Group on Enforced or Involuntary Disappearances

No. 16

PERSONAL DATA

NAME: GERARDO VEGA BARBOSA
NATIONALITY: COSTA RICAN
PROFESSION: UNKNOWN

DESCRIPTION OF EVENTS

Detained April 26, 1981, in El Guasaule, on border with Nicaragua.

ALLEGED RESPONSIBILITY

Honduran Armed Forces; Army Capt. Oscar Barahona

SOURCES

Committee of Relatives of the Detained and Disappeared in Honduras U.N. Working Group on Enforced or Involuntary Disappearances

NO. 17

PERSONAL DATA

NAME: CARLOS ANTONIO RAMIREZ LEMUS (26)
NATIONALITY: GUATEMALAN
PROFESSION: STUDENT

DESCRIPTION OF EVENTS

Secretary of the "Oliverio Castañeda de León" Students Association. Disappeared April 27, 1981. Residence in Guatemala in transit in Honduras, detained by military personnel who told the driver of the bus from the Ticabús comnpany that they were "following orders from superiors." They arrested Ramírez Lemus in front of the bus passengers. Lemus's wife connects this case with that of Gerardo Vega Barbosa, detained and disappeared under similar circumstances.

ALLEGED RESPONSIBILITY

Honduran Armed Forces

SOURCES

Committee for the Defense of Human Rights in Honduras
Amnesty International
UNESCO
U.N. Working Group on Enforced or Involuntary Disappearances

No. 18

PERSONAL DATA

NAME: FIDEL MARTINEZ (40)
NATIONALITY: HONDURAN
PROFESSION: AGRONOMIST

DESCRIPTION OF EVENTS

Detained June 11, 1981, at 3:00 a.m. in Tegucigalpa's El Hogar neighborhood.
Martínez was kidnapped from the house where he was living in El Hogar by six
hooded men and was injured in the operation. *See* Chapter III.

ALLEGED RESPONSIBILITY

FUSEP

SOURCES

Committee for the Defense of Human Rights in Honduras
Amnesty International
U.N. Working Group on Enforced or Involuntary Disappearances

No. 19

PERSONAL DATA

NAME: TOMAS NATIVI GALVEZ (33)

NATIONALITY: HONDURAN
PROFESSION: PROFESSOR

DESCRIPTION OF EVENTS

Detained June 11, 1981, at 3:00 a.m. in Tegucigalpa's El Hogar neighborhood. *See* additional information on this case in Chapter III.

ALLEGED RESPONSIBILITY

FUSEP

SOURCES

Committee for the Defense of Human Rights in Honduras
Amnesty International
U.N. Working Group on Enforced or Involuntary Disappearances

No. 20

PERSONAL DATA

NAME: LUIS ALBERTO REGALADO LEZAMA
NATIONALITY: SALVADORAN
PROFESSION: UNKNOWN

DESCRIPTION OF EVENTS

Arrested August 5, 1981. He was reportedly part of a group of 15 Salvadoran refugees in Honduras detained by the First Infantry Battalion. This case is related to the cases of JORGE MAXIMILIANO HERNANDEZ PAREDES, MATILDE QUINTANILLA MELGAR, MARIO VALLADARES BATRES AND DOMINGO RODRIGUEZ, among others.

ALLEGED RESPONSIBILITY

DNI

SOURCES

Human Rights Commission of El Salvador
Amnesty International
U.N. Working Group on Enforced or Involuntary Disappearances

No. 21

PERSONAL DATA

NAME: EDUARDO GARCIA
NATIONALITY: VENEZUELAN
PROFESSION: UNKNOWN

DESCRIPTION OF EVENTS

Detained August 5, 1981, in Tegucigalpa.

ALLEGED RESPONSIBILITY

DNI

SOURCES

Committee for the Defense of Human Rights in Honduras
U.N. Working Group on Enforced or Involuntary Disappearances

No. 22

PERSONAL DATA

NAME: JORGE MAXIMILIANO HERNANDEZ PAREDES (44)
NATIONALITY: SALVADORAN
PROFESSION: PILOT

DESCRIPTION OF EVENTS

Detained August 5, 1981, in Tegucigalpa. Source reports that Hernández Paredes was a Salvadoran refugee in Honduras. He was reportedly detained by the First Infantry Battalion.

ALLEGED RESPONSIBILITY

DNI

SOURCES

Committee for the Defense of Human Rights in Honduras
Amnesty International
Committee of the Relatives of the Detained and Disappeared in Honduras
U.N. Working Group on Enforced or Involuntary Disappearances

No. 23

PERSONAL DATA

NAME: JORGE ENRIQUE JIMENEZ ARGUETA
NATIONALITY: SALVADORAN
PROFESSION: UNKNOWN

DESCRIPTION OF EVENTS

Detained August 5, 1981, in San Pedro Sula, department of Cortés. The Honduran Government informed the Working Group that Jiménez had not been detained. The Honduran Permanent Mission in Geneva stated, according to immigration records, Jiménez had been deported to El Salvador.

ALLEGED RESPONSIBILITY

DNI

SOURCES

Committee for the Defense of Human Rights in Honduras
U.N. Working Group on Enforced or Involuntary Disappearances

No. 24

PERSONAL DATA

NAME: SOFIA JIMENEZ
NATIONALITY: SALVADORAN
PROFESSION: UNKNOWN

DESCRIPTION OF EVENTS

Detained August 5, 1981, in Tegucigalpa. Source reports that Jiménez was taken to an unknown location. The Honduran Permanent Mission in Geneva claimed Jiménez had never entered the country.

ALLEGED RESPONSIBILITY

DNI

SOURCES

Committee of Relatives of the Detained and Disappeared in Honduras U.N. Working Group on Enforced or Involuntary Disappearances

No. 25

PERSONAL DATA

NAME: ENRIQUE MENJIVAR
NATIONALITY: SALVADORAN
PROFESSION: UNKNOWN

DESCRIPTION OF EVENTS

Detained August 5, 1981, in Tegucigalpa

ALLEGED RESPONSIBILITY

DNI

SOURCES

Committee of Relatives of the Detained and Disappeared in Honduras
Committee for the Defense of Human Rights in Honduras
U.N. Working Group on Enforced or Involuntary Disappearances

No. 26

PERSONAL DATA

NAME: MATILDE QUINTANILLA MELGAR
NATIONALITY: SALVADORAN
PROFESSION: UNKNOWN

DESCRIPTION OF EVENTS

A Salvadoran refugee, she was detained August 5, 1981, in Tegucigalpa.

ALLEGED RESPONSIBILITY

DNI

SOURCES

Committee for the Defense of Human Rights in Honduras
U.N. Working Group on Enforced or Involuntary Disappearances

No. 27

PERSONAL DATA

NAME: RAFAEL ANTONIO RODRIGUEZ
NATIONALITY: SALVADORAN
PROFESSION: UNKNOWN

DESCRIPTION OF EVENTS

Detained August 5, 1981, in Tegucigalpa, presumably by DNI agents.

ALLEGED RESPONSIBILITY

DNI

SOURCES

Committee of Relatives of the Detained-Disappeared in Honduras
U.N. Working Group on Enforced or Involuntary Disappearances

No. 28

PERSONAL DATA

NAME: YADIRA VILLALTA
NATIONALITY: SALVADORAN
PROFESSION: UNKNOWN

DESCRIPTION OF EVENTS

Detained August 5, 1981, in Tegucigalpa. Villalta had been detained earlier in El Salvador, where she had been cruelly tortured.

ALLEGED RESPONSIBILITY

DNI

SOURCES

Committee for the Defense of Human Rights in Honduras
U.N. Working Group on Enforced or Involuntary Disappearances

No. 29

PERSONAL DATA

NAME: DOMINGO RODRIGUEZ
NATIONALITY: SALVADORAN
PROFESSION: UNKNOWN

DESCRIPTION OF EVENTS

Detained August 5, 1981, in Tegucigalpa, along with a group of other Salvadorans, by DNI agents.

ALLEGED RESPONSIBILITY

DNI

SOURCES

Committee for the Defense of Human Rights in Honduras

No. 30

PERSONAL DATA

NAME: RAFAEL RODRIGUEZ
NATIONALITY: SALVADORAN
PROFESSION: UNKNOWN

DESCRIPTION OF EVENTS

Disappeared August 5, 1981, after being detained by DNI agents in Tegucigalpa

ALLEGED RESPONSIBILITY

Agents of the DNI

SOURCES

Committee for the Defense of Human Rights in Honduras

No. 31

PERSONAL DATA

NAME: JOSE FRANCISCO RIVERA MIRANDA
NATIONALITY: NICARAGUAN
PROFESSION: UNKNOWN

DESCRIPTION OF EVENTS

Detained December 22, 1981, by immigration officials in Choluteca as an undocumented immigrant

ALLEGED RESPONSIBILITY

Immigration officials

SOURCES

Committee for the Defense of Human Rights in Honduras

No. 32

PERSONAL DATA

NAME: RAFAEL TORRES RODRIGUEZ
NATIONALITY: SALVADORAN
PROFESSION: UNKNOWN

DESCRIPTION OF EVENTS

Detained August 7, 1981, in San Pedro Sula, Department of Cortés. Torres Rodríguez was part of a group of 15 people arrested by the Honduran army in an operation in San Pedro Sula and Tegucigalpa at the time. Torres Rodríguez was a Salvadoran refugee living in Honduras.

ALLEGED RESPONSIBILITY

Honduran Armed Forces; DNI

SOURCES

Committee for the Defense of Human Rights in Honduras
U.N. Working Group on Enforced or Involuntary Disappearances

No. 33

PERSONAL DATA

NAME: JUAN FRANCISCO ALVARENGA GARCIA
NATIONALITY: HONDURAN
PROFESSION: UNKNOWN

DESCRIPTION OF EVENTS

Arrested August 8, 1981, in Tegucigalpa.

ALLEGED RESPONSIBILITY

DNI

SOURCES

Committee of Relatives of the Detained and Disappeared in Honduras
U.N. Working Group on Enforced or Involuntary Disappearances

No. 34

PERSONAL DATA

NAME: JORGE MANUEL MORALES ALVARADO
NATIONALITY: ECUADORAN
PROFESSION: UNKNOWN

DESCRIPTION OF EVENTS

Detained August 8, 1981, in Tegucigalpa. Source reports that Morales Alvarado
was detained along with Marisol Villalta (8) and Antonio Villalta (5). The
children were later left at their home by female military personnel.

ALLEGED RESPONSIBILITY

DNI; Honduran Armed Forces

SOURCES

Committee for the Defense of Human Rights in Honduras
U.N. Working Group on Enforced or Involuntary Disappearances

No. 35

PERSONAL DATA

NAME: OSCAR GUILLERMO RODRIGUEZ
NATIONALITY: HONDURAN
PROFESSION: UNKNOWN

DESCRIPTION OF EVENTS

Detained August 8, 1981, in the "Alto Verde" mechanic shop in San Lorenzo, Department of Valle. Rodríguez was detained along with Domingo Eleuterio Rodríguez and Andrés Vásquez Rodríguez.

ALLEGED RESPONSIBILITY

DNI

SOURCES

Committee for the Defense of Human Rights in Honduras
Committee of Relatives of the Detained and Disappeared in Honduras
U.N. Working Group on Enforced or Involuntary Disappearances

No. 36

PERSONAL DATA

NAME: DOMINGO ELEUTERIO RODRIGUEZ CABRERA (32)
NATIONALITY: HONDURAN
PROFESSION: MECHANIC

DESCRIPTION OF EVENTS

Detained August 8, 1981, in San Lorenzo, Department of Valle. Rodríguez Cabrera was detained along with his nephew, Oscar Guillermo, by DNI agents.

ALLEGED RESPONSIBILITY

DNI

SOURCES

Committee for the Defense of Human Rights in Honduras
Committee of Relatives of the Detained and Disappeared in Honduras Amnesty
International
U.N. Working Group on Enforced or Involuntary Disappearances

No. 37

PERSONAL DATA

NAME: JORGE ZAVALA EURAKE
NATIONALITY: HONDURAN
PROFESSION: UNKNOWN

DESCRIPTION OF EVENTS

Detained August 8, 1981, in Tegucigalpa by DNI agents.

ALLEGED RESPONSIBILITY

DNI

SOURCES

Committee for the Defense of Human Rights in Honduras
U.N. Working Group on Enforced or Involuntary Disappearances

No. 38

PERSONAL DATA

NAME: DAVID AYALA
NATIONALITY: HONDURAN
PROFESSION: UNKNOWN

DESCRIPTION OF EVENTS

Detained August 10, 1981, in San Pedro Sula, Department of Cortés. His whereabouts are still unknown.

ALLEGED RESPONSIBILITY

DNI

SOURCES

Committee of Relatives of the Detained and Disappeared in Honduras
Committee for the Defense of Human Rights in Honduras
U.N. Working Group on Enforced or Involuntary Disappearances

No. 39

PERSONAL DATA

NAME: JOSE EDUARDO GONZALEZ
NATIONALITY: HONDURAN
PROFESSION: UNKNOWN

DESCRIPTION OF EVENTS

Detained August 10, 1981 in Comayagüela.

ALLEGED RESPONSIBILITY

DNI

SOURCES

Committee for the Defense of Human Rights in Honduras
U.N. Working Group on Enforced or Involuntary Disappearances

No. 40

PERSONAL DATA

NAME: JORGE EDUARDO MORALES
NATIONALITY: SALVADORAN
PROFESSION: UNKNOWN

DESCRIPTION OF EVENTS

Detained August 10, 1981, in San Pedro Sula, Department of Cortés. Source reports that Morales was one of 15 people arrested by the Honduran Armed Forces in San Pedro Sula and Tegucigalpa at the time. Morales was a Salvadoran refugee living in Honduras.

ALLEGED RESPONSIBILITY

Honduran Armed Forces

SOURCES

Committee for the Defense of Human Rights in Honduras
U.N. Working Group on Enforced or Involuntary Disappearances

No. 41

PERSONAL DATA

NAME: FLAVIO NARCISO LOPEZ AYALA
NATIONALITY: SALVADORAN
PROFESSION: UNKNOWN

DESCRIPTION OF EVENTS

Detained August 10, 1981, in San Pedro Sula. López Ayala was a Salvadoran refugee in Honduras.

ALLEGED RESPONSIBILITY

DNI

SOURCES

Committee for the Defense of Human Rights in Honduras
Amnesty International
U.N. Working Group on Enforced or Involuntary Disappearances

No. 42

PERSONAL DATA

NAME: OSCAR ALEXIS COLINDRES
NATIONALITY: HONDURAN
PROFESSION: STUDENT

DESCRIPTION OF EVENTS

Detained September 5, 1981, in Tegucigalpa, by members of the Transit Police.

ALLEGED RESPONSIBILITY

Transit Police

SOURCES

Committee for the Defense of Human Rights in Honduras
U.N. Working Group on Enforced or Involuntary Disappearances

No. 43

PERSONAL DATA

NAME: JULIO DIAZ RUIZ
NATIONALITY: HONDURAN
PROFESSION: UNKNOWN

DESCRIPTION OF EVENTS

Detained September 8, 1981, in Tegucigalpa.

ALLEGED RESPONSIBILITY

DNI

SOURCES

Committee of Relatives of the Detained and Disappeared in Honduras
U.N. Working Group on Enforced or Involuntary Disappearances

No. 44

PERSONAL DATA

NAME: JOSE MARIO MARTINEZ
NATIONALITY: SALVADORAN
PROFESSION: UNKNOWN

DESCRIPTION OF EVENTS

Detained September 8, 1981, in Tegucigalpa.

ALLEGED RESPONSIBILITY

DNI

SOURCES

Committee for the Defense of Human Rights in Honduras
U.N. Working Group on Enforced or Involuntary Disappearances

No. 45

PERSONAL DATA

NAME: TOMAS VIJIL
NATIONALITY: HONDURAN
PROFESSION: UNKNOWN

DESCRIPTION OF EVENTS

Detained September 8, 1981, in Tegucigalpa.

ALLEGED RESPONSIBILITY

DNI

SOURCES

Committee of Relatives of the Detained and Disappeared in Honduras
Committee for the Defense of Human Rights in Honduras
U.N. Working Group on Enforced or Involuntary Disappearances

No. 46

PERSONAL DATA

NAME: ANGEL MANFREDO VELASQUEZ RODRIGUEZ (35)
NATIONALITY: HONDURAN
PROFESSION: STUDENT

DESCRIPTION OF EVENTS

Detained September 12, 1981, close to the Palace and Lido cinemas in Tegucigalpa. The Inter-American Court of Human Rights condemned the Honduran Government as responsible for the disappearance of Velásquez Rodríguez and ordered it to pay just compensation for his disappearance.

ALLEGED RESPONSIBILITY

Six agents from the DNI

SOURCES

Committee for the Defense of Human Rights in Honduras
Amnesty International
U.N. Working Group on Enforced or Involuntary Disappearances

No. 47

PERSONAL DATA

NAME: ANTONIO ZUÑIGA
NATIONALITY: HONDURAN
PROFESSION: UNKNOWN

DESCRIPTION OF EVENTS

Detained September 19, 1981, in Danlí, Department of El Paraíso.

SOURCES

Committee for the Defense of Human Rights in Honduras
U.N. Working Group on Enforced or Involuntary Disappearances

No. 48

PERSONAL DATA

NAME: MARIO VALLADARES BATRES (33)
NATIONALITY: SALVADORAN
PROFESSION: MECHANIC

DESCRIPTION OF EVENTS

Detained October 8, 1981, in the Department of Valle. Valladares Batres was a Salvadoran refugee in Honduras.

ALLEGED RESPONSIBILITY

DNI

SOURCES

Committee for the Defense of Human Rights in Honduras
Amnesty International
U.N. Working Group on Enforced or Involuntary Disappearances

No. 49

PERSONAL DATA

NAME: EDUARDO ANIBAL BLANCO ARAYA (23)
NATIONALITY: COSTA RICAN
PROFESSION: UNKNOWN

DESCRIPTION OF EVENTS

Detained November 14, 1981, at 12:00 a.m. in Comayagüela. Sources report that Blanco Araya was detained by men dressed in civilian clothes who identified themselves as members of the DNI.

ALLEGED RESPONSIBILITY

DNI

SOURCES

Amnesty International
Central American Commission for the Defense of Human Rights
U.N. Working Group on Enforced or Involuntary Disappearances

No. 50

PERSONAL DATA

NAME: YOLANDA DEL CARMEN SOLIS CORRALES (28)
NATIONALITY: COSTA RICAN
PROFESSION: TEACHER

DESCRIPTION OF EVENTS

Disappeared December 11, 1981, while travelling through Honduras on her way to Mexico. [*Editor's note:* The Inter-American Court of Human Rights in a March 15, 1989 ruling, found "insufficient evidence to relate the disappearance of Francisco Fairén Garbi (see below) and Yolando Solís Corrales to the governmental practice of disappearances." (Inter-American Court of Human Rights, *Fairén Garbi and Solís Corrales Case,* Judgment of March 15, 1989, Series C, No. 6, para.158. The decision noted, however, the government of Honduras's "lack of diligence, approaching obstructionism" (para. 160) in failing to respond to repeated requests for an exhumation of a body believed to belong to Fairén which was found in a place called "La Montañita" believed. The fate of Solís Corrales and Fairén Garbi remains unknown.]

ALLEGED RESPONSIBILITY

DNI

SOURCES

Amnesty International
Pax Romana
U.N. Working Group on Enforced or Involuntary Disappearances

No. 51

PERSONAL DATA

NAME: FRANCISCO FAIREN GARBI (28)
NATIONALITY: COSTA RICAN, PASSPORT NO. 9.048.377
PROFESSION: STUDENT

DESCRIPTION OF EVENTS

Disappeared December 11, 1981, while travelling through Honduras on his way
to Mexico. [*See Editor's note, above*] For further information on this case, *see*
Inter-American Court of Human Rights, *Fairén Garbi and Solís Corrales Case,*
Judgment of March 15, 1989, Series C, No. 6, para.158.]

ALLEGED RESPONSIBILITY

DNI

SOURCES

Amnesty International
Pax Romana
Francisco Fairén Almengor (father)
U.N. Working Group on Enforced or Involuntary Disappearances
Committee for the Defense of Human Rights in Honduras

No. 52

PERSONAL DATA

NAME: ALFREDO DUARTE, "EL CHAPIN"
NATIONALITY: GUATEMALAN
PROFESSION: LAY WORKER

DESCRIPTION OF EVENTS

Detained December 20, 1981, while travelling on bus No. 52 of the Impala bus company from San Pedro Sula to Choloma, Department of Cortés. According to sources, witnesses reported that Duarte was detained along with his employer, JOSE FRECH GUTIERREZ, during an operation of inspection of the identification of passengers along the San Pedro Sula-Choloma route.

ALLEGED RESPONSIBILITY

Honduran Armed Forces

SOURCES

Committee of Relatives of the Detained and Disappeared in Honduras
U.N. Working Group on Enforced or Involuntary Disappearances

No. 53

PERSONAL DATA

NAME: JOSE FRECH GUTIERREZ
NATIONALITY: HONDURAN
PROFESSION: MERCHANT

DESCRIPTION OF EVENTS

Detained December 20, 1981 while travelling on bus No. 52 of the Impala bus company from San Pedro Sula to Choloma, Department of Cortés.

ALLEGED RESPONSIBILITY

DNI

SOURCES

Committee for the Defense of Human Rights in Honduras
Committee of Relatives of the Detained and Disappeared in Honduras
U.N. Working Group on Enforced or Involuntary Disappearances

No. 54

PERSONAL DATA

NAME: VICTOR HUGO ALAS HERRERA
NATIONALITY: COSTA RICAN
PROFESSION: UNION LEADER

DESCRIPTION OF EVENTS

Disappeared December 24, 1981, after being arrested in the home of Ricardo Escalón in San Pedro Sula.

SOURCES

Committee for the Defense of Human Rights in Honduras

1982

No. 55

PERSONAL DATA

NAME: MARIA EDILTRUDIS MONTES GIRON (25)
NATIONALITY: HONDURAN
PROFESSION: UNKNOWN

DESCRIPTION OF EVENTS

Detained January 24, 1982, in El Guasaule, border with Nicaragua.

ALLEGED RESPONSIBILITY

DNI

SOURCES

Committee for the Defense of Human Rights in Honduras
U.N. Working Group on Enforced or Involuntary Disappearances

No. 56

PERSONAL DATA

NAME: JULIO CESAR ZAVALA MENDEZ (21)
NATIONALITY: HONDURAN
PROFESSION: STUDENT

DESCRIPTION OF EVENTS

Detained January 24, 1982, in El Guasaule, when he entered the country.

ALLEGED RESPONSIBILITY

DNI

SOURCES

Committee for the Defense of Human Rights in Honduras (Case registered as Julio César Méndez Zavala)
U.N. Working Group on Enforced or Involuntary Disappearances

No. 57

PERSONAL DATA

NAME: SAMUEL PEREZ
NATIONALITY: HONDURAN
PROFESSION: UNKNOWN

DESCRIPTION OF EVENTS

Arrested January 24, 1982, in El Guasaule, by members of the DNI when he entered the country on a Ticabús vehicle.

ALLEGED RESPONSIBILITY

DNI

SOURCES

Committee for the Defense of Human Rights in Honduras
U.N. Working Group on Enforced or Involuntary Disappearances

No. 58

PERSONAL DATA

NAME: ENRIQUE LOPEZ HERNANDEZ

NATIONALITY: HONDURAN
PROFESSION: UNKNOWN

DESCRIPTION OF EVENTS

Disappeared January 24, 1982 after being detained at customs in El Guasaule, a border checkpoint with Nicaragua, while travelling on a Ticabús vehicles.

SOURCES

Committee for the Defense of Human Rights in Honduras

No. 59

PERSONAL DATA

NAME: NELSON MACKAY CHAVARRIA
NATIONALITY: HONDURAN
PROFESSION: LAWYER

DESCRIPTION OF EVENTS

Detained February 21, 1982, in the village of Triunfo de la Cruz and later taken to Tegucigalpa. Mackay Chavarría was detained along with his family, as well as the family of José Dolores Rodríguez, Cresencio Rodríguez, and José Ernesto Velásquez. They were all taken to the DNI headquarters in Choluteca, where the women were released and the men transferred to DNI headquarters in Tegucigalpa.

ALLEGED RESPONSIBILITY

Honduran Armed Forces

SOURCES

Committee for the Defense of Human Rights in Honduras

U.N. Working Group on Enforced or Involuntary Disappearances

No. 60

PERSONAL DATA

NAME: GUADALUPE CARRILLO COLEMAN (35)
NATIONALITY: HONDURAN
PROFESSION: UNKNOWN

DESCRIPTION OF EVENTS

Detained June 11, 1982 in Puerto Lempira, Department of Gracias a Dios. Sources report that Carrillo Coleman was detained along with his relative, Eduardo Reynaldo Coleman Martínez. Both were taken to cells in FUSEP's headquarters in Puerto Lempira and later transferred to an unknown location.

ALLEGED RESPONSIBILITY

FUSEP

SOURCES

Committee for the Defense of Human Rights in Honduras
Committee of Relatives of the Detained and Disappeared in Honduras
U.N. Working Group on Enforced or Involuntary Disappearances

No. 61

PERSONAL DATA

NAME: EDUARDO COLEMAN MARTINEZ (56)
NATIONALITY: HONDURAN
PROFESSION: UNKNOWN

DESCRIPTION OF EVENTS

Detained June 11, 1982, in Puerto Lempira, Department of Gracias a Dios.

ALLEGED RESPONSIBILITY

FUSEP

SOURCES

Committee for the Defense of Human Rights in Honduras
Committee of Relatives of the Detained and Disappeared in Honduras U.N.
Working Group on Enforced or Involuntary Disappearances

No. 62

PERSONAL DATA

NAME: REYNALDO COLEMAN MARTINEZ (65)
NATIONALITY: HONDURAN
PROFESSION: UNKNOWN

DESCRIPTION OF EVENTS

Detained June 11, 1982, in Puerto Lempira, Department of Gracias a Dios.

ALLEGED RESPONSIBILITY

FUSEP

SOURCES

Committee for the Defense of Human Rights in Honduras
Committee of Relatives of the Detained and Disappeared in Honduras
U.N. Working Group on Enforced or Involuntary Disappearances

No. 63

PERSONAL DATA

NAME: AMADO ESPINOZA PAZ
NATIONALITY: NICARAGUAN
PROFESSION: MECHANIC

DESCRIPTION OF EVENTS

Detained June 12, 1982, in Choluteca

ALLEGED RESPONSIBILITY

DNI; FUSEP; Fermín Macotto, agent of the Immigration Bureau

SOURCES

Committee of Relatives of the Detained and Disappeared in Honduras
Committee for the Defense of Human Rights in Honduras
U.N. Working Group on Enforced or Involuntary Disappearances

No. 64

PERSONAL DATA

NAME: ADAN VILLANUEVA
NATIONALITY: HONDURAN
PROFESSION: MERCHANT

DESCRIPTION OF EVENTS

Detained June 12, 1982, in Choluteca, by DNI and FUSEP agents along with
Amado Espinoza Paz.

ALLEGED RESPONSIBILITY

DNI; FUSEP; Immigration Agent Fermín Macotto

SOURCES

Committee for the Defense of Human Rights in Honduras
Committee of Relatives of the Detained and Disappeared in Honduras U.N.
Working Group on Enforced or Involuntary Disappearances

No. 65

PERSONAL DATA

NAME: HANS ALBERT MADISSON LOPEZ
NATIONALITY: HONDURAN
PROFESSION: STUDENT

DESCRIPTION OF EVENTS

Detained July 8, 1982, in Tegucigalpa's Florencia neighborhood.

ALLEGED RESPONSIBILITY

Honduran Armed Forces

SOURCES

Committee for the Defense of Human Rights in Honduras
U.N. Working Group on Enforced or Involuntary Disappearances

No. 66

PERSONAL DATA

NAME: JOSE SAUL GODINEZ CRUZ (32)
NATIONALITY: HONDURAN
PROFESSION: TEACHER

DESCRIPTION OF EVENTS

Detained July 22, 1982, at 6:30 a.m. in Santa Elena de la Cruz, Choluteca. The Inter-American Court of Human Rights determined that there was sufficient evidence in this case to declare the State of Honduras responsible for the involuntary disappearance of Saúl Godínez and determined that the Honduran Government should pay compensation to his family.

ALLEGED RESPONSIBILITY

Security Forces

SOURCES

Committee of Relatives of the Detained and Disappeared in Honduras U.N. Working Group on Enforced or Involuntary Disappearances Committee for the Defense of Human Rights in Honduras

No. 67

PERSONAL DATA

NAME: JOSE EDUARDO BECERRA LANZA
NATIONALITY: HONDURAN
PROFESSION: STUDENT

DESCRIPTION OF EVENTS

Detained August 1, 1982, at 10:00 p.m. near the Regis Pharmacy in Tegucigalpa. *See* Chapter III for more information on this case.

ALLEGED RESPONSIBILITY

DNI

SOURCES

Amnesty International

Committee for the Defense of Human Rights in Honduras
U.N. Working Group on Enforced or Involuntary Disappearances

No. 68

PERSONAL DATA

NAME: GERMAN PEREZ ALEMAN
NATIONALITY: HONDURAN
PROFESSION: UNION LEADER

DESCRIPTION OF EVENTS

Detained August 18, 1982, in Tegucigalpa by six hooded agents. Pérez Alemán was a leader of the union of maintenance workers in airports and terminals. *See* additional information on this case in Chapter III.

ALLEGED RESPONSIBILITY

Six hooded plainclothesmen; DNI

SOURCES

Committee for the Defense of Human Rights in Honduras

No. 69

PERSONAL DATA

NAME: TERESA DE JESUS SIERRA ALVARENGA (25)
NATIONALITY: HONDURAN
PROFESSION: SECRETARY

DESCRIPTION OF EVENTS

She disappeared August 31, 1982, after being kidnapped by unknown individuals.

SOURCE

Committee for the Defense of Human Rights in Honduras

No. 70

PERSONAL DATA

NAME: RAFAEL ANTONIO PACHECO
NATIONALITY: HONDURAN
PROFESSION: CARITAS RELIGIOUS VOLUNTEER

DESCRIPTION OF EVENTS

Disappeared after being detained September 1, 1982, in Belén, Gualcho, Ocotepeque, by soldiers from the Seventh Battalion.

ALLEGED RESPONSIBILITY

Honduran Armed Forces, Seventh Battalion

SOURCE

Committee for the Defense of Human Rights in Honduras

No. 71

PERSONAL DATA

NAME: HECTOR HERNANDEZ (28)
NATIONALITY: HONDURAN
PROFESSION: MERCHANT

DESCRIPTION OF EVENTS

Detained December 24, 1982, in San Pedro Sula. Hernández was President of the Bemis Handal Textiles Union.

ALLEGED RESPONSIBILITY

DNI

SOURCES

Committee for the Defense of Human Rights in Honduras
Committee of Relatives of the Detained and Disappeared in Honduras U.N.
Working Group on Enforced or Involuntary Disappearances

No. 72

PERSONAL DATA

NAME: JOSE CELESTINO MEDINA (52)
NATIONALITY: HONDURAN
PROFESSION: SHOEMAKER

DESCRIPTION OF EVENTS

Disappeared December 24, 1982, after being captured by unknown suspects.

SOURCE

Committee for the Defense of Human Rights in Honduras

1983

No. 73

PERSONAL DATA

NAME: CASIMIRO CASTELLANOS
NATIONALITY: HONDURAN
PROFESSION: UNKNOWN

DESCRIPTION OF EVENTS

Disappeared after being recruited by the Honduran Armed Forces' "Ojo de Agua" Battalion sometime in 1983.

ALLEGED RESPONSIBILITY

Honduran Armed Forces

SOURCE

Committee for the Defense of Human Rights in Honduras

No. 74

PERSONAL DATA

NAME: PEDRO JOSE AMADOR MEZA
NATIONALITY: HONDURAN
PROFESSION: PEASANT

DESCRIPTION OF EVENTS

Detained January 22, 1983, in Namasigue, department of Choluteca. Sources report that Amador Meza was arrested by a group of men who identified themselves as members of the Nicaraguan Democratic Forces (FDN).

ALLEGED RESPONSIBILITY

Nicaraguan contras operating from Honduras

SOURCES

Committee for the Defense of Human Rights in Honduras
Committee of Relatives of the Detained and Disappeared in Honduras U.N.
Working Group on Enforced or Involuntary Disappearances

No. 75

PERSONAL DATA

NAME: MARIA MARTHA VENTURA GARCIA (26)
NATIONALITY: SALVADORAN
PROFESSION: UNKNOWN

DESCRIPTION OF EVENTS

Detained February 17, 1983, at 5:00 p.m. in Tegucigalpa while travelling to the
city from the border of Ocotepeque. Soldiers took her to an unknown location.

ALLEGED RESPONSIBILITY

Honduran Armed Forces

SOURCES

Committee for the Defense of Human Rights in Honduras
Committee of Relatives of the Detained and Disappeared
U.N. Working Group on Enforced or Involuntary Disappearances

No. 76

PERSONAL DATA

NAME: DOLORES GERALDINA GARCIA ZELAYA (24)

NATIONALITY: HONDURAN
PROFESSION: UNKNOWN

DESCRIPTION OF EVENTS

Disappeared after going out with Edwin Reineri Castro, who was found dead February 25, 1983.

SOURCE

Committee for the Defense of Human Rights in Honduras

No. 77

PERSONAL DATA

NAME: MELBA CACERES MONDRAGON
NATIONALITY: NICARAGUAN
PROFESSION: UNKNOWN

DESCRIPTION OF EVENTS

Detained March 15, 1983, in the hamlet of San Francisco, San Marcos de Colón, Department of Choluteca. Sources report that Cáceres Mondragón was residing legally in Honduras. A former member of Battalion 3-16, Florencio Caballero, stated in a 1987 public hearing before the Inter-American Court of Human Rights that he participated in Cáceres Mondragón's detention and indicated that she was first taken to a clandestine jail near INDUMIL and later transferred to a clandestine detention center, known as "El Manchén." Her whereabouts are still unknown.

ALLEGED RESPONSIBILITY

Honduran Armed Forces

SOURCES

Committee for the Defense of Human Rights in Honduras

Committee of Relatives of the Detained and Disappeared in Honduras U.N. Working Group on Enforced or Involuntary Disappearances

No. 78

PERSONAL DATA

NAME: JOSE MARTINEZ VASQUEZ
NATIONALITY: HONDURAN
PROFESSION: UNKNOWN

DESCRIPTION OF EVENTS

Detained March 17, 1983, in Comayagüela. Source reports that Martínez Vásquez remains disappeared.

ALLEGED RESPONSIBILITY

FUSEP

SOURCES

Committee for the Defense of Human Rights in Honduras
Committee of Relatives of the Detained and Disappeared in Honduras
U.N. Working Group on Enforced or Involuntary Disappearances

No. 79

PERSONAL DATA

NAME: FILIBERTO FLORES ZUÑIGA
NATIONALITY: HONDURAN
PROFESSION: MERCHANT

DESCRIPTION OF EVENTS

Detained April 13, 1983, in Tegucigalpa. Sources report the Flores Zúñiga was detained by five armed men dressed in civilian clothes who were driving a vehicle without license plates.

ALLEGED RESPONSIBILITY

FUSEP

SOURCES

Committee for the Defense of Human Rights in Honduras
U.N. Working Group on Enforced or Involuntary Disappearances

No. 80

PERSONAL DATA

NAME: VICTOR MANUEL TORRES LOPEZ
NATIONALITY: HONDURAN
PROFESSION: HOSPITAL SCHOOL EMPLOYEE

DESCRIPTION OF EVENTS

Disappeared April 13, 1983, while returning home.

SOURCE

Committee for the Defense of Human Rights in Honduras

No. 81

PERSONAL DATA

NAME: LUIS ALONSO ROMERO ORTIZ

NATIONALITY: GUATEMALAN
PROFESSION: UNKNOWN

DESCRIPTION OF EVENTS

Disappeared April 24, 1983.

SOURCE

Committee for the Defense of Human Rights in Honduras

No. 82

PERSONAL DATA

NAME: DANIEL VELASQUEZ NUÑEZ
NATIONALITY: HONDURAN
PROFESSION: MERCHANT

DESCRIPTION OF EVENTS

Detained May 4, 1983, in Santa Cruz de Yojoa, by four hooded and armed FUSEP agents.

ALLEGED RESPONSIBILITY

FUSEP

SOURCES

Committee for the Defense of Human Rights in Honduras
Committee of Relatives of the Detained and Disappeared in Honduras U.N. Working Group on Enforced or Involuntary Disappearances

No. 83

PERSONAL DATA

NAME: JOSE ELOY TORRES BARAHONA
NATIONALITY: HONDURAN
PROFESSION: UNKNOWN

DESCRIPTION OF EVENTS

Detained June 1, 1983, in the Tepeyac neighborhood of San Pedro Sula.

ALLEGED RESPONSIBILITY

Agents dressed in civilian clothes

SOURCES

Committee for the Defense of Human Rights in Honduras
U.N. Working Group on Enforced or Involuntary Disappearances

No. 84

PERSONAL DATA

NAME: VICTOR MANUEL RAMOS
NATIONALITY: HONDURAN
PROFESSION: UNKNOWN

DESCRIPTION OF EVENTS

Detained June 10, 1983, in Tegucigalpa by armed men who identified themselves as DNI agents.

ALLEGED RESPONSIBILITY

DNI

SOURCES

Committee for the Defense of Human Rights in Honduras
Committee of Relatives of the Detained and Disappeared in Honduras U.N.
Working Group on Enforced or Involuntary Disappearances

No. 85

PERSONAL DATA

NAME: JOSE AMILCAR MARADIAGA (43)
NATIONALITY: HONDURAN
PROFESSION: PEASANT

DESCRIPTION OF EVENTS

Disappeared July 1, 1983, reportedly kidnapped by members of the Nicaraguan
contras in Jacaleapa, Department of El Paraíso.

SOURCE

Committee for the Defense of Human Rights in Honduras

No. 86

PERSONAL DATA

NAME: MARCO ANTONIO MARIN AGUILAR (19)
NATIONALITY: HONDURAN
PROFESSION: STUDENT

DESCRIPTION OF EVENTS

Detained in August 1983, in Río Patuca, Olancho, while travelling from
Nicaragua to Honduras. Marín Aguilar was a member of an armed group that
entered Honduras from Nicaragua, according to testimony given by Florencio
Caballero to the Inter-American Court of Human Rights.

ALLEGED RESPONSIBILITY

Honduran Armed Forces, Lt. Col. Ricardo Luque Portillo, Maj. Lima Bueso, Maj. Andino Benítez and Col. Hernández Chávez; Honduran Air Force helicopter and plane also used.

SOURCES

Marco Antonio Marín (father)
U.N. Working Group on Enforced or Involuntary Disappearances

No. 87

PERSONAL DATA

NAME: RAMON ADONAY BUSTILLO JIMENEZ
NATIONALITY: HONDURAN
PROFESSION: TRADE EXPERT, PUBLIC ACCOUNTANT

DESCRIPTION OF EVENTS

Disappeared September 9, 1983.

SOURCES

Committee for the Defense of Human Rights in Honduras

No. 88

PERSONAL DATA

NAME: PABLO ROBERTO MUNGUIA
NATIONALITY: HONDURAN
PROFESSION: UNKNOWN

DESCRIPTION OF EVENTS

Disappeared September 28, 1983 after being captured by DNI agents
investigating robbery in his house.

ALLEGED RESPONSIBILITY

DNI

SOURCE

Committee for the Defense of Human Rights in Honduras

No. 89

PERSONAL DATA

NAME: MARIO MEJIA MATEO (22)
NATIONALITY: HONDURAN
PROFESSION: NURSE

DESCRIPTION OF EVENTS

Detained October 1, 1983, along with a co-worker, José Melanio Valle
Alvarado, in Danlí, Department of El Paraíso, by members of the FDN.

ALLEGED RESPONSIBILITY

FDN

SOURCES

Committee for the Defense of Human Rights in Honduras
Committee of Relatives of the Detained and Disappeared in Honduras
U.N. Working Group on Enforced or Involuntary Disappearances

No. 90

PERSONAL DATA

NAME: JOSE MELANIO VALLE ALVARADO (20)
NATIONALITY: HONDURAN
PROFESSION: NURSE

DESCRIPTION OF EVENTS

Detained October 1, 1983, in Danlí, Department of El Paraíso, along with Mario Mejía Mateos by members of the FDN.

ALLEGED RESPONSIBILITY

FDN

SOURCES

Committee for the Defense of Human Rights in Honduras
Committee of Relatives of the Detained and Disappeared in Honduras U.N. Working Group on Enforced or Involuntary Disappearances

No. 91

PERSONAL DATA

NAME: JAMES FRANCISCO CARNEY (FATHER GUADALUPE)
NATIONALITY: AMERICAN (U.S.)
PROFESSION: PRIEST

DESCRIPTION OF EVENTS

Disappeared after being captured, along with Dr. Reyes Mata, in the beginning of December 1983, after entering the country from Nicaragua with a guerrilla column.

ALLEGED RESPONSIBILITY

Honduran Armed Forces

SOURCE

Committee for the Defense of Human Rights in Honduras

No. 92

PERSONAL DATA

NAME: JUAN BAUTISTA CANALES H.
NATIONALITY: HONDURAN
PROFESSION: ELECTRICIAN

DESCRIPTION OF EVENTS

Detained December 15, 1983, at 7:15 p.m. in the Satélite neighborhood in San Pedro Sula. Canales was detained by three agents dressed in civilian clothes and driving a Toyota van, license plate P-3195.

ALLEGED RESPONSIBILITY

Three plainclothesmen

SOURCES

Committee for the Defense of Human Rights in Honduras
U.N. Working Group on Enforced or Involuntary Disappearances

1984

No. 93

PERSONAL DATA

NAME: MARCELINO MONCADA BUSTAMANTE
NATIONALITY: HONDURAN
PROFESSION: UNKNOWN

DESCRIPTION OF EVENTS

Detained February 18, 1984, at 8:00 a.m. in front of the Guaymuras radio station in Santa Clara, Department of Paraíso, by members of the Nicaraguan contras. One of his captors was named Armando (Commander Toño).

ALLEGED RESPONSIBILITY

Nicaraguan contras, Commander "Toño"

SOURCES

Committee for the Defense of Human Rights in Honduras
Central American Commission for the Defense of Human Rights
U.N. Working Group on Enforced or Involuntary Disappearances

No. 94

PERSONAL DATA

NAME: GUSTAVO ADOLFO MORALES FUNES
NATIONALITY: HONDURAN
PROFESSION: ECONOMIST

DESCRIPTION OF EVENTS

Detained March 18, 1984, on La Paz Avenue in Tegucigalpa by six armed men dressed in civilian clothes.

ALLEGED RESPONSIBILITY

FUSEP

SOURCES

Committee for the Defense of Human Rights in Honduras
Amnesty International
U.N. Working Group on Enforced or Involuntary Disappearances

No. 95

PERSONAL DATA

NAME: ROLANDO VINDEL GONZALEZ
NATIONALITY: HONDURAN
PROFESSION: UNION LEADER

DESCRIPTION OF EVENTS

Detained March 18, 1984, in Tegucigalpa. Vindel González was president of the
electrical workers union.

ALLEGED RESPONSIBILITY

FUSEP

SOURCES

Committee for the Defense of Human Rights in Honduras
Amnesty International
U.N. Working Group on Enforced or Involuntary Disappearances

No. 96

PERSONAL DATA

NAME: FRANCISCO GARCIA
NATIONALITY: HONDURAN
PROFESSION: JOURNALIST

DESCRIPTION OF EVENTS

Detained July 9, 1984, in Nahuaterique, Department of La Paz.

ALLEGED RESPONSIBILITY

Honduran Armed Forces

SOURCES

Committee for the Defense of Human Rights in Honduras
U.N. Working Group on Enforced or Involuntary Disappearances

No. 97

PERSONAL DATA

NAME: FRANCISCO OSORTO (30)
NATIONALITY: HONDURAN
PROFESSION: PEASANT

DESCRIPTION OF EVENTS

Detained July 9, 1984, near Cerro El Alumbrador, 500 meters from the
Salvadoran border, by soldiers from the Honduran Army.

ALLEGED RESPONSIBILITY

Honduran Armed Forces

SOURCES

Committee for the Defense of Human Rights in Honduras
U.N. Working Group on Enforced or Involuntary Disappearances

No. 98

PERSONAL DATA

NAME: ALBERTO GARCIA
NATIONALITY: HONDURAN
PROFESSION: UNKNOWN

DESCRIPTION OF EVENTS

Detained July 9, 1984 in Nahuaterique, Department of La Paz.

ALLEGED RESPONSIBILITY

Honduran Armed Forces

SOURCE

Committee for the Defense of Human Rights in Honduras

No. 99

PERSONAL DATA

NAME: ELSA MARINA PERDOMO (10)
NATIONALITY: HONDURAN
PROFESSION: UNKNOWN

DESCRIPTION OF EVENTS

Detained August 12, 1984 in Santa Bárbara, Villa Los Planes by men in a green pickup truck. Sources report that she was kidnapped along with her sister

Rosaura Perdomo (12) close to their home. According to neighbors who witnessed the events, the two girls were forced to get into the truck by a man who threatened them with a gun. A spokesperson for the DNI indicated that the girls left their home because they were being abused by their father.

ALLEGED RESPONSIBILITY

Agents dressed in civilian clothing driving a green pickup truck

SOURCES

Committee for the Defense of Human Rights in Honduras
DNI

No. 100

PERSONAL DATA

NAME: JUAN ALBERTO VILLEDA
NATIONALITY: HONDURAN
PROFESSION: PEASANT

DESCRIPTION OF EVENTS

Disappeared September 25, 1984.

SOURCE

Committee for the Defense of Human Rights in Honduras

No. 101

PERSONAL DATA

NAME: LUIS RAMON BLANDON ZEAS (22)
NATIONALITY: NICARAGUAN
PROFESSION: TEACHER

DESCRIPTION OF EVENTS

Detained September 28, 1984, in the locality of Las Cruces, in the city of Pantasma, Department of Jinotega, Nicaragua by guerrillas under the Diriangen Region command of the FDN, based in Honduras.

ALLEGED RESPONSIBILITY

FDN

SOURCES

National Commission for the Promotion and Protection of Human Rights, Managua, Nicaragua
Amnesty International
Americas Watch [now Human Rights Watch/Americas]
U.N. Working Group on Enforced or Involuntary Disappearances

No. 102

PERSONAL DATA

NAME: ELMAN LUIS CORTES SIEZA (20)
NATIONALITY: NICARAGUAN
PROFESSION: TEACHER

DESCRIPTION OF EVENTS

Detained September 28, 1984, at 4:00 p.m. in Las Cruces, Pantasma, Department of Jinotega, Nicaragua, and taken to Honduras.

ALLEGED RESPONSIBILITY

FDN

SOURCES

National Commission for the Promotion and Protection of Human Rights, Managua, Nicaragua
Amnesty International
Americas Watch [now Human Rights Watch/Americas]
U.N. Working Group on Enforced or Involuntary Disappearances

No. 103

PERSONAL DATA

NAME: MARCIA MERCEDES CHAMORRO MORALES (18)
NATIONALITY: NICARAGUAN
PROFESSION: TEACHER

DESCRIPTION OF EVENTS

Detained October 5, 1984, at 6:00 a.m. in Bocaycito, Nicaragua. Sources report that Chamorro Morales, a volunteer teacher in Bocaycito, Jinotega, Nicaragua, was kidnapped while she was travelling with her mother from Jinotega to Bocaycito by a group of contras led by a commander with the nickname "Black Hand" (*Mano Negra*). Chamorro Morales was reportedly taken toward Honduras.

ALLEGED RESPONSIBILITY

Nicaraguan contras operating from Honduras; Contra commander "Black Hand"

SOURCES

National Commission for the Promotion and Protection of Human Rights, Managua, Nicaragua
Amnesty International
Americas Watch [now Human Rights Watch/Americas]
U.N. Working Group on Enforced or Involuntary Disappearances

No. 104

PERSONAL DATA

NAME: ESTANISLAO VASQUEZ M.
NATIONALITY: HONDURAN
PROFESSION: DAY LABORER

DESCRIPTION OF EVENTS

Detained October 22, 1984, on the Santa Elena plantation, Department of La Paz. Vásquez was detained at his place of employment along with other people who the Armed Forces described as militants of the "Lorenzo Zelaya" Revolutionary Forces.

ALLEGED RESPONSIBILITY

Honduran Armed Forces

SOURCES

Committee for the Defense of Human Rights in Honduras
U.N. Working Group on Enforced or Involuntary Disappearances

No. 105

PERSONAL DATA

NAME: JOAQUIN
NATIONALITY: HONDURAN
PROFESSION: LABORER

DESCRIPTION OF EVENTS

Disappeared October 22, 1984, along with Estanislao Vásquez M.

SOURCE

Committee for the Defense of Human Rights in Honduras

No. 106

PERSONAL DATA

NAME: REYNALDO CACERES LOPEZ (16)
NATIONALITY: HONDURAN
PROFESSION: UNKNOWN

DESCRIPTION OF EVENTS

Detained October 28, 1984, in the cemetery in San Pedro Sula, Department of Cortés. Cáceres López's detention was witnessed by MARCO TULIO JIMENEZ.

ALLEGED RESPONSIBILITY

Two armed plainclothesmen

SOURCES

Committee for the Defense of Human Rights in Honduras
U.N. Working Group on Enforced or Involuntary Disappearances

No. 107

PERSONAL DATA

NAME: ESTANISLAO MARTINEZ LOPEZ (17)
NATIONALITY: HONDURAN
PROFESSION: PEASANT

DESCRIPTION OF EVENTS

Detained October 31, 1984, in Quiscamote, Santa Elena, Department of La Paz.

ALLEGED RESPONSIBILITY

Treasury Police: Sergeant with the nickname "Gado," Sgt. Tiburcio Domínguez, Cpl. Carlos Martínez and Cpl. Santos Martínez Gómez.

SOURCES

Committee for the Defense of Human Rights in Honduras
U.N. Working Group on Enforced or Involuntary Disappearances

No. 108

PERSONAL DATA

NAME: MARITZA CUBILLO MOLINA (31)
NATIONALITY: NICARAGUAN
PROFESSION: TEACHER

DESCRIPTION OF EVENTS

Detained November 4, 1984 at 4:00 a.m. in Wiwili, Department of Jinotega, Nicaragua, and taken to Honduras.

ALLEGED RESPONSIBILITY

Nicaraguan contras operating from Honduras

SOURCES

Amnesty International
Americas Watch [now Human Rights Watch/Americas]
National Commission for the Promotion and Protection of Human Rights, Managua, Nicaragua
U.N. Working Group on Enforced or Involuntary Disappearances

No. 109

PERSONAL DATA

NAME: JOSE ISABEL SALGADO (43)
NATIONALITY: HONDURAN
PROFESSION: DRIVER

DESCRIPTION OF EVENTS

Disappeared November 20, 1984, while travelling in the southern part of the country.

SOURCE

Committee for the Defense of Human Rights in Honduras

No. 110

PERSONAL DATA

NAME: JOSE EDUARDO LOPEZ (38)
NATIONALITY: HONDURAN
PROFESSION: STUDENT

DESCRIPTION OF EVENTS

Detained December 24, 1984 in San Pedro Sula. López had been the past president of the Cortés regional section of the Committee for the Defense of Human Rights in Honduras.

ALLEGED RESPONSIBILITY

DNI

SOURCES

Committee for the Defense of Human Rights in Honduras
U.N. Working Group on Enforced or Involuntary Disappearances

1985

No. 111

PERSONAL DATA

NAME: ROSE NELLY MATAMOROS (22)
NATIONALITY: HONDURAN
PROFESSION: UNKNOWN

DESCRIPTION OF EVENTS

Disappeared in January 1985. Last seen accompanied by Santos Martínez, believed to be a DNI agent.

SOURCE

Committee for the Defense of Human Rights in Honduras

No. 112

PERSONAL DATA

NAME: JESUS REYES ESCOBAR (59)
NATIONALITY: HONDURAN
PROFESSION: UNKNOWN

DESCRIPTION OF EVENTS

Detained March 24, 1985, in La Virtud, Department of Lempira.

ALLEGED RESPONSIBILITY

Honduran Armed Forces

SOURCES

Committee for the Defense of Human Rights in Honduras
U.N. Working Group on Enforced or Involuntary Disappearances

No. 113

PERSONAL DATA

NAME: ROLANDO ISMAEL AMAYA HERNANDEZ
NATIONALITY: HONDURAN
PROFESSION: PAINTER

DESCRIPTION OF EVENTS

Detained June 1, 1985, at 12:00 in front of the Olivera Radio repair shop in the
Flores de Juticalpa neighborhood, Department of Olancho. Sources report that
Amaya Hernández was kidnapped by four men, one of whom was identified by
witnesses as HUMBERTO SARMIENTO BONILLA.

ALLEGED RESPONSIBILITY

Four agents dressed as civilians, denounced as collaborators of the DNI

SOURCES

Committee for the Defense of Human Rights in Honduras
U.N. Working Group on Enforced or Involuntary Disappearances

No. 114

PERSONAL DATA

NAME: RIGOBERTO SANCHEZ (36)
NATIONALITY: HONDURAN
PROFESSION: DRIVER

DESCRIPTION OF EVENTS

Disappeared June 5, 1985.

SOURCE

Committee for the Defense of Human Rights in Honduras

No. 115

PERSONAL DATA

NAME: LUIS AGUILAR OLIVAS (15)
NATIONALITY: NICARAGUAN
PROFESSION: PEASANT

DESCRIPTION OF EVENTS

Arrested September 19, 1985, along with 21 other people, in Las Lajitas, Department of Chinandega, Nicaragua, and later taken to Honduras.

ALLEGED RESPONSIBILITY

Nicaraguan contras operating from Honduras

SOURCES

National Commission for the Promotion and Protection of Human Rights, Managua, Nicaragua
U.N. Working Group on Enforced or Involuntary Disappearances.

No. 116

PERSONAL DATA

NAME: REYNALDO AGUILAR RIVERA (25)
NATIONALITY: NICARAGUAN
PROFESSION: PEASANT

DESCRIPTION OF EVENTS

Arrested September 19, 1985, in Las Lajitas, Department of Chinandega, Nicaragua.

ALLEGED RESPONSIBILITY

Nicaraguan contras operating from Honduras

SOURCES

National Commission for the Promotion and Protection of Human Rights, Managua, Nicaragua
U.N. Working Group on Enforced or Involuntary Disappearances

No. 117

PERSONAL DATA

NAME: SANTOS AMADOR MEDINA (25)
NATIONALITY: HONDURAN
PROFESSION: PEASANT

DESCRIPTION OF EVENTS

Detained September 19, 1985, in El Nancital, Department of Chinandega, Nicaragua.

ALLEGED RESPONSIBILITY

Nicaraguan contras operating from Honduras

SOURCES

National Commission for the Protection and Promotion of Human Rights, Managua, Nicaragua
U.N. Working Group on Enforced or Involuntary Disappearances

No. 118

PERSONAL DATA

NAME: URSULO ARCE ROMERO
NATIONALITY: NICARAGUAN
PROFESSION: PEASANT

DESCRIPTION OF EVENTS

Detained September 19, 1985, in Pado Hondo, Department of Chinandega, Nicaragua.

ALLEGED RESPONSIBILITY

Nicaraguan contras operating from Honduras

SOURCES

National Commission for the Protection and Promotion of Human Rights, Managua, Nicaragua
U.N. Working Group on Enforced or Involuntary Disappearances

No. 119

PERSONAL DATA

NAME: OSCAR GARACHE ESPINOZA (28)
NATIONALITY: NICARAGUAN

PROFESSION: PEASANT

DESCRIPTION OF EVENTS

Detained September 19, 1985, in El Nancital, Department of Chinandega, Nicaragua, and taken by his captors to Honduras.

No. 120

PERSONAL DATA

NAME: NEMECIO MARADIAGA MARTINEZ (26)
NATIONALITY: NICARAGUAN
PROFESSION: PEASANT

DESCRIPTION OF EVENTS

Detained September 19, 1985, in Fragua, Department of Chinandega, Nicaragua, by a group of contras and later taken to Honduras.

ALLEGED RESPONSIBILITY

Nicaraguan contras operating from Honduras

SOURCES

National Commission for the Promotion and Protection of Human Rights, Managua, Nicaragua
U.N. Working Group on Enforced or Involuntary Disappearances

No. 121

PERSONAL DATA

NAME: SABAS MARTINEZ (40)
NATIONALITY: NICARAGUAN
PROFESSION: PEASANT

DESCRIPTION OF EVENTS

Detained September 19, 1985, in Fragua, Department of Chinandega, Nicaragua, by a group of Nicaraguan contras and later brought to Honduras.

ALLEGED RESPONSIBILITY

Nicaraguan contras operating from Honduras

SOURCES

National Commission for the Promotion and Protection of Human Rights, Managua, Nicaragua
U.N. Working Group on Enforced or Involuntary Disappearances

No. 122

PERSONAL DATA

NAME: LUGERIO MEDINA OSORIO (12)
NATIONALITY: NICARAGUAN
PROFESSION: PEASANT

DESCRIPTION OF EVENTS

Detained September 19, 1985, in El Nancital, Department of Chinandega, Nicaragua, by a group of Nicaraguan contras and later brought to Honduras.

ALLEGED RESPONSIBILITY

Nicaraguan contras operating from Honduras

SOURCES

National Commission for the Promotion and Protection of Human Rights, Managua, Nicaragua
U.N. Working Group on Enforced or Involuntary Disappearances

No. 123

PERSONAL DATA

NAME: CRISTINO MEDINA SANCHEZ
NATIONALITY: NICARAGUAN
PROFESSION: PEASANT

DESCRIPTION OF EVENTS

Detained September 19, 1985, in El Zapote, Department of Chinandega, Nicaragua by a group of Nicaraguan contras and later brought to Honduras.

ALLEGED RESPONSIBILITY

Nicaraguan contras operating from Honduras

SOURCES

National Commission for the Promotion and Protection of Human Rights, Managua, Nicaragua
U.N. Working Group on Enforced or Involuntary Disappearances

No. 124

PERSONAL DATA

NAME: MARVIN MEDINA SANCHEZ (25)
NATIONALITY: NICARAGUAN
PROFESSION: PEASANT

DESCRIPTION OF EVENTS

Detained September 19, 1985, in El Zapote, Department of Chinandega, Nicaragua by a group of Nicaraguan contras and later brought to Honduras

ALLEGED RESPONSIBILITY

Nicaraguan contras operating from Honduras

SOURCES

National Commission for the Promotion and Protection of Human Rights, Managua, Nicaragua
U.N. Working Group on Enforced or Involuntary Disappearances

No. 125

PERSONAL DATA

NAME: VICTORINO MEDINA SANCHEZ (45)
NATIONALITY: NICARAGUAN
PROFESSION: PEASANT

DESCRIPTION OF EVENTS

Detained September 19, 1985, in El Zapote, Department of Chinandega, Nicaragua by a group of Nicaraguan contras and later brought to Honduras.

ALLEGED RESPONSIBILITY

Nicaraguan contras operating from Honduras

SOURCES

National Commission for the Promotion and Protection of Human Rights, Managua, Nicaragua
U.N. Working Group on Enforced or Involuntary Disappearances

No. 126

PERSONAL DATA

NAME: SANTIR OSORIO MEDINA (32)
NATIONALITY: NICARAGUAN
PROFESSION: PEASANT

DESCRIPTION OF EVENTS

Kidnapped September 19, 1985, in the Department of Chinandega, Nicaragua, by a group of Nicaraguan contras operating from Honduras. She was later taken to Honduras.

ALLEGED RESPONSIBILITY

Nicaraguan contras operating from Honduras

SOURCES

National Commission for the Promotion and Protection of Human Rights, Managua, Nicaragua
U.N. Working Group on Enforced or Involuntary Disappearances

No. 127

PERSONAL DATA

NAME: RAFAEL PINEDA SANCHEZ (45)
NATIONALITY: NICARAGUAN
PROFESSION: PEASANT

DESCRIPTION OF EVENTS

Detained September 19, 1985, in El Nancital, Department of Chinandega, Nicaragua, by a group of Nicaraguan contras and later taken to Honduras.

ALLEGED RESPONSIBILITY

Nicaraguan contras operating from Honduras

SOURCES

National Commission for the Promotion and Protection of Human Rights, Managua, Nicaragua
U.N. Working Group on Enforced or Involuntary Disappearances

No. 128

PERSONAL DATA

NAME: MARTIN RIVERA MARTINEZ (29)
NATIONALITY: NICARAGUAN
PROFESSION: PEASANT

DESCRIPTION OF EVENTS

Detained September 19, 1985 in La Bolsa, Department of Chinandega, Nicaragua, by a group of Nicaraguan contras and later taken to Honduras.

ALLEGED RESPONSIBILITY

Nicaraguan contras operating from Honduras

SOURCES

National Commission for the Promotion and Protection of Human Rights, Managua, Nicaragua
U.N. Working Group on Enforced or Involuntary Disappearances

No. 129

PERSONAL DATA

NAME: MANUEL RODRIGUEZ BENAVIDES (44)
NATIONALITY: NICARAGUAN
PROFESSION: PEASANT

DESCRIPTION OF EVENTS

Detained September 19, 1985, in La Bolsa, Department of Chinandega, Nicaragua, by a group of Nicaraguan contras and later taken to Honduras.

ALLEGED RESPONSIBILITY

Nicaraguan contras operating from Honduras

SOURCES

National Commission for the Promotion and Protection of Human Rights, Managua, Nicaragua
U.N. Working Group on Enforced or Involuntary Disappearances

No. 130

PERSONAL DATA

NAME: SILVANO RODRIGUEZ PEREZ (18)
NATIONALITY: NICARAGUAN
PROFESSION: PEASANT

DESCRIPTION OF EVENTS

Detained September 19, 1985, in La Flor, Department of Chinandega, Nicaragua, by a group of Nicaraguan contras and later taken to Honduras.

ALLEGED RESPONSIBILITY

Nicaraguan contras operating from Honduras

SOURCES

Committee for the Defense of Human Rights in Honduras
U.N. Working Group on Enforced or Involuntary Disappearances

No. 131

PERSONAL DATA

NAME: VALENTIN SANCHEZ SIERRA (19)
NATIONALITY: NICARAGUAN
PROFESSION: PEASANT

DESCRIPTION OF EVENTS

Detained September 19, 1985, in El Nancital, Department of Chinandega, Nicaragua, by a group of Nicaraguan contras and later taken to Honduras.

ALLEGED RESPONSIBILITY

Nicaraguan contras operating from Honduras

SOURCES

National Commission for the Promotion and Protection of Human Rights, Managua, Nicaragua
U.N. Working Group on Enforced or Involuntary Disappearances

No. 132

PERSONAL DATA

NAME: ADIN SORIANO ZELAYA (26)
NATIONALITY: NICARAGUAN
PROFESSION: PEASANT

DESCRIPTION OF EVENTS

Detained September 19, 1985, in El Espino, Department of Chinandega, Nicaragua, by a group of Nicaraguan contras and later taken to Honduras.

ALLEGED RESPONSIBILITY

Nicaraguan contras operating from Honduras

SOURCES

National Commission for the Promotion and Protection of Human Rights, Managua, Nicaragua
U.N. Working Group on Enforced or Involuntary Disappearances

No. 133

PERSONAL DATA

NAME: JOSE ADALBERTO VARELA ORDOÑEZ (22)
NATIONALITY: NICARAGUAN
PROFESSION: PEASANT

DESCRIPTION OF EVENTS

Detained September 19, 1985, in Paso Hondo, Department of Chinandega, Nicaragua, by a group of Nicaraguan contras and later taken to Honduras.

ALLEGED RESPONSIBILITY

Nicaraguan contras operating from Honduras

SOURCES

National Commission for the Promotion and Protection of Human Rights, Managua, Nicaragua
U.N. Working Group on Enforced or Involuntary Disappearances

No. 134

PERSONAL DATA

NAME: MANUEL ARISTIDES VARELA ORDONEZ (18)
NATIONALITY: NICARAGUAN
PROFESSION: PEASANT

DESCRIPTION OF EVENTS

Detained September 19, 1985, in Paso Hondo, Department of Chinandega, Nicaragua, by a group of Nicaraguan contras and later taken to Honduras.

ALLEGED RESPONSIBILITY

Nicaraguan contras operating from Honduras

SOURCES

National Commission for the Promotion and Protection of Human Rights, Managua, Nicaragua
U.N. Working Group on Enforced or Involuntary Disappearances

No. 135

PERSONAL DATA

NAME: ELISEO PADILLA
NATIONALITY: HONDURAN
PROFESSION: JUDGE

DESCRIPTION OF EVENTS

Disappeared after being detained September 26, 1985, along with his son Constantino Padilla, by police in Santa Rita, Santa Bárbara.

ALLEGED RESPONSIBILITY

DNI

SOURCE

Committee for the Defense of Human Rights in Honduras

No. 136

PERSONAL DATA

NAME: CONSTANTINO PADILLA
NATIONALITY: HONDURAN
PROFESSION: UNKNOWN

DESCRIPTION OF EVENTS

Disappeared along with his father, Eliseo Padilla, September 26, 1985 in Santa Rita, Santa Bárbara.

ALLEGED RESPONSIBILITY

DNI

SOURCE

Committee for the Defense of Human Rights in Honduras

1986

No. 137

PERSONAL DATA

NAME: JUAN CARLOS NIETO
NATIONALITY: HONDURAN
PROFESSION: MERCHANT

DESCRIPTION OF EVENTS

Detained March 16, 1986, at 8:00 p.m. in Intibucá, Honduras. Source reports that several individuals witnessed Nieto's arrest, which was carried out by members of the Tenth Battalion, based in Marcala, La Paz.

ALLEGED RESPONSIBILITY

Honduran Armed Forces, Tenth Battalion

SOURCES

Committee for the Defense of Human Rights in Honduras
U.N. Working Group on Enforced or Involuntary Disappearances

No. 138

PERSONAL DATA

NAME: NOEMI ORDOÑEZ FLORES
NATIONALITY: HONDURAN
PROFESSION: MERCHANT

DESCRIPTION OF EVENTS

Detained March 16, 1986, in San Isidro, Department of Intibucá. Several people witnessed her arrest, which was effectuated by members of the Tenth Battalion based in Marcala, La Paz.

ALLEGED RESPONSIBILITY

Honduran Armed Forces, Tenth Battalion

SOURCES

Committee for the Defense of Human Rights in Honduras
U.N. Working Group on Enforced or Involuntary Disappearances

No. 139

PERSONAL DATA

NAME: SANDRA LIZETH GALLARDO ROSALES (28)
NATIONALITY: HONDURAN
PROFESSION: SECRETARY

DESCRIPTION OF EVENTS

Disappeared June 20, 1986. Last seen in the company of U.S. citizens Jim Boesh and West Morris, who were accused by Gallardo Rosales's father of being agents of the U.S. Embassy. The U.S. Embassy later indicated that the two men were communication specialists working for the U.S. Defense Department and assigned to the radar station in La Mola, Francisco Morazán.

SOURCE

Committee for the Defense of Human Rights in Honduras

No. 140

PERSONAL DATA

NAME: CORINA CRUZ PINEDA (17)
NATIONALITY: HONDURAN
PROFESSION: UNKNOWN

DESCRIPTION OF EVENTS

Detained October 8, 1986, in the village of El Castaño, Department of Intibucá. Sources report that Cruz Pineda was detained October 7, 1986, by Lt. Vaquero of the Fifth Infantry Battalion and released the same day. The following day, she was detained again by the same lieutenant and taken to San Antonio de Intibucá. She was transferred to the headquarters of the Marcala Battalion on October 10, 1986. Her whereabouts have been unknown since then.

ALLEGED RESPONSIBILITY

Honduran Armed Forces; Lt. Vaquero

SOURCES

Committee for the Defense of Human Rights in Honduras
U.N. Working Group on Enforced or Involuntary Disappearances

1987

No. 141

PERSONAL DATA

NAME: MARIA CANDELARIA MUNOZ (32)
NATIONALITY: HONDURAN
PROFESSION: STUDENT

DESCRIPTION OF EVENTS

Disappeared in 1987 from the grounds of the Technical Institute for Business Administration (*Instituto Tecnológico de Administración de Empresas*).

SOURCE

Committee for the Defense of Human Rights in Honduras

No. 142

PERSONAL DATA

NAME: ISRAEL BONILLA (24)
NATIONALITY: HONDURAN
PROFESSION: FORMER FUSEP AGENT

DESCRIPTION OF EVENTS

Disappeared in 1987.

SOURCES

Committee for the Defense of Human Rights in Honduras

No. 143

PERSONAL DATA

NAME: ISRAEL RODRIGUEZ RUBIO
NATIONALITY: HONDURAN
PROFESSION: TRADE EXPERT, PUBLIC ACCOUNTANT

DESCRIPTION OF EVENTS

Disappeared January 21, 1987, in Tegucigalpa.

SOURCE

Committee for the Defense of Human Rights in Honduras

No. 144

PERSONAL DATA

NAME: LUIS ANTONIO RODRIGUEZ (22)
NATIONALITY: HONDURAN
PROFESSION: UNKNOWN

DESCRIPTION OF EVENTS

Disappeared March 2, 1987, in Tegucigalpa.

SOURCE

Committee for the Defense of Human Rights in Honduras

No. 145

PERSONAL DATA

NAME: SAMY LEONEL SANCHEZ (20)

NATIONALITY: HONDURAN
PROFESSION: UNKNOWN

DESCRIPTION OF EVENTS

Disappeared March 11, 1987, according to a complaint made by his parents.

SOURCES

Committee for the Defense of Human Rights in Honduras

No. 146

PERSONAL DATA

NAME: PEDRO SEBASTIAN LOPEZ (38)
NATIONALITY: HONDURAN
PROFESSION: MERCHANT

DESCRIPTION OF EVENTS

Disappeared March 15, 1987.

SOURCES

Committee for the Defense of Human Rights in Honduras

No. 147

PERSONAL DATA

NAME: MARIA DE JESUS ANDRADE DIAZ (30)
NATIONALITY: HONDURAN
PROFESSION: HOUSE WIFE

DESCRIPTION OF EVENTS

The wife of Pedro Sebastián López (Case No. 146), she disappeared on March 15 or 16, 1987, after going to the police station to look for her husband who had been detained.

SOURCES

Committee for the Defense of Human Rights in Honduras

No. 148

PERSONAL DATA

NAME: COSME OSORIO MURILLO (30)
NATIONALITY: HONDURAN
PROFESSION: MARINE TECHNICIAN AND LABORER

DESCRIPTION OF EVENTS

Disappeared March 25, 1987, in San Pedro Sula.

SOURCES

Committee for the Defense of Human Rights in Honduras

No. 149

PERSONAL DATA

NAME: MARTIN ANTONIO LAZO MURILLO (22)
NATIONALITY: HONDURAN
PROFESSION: UNKNOWN

DESCRIPTION OF EVENTS

Last seen in April 1987.

SOURCE

Committee for the Defense of Human Rights in Honduras

No. 150

NAME: JOSE ALBERTO CASTRO (38)
NATIONALITY: HONDURAN
PROFESSION: MECHANIC

DESCRIPTION OF EVENTS

Disappeared April 25, 1987, after leaving his workshop.

SOURCE

Committee for the Defense of Human Rights in Honduras

No. 151

PERSONAL DATA

NAME: JOSE ANTONIO ALVAREZ AVILA (22)
NATIONALITY: HONDURAN
PROFESSION: LABORER

DESCRIPTION OF EVENTS

Disappeared April 30, 1987, in Tegucigalpa.

SOURCE

Committee for the Defense of Human Rights in Honduras

No. 152

PERSONAL DATA

NAME: JULIO LOPEZ (25)
NATIONALITY: HONDURAN
PROFESSION: LABORER

DESCRIPTION OF EVENTS

Disappeared May 10, 1987.

SOURCE

Committee for the Defense of Human Rights in Honduras

No. 153

PERSONAL DATA

NAME: MANUEL ANTONIO GONZALEZ SANCHEZ (18)
NATIONALITY: NICARAGUAN
PROFESSION: UNKNOWN

DESCRIPTION OF EVENTS

Detained June 19, 1987, at 8:00 a.m. in Cano de la Cruz, Cerro/Milambe, Department of Jinotega, Nicaragua, by a group of contras and later taken to Honduras.

ALLEGED RESPONSIBILITY

Five hundred members of the Nicaraguan contras operating from Honduras

SOURCES

Committee for the Defense of Human Rights in Honduras
Socorro Escobar (mother)

U.N. Working Group on Enforced or Involuntary Disappearances

No. 154

PERSONAL DATA

NAME: JOSE ANTONIO HERNANDEZ PERNUDY (23)
NATIONALITY: NICARAGUAN
PROFESSION: UNKNOWN

DESCRIPTION OF EVENTS

Detained June 19, 1987, at 8:00 a.m. in Cano de la Cruz, Cerro/Milambe, Department of Jinotega, Nicaragua. Sources report that about 500 Nicaraguan contras based in Honduras had entered Nicaragua, kidnapping eight young Nicaraguans, all of whom were completing their military service, and forcibly taking them to Honduras. This case is related to the cases of Domingo José Escobar Sánchez, Juan José López Venegas, Richard Lugo, Melvin Humberto Thom Morán, Eliazar Paguaga Mayorga and Franklin Sánchez Jiménez.

ALLEGED RESPONSIBILITY

Five hundred members of the Nicaraguan contras operating from Honduras

SOURCES

Socorro Escobar (mother)
U.N. Working Group on Enforced or Involuntary Disappearances

No. 155

PERSONAL DATA

NAME: JUAN JOSE LOPEZ VENEGAS (22)
NATIONALITY: NICARAGUAN
PROFESSION: UNKNOWN

DESCRIPTION OF EVENTS

Detained June 19, 1987, at 8:00 a.m. in Cano de la Cruz, Cerro/Milambe, Department of Jinotega, Nicaragua by a group of about 500 contras based in Honduras who had entered Nicaragua. This case is related to the cases of Domingo José Escobar Sánchez, José Antonio Hernández Pernudy, Richard Lugo, Melvin Humberto Thom Morán, Eliazar Paguaga Mayorga and Franklin Sánchez Jiménez.

ALLEGED RESPONSIBILITY

Five hundred members of the Nicaraguan contras operating from Honduras

SOURCES

Committee for the Defense of Human Rights in Honduras
U.N. Working Group on Enforced or Involuntary Disappearances

No. 156

PERSONAL DATA

NAME: RICHARD LUGO (17)
NATIONALITY: NICARAGUAN
PROFESSION: UNKNOWN

DESCRIPTION OF EVENTS

Detained June 19, 1987, at 8:00 a.m. in Cano de la Cruz, Cerro/Milambe, Department of Jinotega, Nicaragua, by a group of about 500 contras based in Honduras who had entered Nicaragua. He was later taken to Honduras.

ALLEGED RESPONSIBILITY

Five hundred members of the Nicaraguan contras operating from Honduras

SOURCES

Committee for the Defense of Human Rights in Honduras
U.N. Working Group on Enforced or Involuntary Disappearances

No. 157

PERSONAL DATA

NAME: MELVIN HUMBERTO THOM MORAN (17)
NATIONALITY: NICARAGUAN
PROFESSION: UNKNOWN

DESCRIPTION OF EVENTS

Detained June 19, 1987, in the Department of Jinotega, Nicaragua, by a group
of about 500 Nicaraguan contras and later brought to Honduras.

ALLEGED RESPONSIBILITY

Five hundred members of the Nicaraguan contras operating from Honduras

SOURCES

Committee for the Defense of Human Rights in Honduras
U.N. Working Group on Enforced or Involuntary Disappearances

No. 158

PERSONAL DATA

NAME: ELIAZAR PAGUAGA MAYORGA (17)
NATIONALITY: NICARAGUAN
PROFESSION: UNKNOWN

DESCRIPTION OF EVENTS

Detained June 19, 1987 in the Department of Jinotega, Nicaragua, by about 500 Nicaraguan contras operating from Honduras and later taken to Honduras.

ALLEGED RESPONSIBILITY

Five hundred members of the Nicaraguan contras operating from Honduras

SOURCES

Committee for the Defense of Human Rights in Honduras
U.N. Working Group on Enforced or Involuntary Disappearances

No. 159

PERSONAL DATA

NAME: FRANKLIN SANCHEZ JIMENEZ (18)
NATIONALITY: NICARAGUAN
PROFESSION: UNKNOWN

DESCRIPTION OF EVENTS

Detained June 19, 1987, in the Department of Jinotega, Nicaragua, by about 500 Nicaraguan contras based in Honduras and later taken to Honduras.

ALLEGED RESPONSIBILITY

Five hundred members of the Nicaraguan contras operating from Honduras

SOURCES

Committee for the Defense of Human Rights in Honduras
U.N. Working Group on Enforced or Involuntary Disappearances

No. 160

PERSONAL DATA

NAME: DOMINGO JOSE ESCOBAR SANCHEZ
NATIONALITY: NICARAGUAN
PROFESSION: SOLDIER

DESCRIPTION OF EVENTS

Detained June 19, 1987, in Cano de la Cruz, in Cerro/Milambe, Department of
Jinotega, Nicaragua, by about 500 Nicaraguan contras based in Honduras and
later taken to Honduras.

ALLEGED RESPONSIBILITY

Five hundred members of the Nicaraguan contras operating from Honduras

SOURCES

Committee for the Defense of Human Rights in Honduras
U.N. Working Group on Enforced or Involuntary Disappearances

No. 161

PERSONAL DATA

NAME: STANLEY CASTELLON AMAYA (48)
NATIONALITY: HONDURAN
PROFESSION: UNKNOWN

DESCRIPTION OF EVENTS

Disappeared July 28, 1987, on the highway between Santa Bárbara and San
Pedro Sula.

SOURCE

Committee for the Defense of Human Rights in Honduras

No. 162

PERSONAL DATA

NAME: LINA VEACELY CORTES GRANADOS (13)
NATIONALITY: HONDURAN
PROFESSION: UNKNOWN

DESCRIPTION OF EVENTS

Disappeared December 29, 1987, in Tegucigalpa's Villanueva neighborhood.

SOURCE
Committee for the Defense of Human Rights in Honduras

1988

No. 163

PERSONAL DATA

NAME: OSCAR ORLANDO GARCIA RODRIGUEZ
NATIONALITY: HONDURAN
PROFESSION: SHOE SHINER

DESCRIPTION OF EVENTS

Arrested March 1, 1988 by DNI agents and transferred to the holding cells of the FUSEP of Region VII, in the Belén neighborhood, Comayagüela, until March 15. After that date there is no information as to his whereabouts.

ALLEGED RESPONSIBILITY

FUSEP

SOURCE

Committee for the Defense of Human Rights in Honduras

No. 164

NAME: ROGER SAMUEL GONZALEZ ZELAYA (23)
NATIONALITY: HONDURAN
PROFESSION: STUDENT

DESCRIPTION OF EVENTS

Arrested April 19, 1988, in Tegucigalpa's Central Park and later taken to the headquarters of the DNI in Tegucigalpa. In his testimony, Fausto Reyes Caballero, former agent of the 3-16 Battalion, stated that he saw Roger González Zelaya alive in a military center in May 1988.

ALLEGED RESPONSIBILITY

DNI

SOURCES

Committee for the Defense of Human Rights in Honduras
Amnesty International
Central American Commission for the Defense of Human Rights
World Organization Against Torture
U.N. Working Group on Enforced or Involuntary Disappearances

No. 165

PERSONAL DATA

NAME: HERIBERTO CARRILLOS ESCOBAR (30)
NATIONALITY: HONDURAN
PROFESSION: UNKNOWN

DESCRIPTION OF EVENTS

Disappeared August 7, 1988, after being detained by DNI agents.

SOURCE

Committee for the Defense of Human Rights in Honduras

No. 166

PERSONAL DATA

NAME: OSCAR ALFONSO FLORES CASTOS (28)
NATIONALITY: HONDURAN
PROFESSION: UNKNOWN

DESCRIPTION OF EVENTS

Disappeared after being detained August 22, 1988, by agents of the DNI in the San José de la Peña neighborhood.

SOURCE

Committee for the Defense of Human Rights in Honduras

No. 167

PERSONAL DATA

NAME: CARMEN EUCEDA
NATIONALITY: HONDURAN
PROFESSION: UNKNOWN

DESCRIPTION OF EVENTS

Disappeared August 30, 1988, after she was detained by men believed to be agents of the DNI.

SOURCE

Committee for the Defense of Human Rights in Honduras

No. 168

PERSONAL DATA

NAME: JOSE SANTOS HERNANDEZ GOMEZ (21)
NATIONALITY: HONDURAN
PROFESSION: UNKNOWN

DESCRIPTION OF EVENTS

Missing since September 1988, according to complaints filed by his family members.

SOURCE

Committee for the Defense of Human Rights in Honduras

No. 169

PERSONAL DATA

NAME: JOSE ARNALDO PEREZ MARTINEZ
NATIONALITY: HONDURAN
PROFESSION: UNKNOWN

DESCRIPTION OF EVENTS

Disappeared September 9, 1988.

SOURCE

Committee for the Defense of Human Rights in Honduras

No. 170

PERSONAL DATA

NAME: OSCAR HUMBERTO SANCHEZ
NATIONALITY: HONDURAN
PROFESSION: UNKNOWN

DESCRIPTION OF EVENTS

Disappeared September 9, 1988.

SOURCES

Committee for the Defense of Human Rights in Honduras

No. 171

PERSONAL DATA

NAME: OMAR CALDERON
NATIONALITY: HONDURAN
PROFESSION: UNKNOWN

DESCRIPTION OF EVENTS

Disappeared September 9, 1988.

SOURCE

Committee for the Defense of Human Rights in Honduras

No. 172

PERSONAL DATA

NAME: MARIANO PINEDA CRUZ (32)
NATIONALITY: HONDURAN
PROFESSION: LABORER

DESCRIPTION OF EVENTS

Disappeared September 19, 1988, after leaving his house on his way to the dentist's office.

SOURCE

Committee for the Defense of Human Rights in Honduras

No. 173

PERSONAL DATA

NAME: JOSE LEONEL SUAZO CASTILLO (31)
NATIONALITY: HONDURAN
PROFESSION: STUDENT

DESCRIPTION OF EVENTS

Detained February 2, 1989, at a bus stop on Calle Real street in Comayagüela, Department of Francisco Morazán, by a beige-colored truck with tinted windows and no license plates.

ALLEGED RESPONSIBILITY

FUSEP

SOURCES

Central American Commission for the Defense of Human Rights
World Organization Against Torture
Amnesty International
Rosa Francisca Suazo Castillo (mother)
Committee of Relatives of the Detained and Disappeared in Honduras
U.N. Working Group on Enforced or Involuntary Disappearances

No. 174

PERSONAL DATA

NAME: DIONISIO PORTILLO
NATIONALITY: HONDURAN
PROFESSION: REFUGEE CAMP WORKER

DESCRIPTION OF EVENTS

Arrested February 3, 1989, at 6:00 p.m. in San Marcos de Ocotepeque. *See* additional information on this case in Chapter III.

ALLEGED RESPONSIBILITY

Honduran Armed Forces

SOURCES

Central American Commission for the Defense of Human Rights
World Organization Against Torture
U.N. Working Group on Enforced or Involuntary Disappearances

1992

No. 175

PERSONAL DATA

NAME: JUAN HUMBERTO SANCHEZ (26)
NATIONALITY: HONDURAN
PROFESSION: UNKNOWN

DESCRIPTION OF EVENTS

Detained July 11, 1992, in the hamlet of Santo Domingo, Colomoncagua, Department of Intibucá. Sánchez reportedly had been detained several days earlier, July 9, 1992, by members of the Honduran Armed Forces based in Colomoncagua. He was released July 11 and detained again on the same day in front of his parents. His whereabouts remain unknown.

ALLEGED RESPONSIBILITY

Honduran Armed Forces

SOURCES

Central American Commission for the Defense of Human Rights
U.N. Working Group on Enforced or Involuntary Disappearances

Date Unknown

No. 176

PERSONAL DATA

NAME: JOSE GUSTAVO ARGUETA
NATIONALITY: HONDURAN
PROFESSION: UNKNOWN

DESCRIPTION OF EVENTS

Sources report that Argueta was taken to an unknown location and remains disappeared.

ALLEGED RESPONSIBILITY

DNI

SOURCES

Committee of Relatives of the Detained and Disappeared in Honduras
U.N. Working Group on Enforced or Involuntary Disappearances

No. 177

PERSONAL DATA

NAME: MANUEL DE JESUS RODRIGUEZ SANDOVAL
NATIONALITY: UNKNOWN
PROFESSION: UNKNOWN

DESCRIPTION OF EVENTS

Arrested by DNI agents in Jícaro Galán, Department of Valle.

ALLEGED RESPONSIBILITY

DNI

SOURCE
Committee for the Defense of Human Rights in Honduras

No. 178

PERSONAL DATA

NAME: ALFREDO SILES ROSENDO
NATIONALITY: NICARAGUAN
PROFESSION: UNKNOWN

DESCRIPTION OF EVENTS

Disappeared while prisoner in the Central Penitentiary, Tegucigalpa.

SOURCE
Committee for the Defense of Human Rights in Honduras

No. 179

PERSONAL DATA

NAME: JOSE ENOE CARIAS TROCHEZ (25)
NATIONALITY: HONDURAN
PROFESSION: UNKNOWN

DESCRIPTION OF EVENTS

Disappeared after being detained by DNI agents in the Rivera Hernández
neighborhood.

ALLEGED RESPONSIBILITY

DNI

SOURCE

Committee for the Defense of Human Rights in Honduras

III

FOURTEEN ILLUSTRATIVE
CASES OF DISAPPEARANCES

1. The Pattern of Disappearances

The cases of disappearances presented in this report show similar characteristics and thus indicate that—at least during the period from 1982 to 1984—the practice was systematic. An examination of a few selected cases will help illustrate the pattern of disappearances in Honduras and may explain the motives, methods, results and responsibility for this practice.[1]

Crimes committed by representatives of the state or by people who enjoy its protection are particularly difficult to investigate. The crime of forced disappearances involves a network of people who operate in a clandestine and illegal manner. Unlike members of criminal organizations, those involved in disappearance abuse the power conferred on them as members of the armed forces or police. These actors often seek to legitimize their behavior by arguing that it is motivated by legitimate concern for national security. The pretext of engaging in intelligence operations affords those involved the cover necessary to operate secretly. The domination of mechanisms of control, the enormous power which the quasi-legitimate use of force provides, and the totally clandestine nature of the operations facilitate cover-ups by those responsible and render the search for evidence extremely difficult.

Nevertheless, these crimes leave other traces, especially in the similarity of the acts and their repetition, which may be pursued.

a. Disappearances are repetitive crimes in both their number and characteristics.

These disappearances were not isolated events, particularly in the period

---

[1] The Inter-American Court of Human Rights was the first to establish that "the disappearances [in Honduras] were carried out in a systematic manner," *Velásquez Rodríguez* Case, July 29, 1988, Series C, No. 4, Paragraph 147, Clause (d). The Velásquez Rodríguez case, as well as that of Saúl Godínez Cruz, corresponds to the pattern of disappearances described in this chapter. Given that these cases have already been studied in-depth by the Inter-American Commission and Court of Human Rights, the Commissioner has chosen to analyze other cases.

121

from 1982 to 1984 when they constituted a repetitive and persistent phenomenon.[2] The repetition of these crimes reveals a permanent policy or conduct and may demonstrate that those responsible for one operation could easily have been responsible for all operations.[3] None of these crimes was exceptional: they bear distinct similarities in both the type of victim and the methods employed in their commission. They are not, therefore, isolated incidents or unique acts of violence, as the case may be with common criminal acts.

b. Disappearances are carried out for a similar purpose or end.

Another important element in these disappearances is that the victims were similar, thus revealing the objectives of those carrying out the crimes—to undermine the actions of certain people or groups of people. In particular, the targets of this policy were often union members and students, or protesters of any kind. In the case of our country, those responsible for disappearances sought to obtain information and kill alleged Honduran subversives or sympathizers of the Salvadoran guerrillas or Nicaraguan Sandinistas. Thus "[t]he victims were usually persons whom Honduran officials considered dangerous to State security."[4]

c. Disappearances are conducted by following the same procedures; they share a common modus operandi.

The systematic and repetitive nature of this practice is another element that makes it clear that the authors of these crimes are the same, belong to the same organization or have received the same training. It also demonstrates that there existed a near total control of the situation based on the exercise of official

---

[2] According the Inter-American Court of Human Rights, "During the period 1981 to 1984, 100 to 150 persons disappeared in the Republic of Honduras, and many were never heard from again," Inter-American Court of Human Rights, Case of Velásquez Rodríguez, July 29, 1988, Series C, No. 4, Paragraph 147, Clause a.

[3] Between 1982 and 1992, 179 complaints of cases of forced disappearance were recorded. For more information see the list in Chapter II.

[4] Inter-American Court of Human Rights, Case of Velásquez Rodríguez, July 29, 1988, Series C, No. 4, Paragraph 147, Clause (d), Section (i).

power. In the case of Honduras, the *modus operandi* consisted of: (i) surveillance and identification of the victim; (ii) the victim(s)' prior arrest(s) by the police, military, intelligence services, or in some cases the National Investigations Directorate (DNI) or Public Security Force (FUSEP); (iii) detention of the victim, in public or in the person's home, with total impunity, by armed men dressed in civilian clothes, using automobiles with similar characteristics; (iv) the use of official resources and authority to carry out kidnappings and to avoid interference by other security branches; (v) the total indifference or subordination of any authority that may have witnessed the kidnapping.[5]

d. The kidnappings and illegal detentions have a common result.

The majority of the cases of illegal detentions ended with the permanent disappearance of the person, and the absence of any information as to the victim's whereabouts or the whereabouts of her or his corpse. Cases in which the detained person reappears were extremely rare. When they occurred, they could be attributed to unusual circumstances, such as the nationality of the victim, the notoriety or status of the victim or the victim's family, or international pressure.

e. Members of investigation and military intelligence units are repeatedly implicated as responsible for the disappearances.

In a majority of the cases, information received from witnesses, victims who survived, family members and the press points to specialized units, such as the DNI and the 3-16 Intelligence Battalion,[6] as having direct responsibility for the disappearances. The G-2 and other military units are also mentioned. Although Battalion 3-16 has been described as a special unit dedicated to investigating and producing intelligence reports about subversive activities in

---

[5] The Court calls attention to some of these characteristics. *See Velásquez Rodríguez Case*, July 29, 1988, Series C, No. 4, Paragraph 147, Clause d).

[6] See the agreements signed by the commander-in-chief of the armed forces in relation to the officers in the 3-16 Intelligence Battalion, appendix.

Honduras,[7] it did not produce strategic intelligence reports. Instead, the battalion gathered information on Hondurans who were suspected by the Armed Forces of involvement with subversion.

f. Judicial protection and guarantees are not available.

Mechanisms of constitutional protection such as *habeas corpus* failed to secure the release of anyone who had been disappeared. The justice system consistently failed to act to determine the whereabouts of the victims.

g. There is no serious effort to investigate or sanction those responsible for these crimes.

The justice system has done nothing to prevent or investigate disappearances. Despite the obvious nature in which disappearances were carried out, the judiciary was absolutely incapable of investigating or sanctioning those responsible for these crimes.

h. The official investigations are inconclusive or cover up the facts and those responsible; they are formalities which offer no evidence as to the whereabouts of the disappeared or their fate.

The investigations carried out with the participation of official institutions that may have been responsible for the commission of these crimes offer no evidence nor do they even suggest that the search for the disappeared was carried out in a serious and detailed manner.

One example of these inconclusive reports was that which the "Special Commission to Investigate Complaints of People Disappeared in Honduran Territory" drafted.[8] Despite the numerous testimonies, the repetitive nature of

---

[7] Statement by Gen. Walter López before the National Commissioner for the Protection and Defense of Human Rights, Tegucigalpa, December 23, 1993.

[8] This commission was created by the order of the commander-in-chief of the Honduran Armed Forces by Defense Ministry Accord No. 232 of June 14, 1984. The members of the commission who signed the report were: Col. Manuel Enrique Suárez Benavides (president); Col. Guillermo Thumann Cordón (member); Air Force Col. Francisco Zepeda Andino (member); Col. Diego Arturo Landa Celano (member); Col. Humberto Regalado Hernández (member); Col. Roberto Martínez Avila (member) and

the acts committed, and the obvious participation of official agents in the detentions and subsequent disappearances of the victims, the commission concluded that it could not make a definitive statement on disappearances.[9] The commission concluded: "based on the information obtained, this commission believes that it is impossible to state with absolute certainty regarding the disappearance of persons as a consequence of acts attributable to government authorities and, in the case that they could be so attributed, identify those responsible; on the other hand, the commission has encountered resistance to cooperation on the part of some of the people interviewed, apparently out of fear."[10] Many doubts were raised as to whether this report was really an attempt at a cover-up. It was, and remains very difficult to believe that a commission composed of six colonels from the Honduran Armed Forces wrote a report with no conclusions and only ten pages in length. At the time the report was written there were already dozens of cases of disappearances.

The crimes committed by non-military personnel, especially the Nicaraguan contras,[11] are also similar in nature. When a disappearance was carried out by a private group with official protection, as was the case with the contras, the *modus operandi* was as follows: (i) kidnapping of people tied to the Sandinista government; (ii) their use as human shields in confrontations; (iii) their forced transfer to Honduran territory with the objective of intimidating their fellow citizens and comrades and to obtain information; (iv) absolute

---

Second Lt. of Military Justice Mario Enrique Boquín Hernández (secretary). *See Report of the Special Commission to Investigate Complaints of People Disappeared in Honduran Territory*, June 28, 1984 (10 pages).

[9] The commission stated, among other conclusions, that "there are suspicions that some of the people reported as disappeared could have been victims of vendettas by non-Honduran armed groups on the left and right that have operated clandestinely in national territory in the past," *Ibid.*, p. 8.

[10] *Ibid.*

[11] *Editor's note*: The "contras" were a Nicaraguan guerrilla force backed by the United States which sought to overthrow the Sandinista government in Nicaragua, using Honduran territory as a base.

inaction on the part of the Honduran forces of order in the face of these actions.[12]

2. Investigation of Disappearances

It is very important for this investigation to establish the special nature of the crimes analyzed. These are crimes which presume the active participation of agents of the state's own security forces, including those in charge of enforcing the law or investigating these crimes. These facts render investigation quite complicated and facilitate cover-ups. For these reasons, it is critical that the testimonies of the victims and their relatives and those of former perpetrators of these crimes be accorded particular value.

In an investigation of these crimes it is very difficult to obtain documentation. The order to have someone disappeared is invariably oral, thus leaving no written traces. The truth is to be found in the various accounts of the crime; credence should be accorded those elements of these accounts that are corroborated in the distinct versions. The logic here is quite clear: there is always the possibility that someone may lie or that several people may agree to render the same version of certain facts. Nevertheless, it is difficult to deny the validity of hundreds of testimonies of people who do not know each other and who have not had access to each other's statements. It is impossible to maintain that these people have invented a reality so identical in all its gruesome extremes.

The following cases, in which the testimonies of victims, their families and human rights organizations that have gathered information over the years have been accorded due weight, permit a detailed examination of the systematic pattern and principal characteristics of all the cases of disappearances. They also provide the opportunity to determine responsibility, as much for the crimes themselves as for their cover-up.

---

[12] It was only in 1984, under the command of Gen. Walter López Reyes, that some steps were taken to control the contras. Gen. López ordered the capture of a Nicaraguan rebel leader known as "Chino Lau," who had been implicated in various attacks against Honduran citizens. Gen. López stated that he could not be certain if his orders were effectively carried out and if all the foreign units operating in Honduras had been stopped. Statement of Gen. Walter López Reyes before the National Commissioner for the Protection of Human Rights, Tegucigalpa, December 23, 1993.

3. Illustrative Cases

These case represent only a handful of those that the Commissioner has reviewed. Selected because they constitute paradigmatic examples, they reflect what happened in dozens of other cases.

a. Estanislao Maradiaga Linares (1980)

Maradiaga Linares lived in Choluteca and was 39 years old when he was disappeared. He was a leader of the National Autonomous Service of Aqueducts and Sewers Employees' Union (Sindicato de Trabajadores del Servicio Autónomo Nacional de Acueductos y de Alcantarillado-SITRASANAA). He was also a veteran of the Honduran Army.

Maradiaga was disappeared May 24, 1980, kidnapped by five armed men. According to his mother, he "disappeared May 24 from his house, which faced the airstrip near the Pan-American Highway. My son was taken away by five heavily armed men who identified themselves as authorities. My son was wearing grey pants and a white shirt."[13] According to some reports, Salomóm Herrera was one of the agents who took part in the operation to detain Maradiaga.

In this case, as in other cases of forced disappearances, at one point there was an attempt to deny that the victim ever existed. In Maradiaga's case, any doubts were removed by a certificate issued by the mayor and municipal secretary of Santa Ana de Yusguare, Choluteca, Honduras. The certificate states that Maradiago, born November 16, 1940, was the natural son of Dolores Maradiaga.[14]

> Maradiaga's relatives filed all relevant legal petitions. As they relate:
> After he was taken away we asked the authorities for help. Maj. Peña Mejía was in charge, but he wasn't there when we arrived. As soon as he arrived he said 'not one patrol is to leave.' At that moment we left thinking that they had him. I remember that on (May) 27, Maj. Peña sent word that I should show up to talk at 2:00 in the afternoon. I

---

[13] Letter from María Dolores de Maradiaga (mother) and Josefina Maradiaga (sister), April 24, 1984.

[14] Certificate from the municipal secretary of Santa Ana de Yusguare, issued May 25, 1959.

received his request and I was there on time. He later sent word that he could not see me. Then, my daughter and I went to see Col. Bodden. He talked to us and sent us to talk to Peña Mejía. When we went back, Peña Mejía told us to talk to Bodden. They kept lying to us the whole time. We also went to see the DNI. They told us that they didn't have him. We went to [the] Casamata [Military base] and to the P.C., [Central Penitentiary] but we didn't find him. The only place we didn't go was to the First Infantry Battalion. Later, we went to the Supreme Court and we spoke to the president of the court who told us they didn't have him. Two people who investigated what happened (to my son) said that it was authorities who took him away. They didn't want their names used because they are afraid for their lives. They told us he was captured by Interpol because one of them knew one of kidnappers. We are always asking God that he return to his mother because only his mother and his brothers and sisters suffer the pain. But by the power of God, he'll return."[15]

Maradiaga's wife, Isolina Contreras de Maradiaga, also took steps to locate Maradiaga, such as denouncing the disappearances before the First Criminal Court. She, too, was unsuccessful in her search.

The fate of Estanislao Maradiaga Linares remains unknown. Neither he nor his body has been found.

2. Nora Trinidad Gómez de Barillas (1981)

Gómez de Barillas, a Salvadoran, was a close colleague of, and secretary to Salvadoran Archbishop Oscar Arnulfo Romero before his assassination. She was also a former secretary of the department of humanities at the Central American University (Universidad Centroamericana-UCA). She was temporarily living in Tegucigalpa when she was disappeared April 22, 1981, arrested by DNI agents in Tegucigalpa.[16]

---

[15] Letter by María Dolores Maradiaga (mother) and Josefina Maradiaga (sister), sent to Dr. Ramón Custodio of CODEH, April 27, 1984.

[16] This case was mentioned in congressional hearings in Washington, D.C. *Hearings Before the Subcommittee on Inter-American Affairs, of the Committee on Foreign Affairs of the House of Representatives,* December 17, 1981, p. 11 (Testimony of Rev. William Wipfler, National Council of Churches).

Her case was presented to the U.N. Working Group on Enforced or Involuntary Disappearances (case No. 007625). Gómez was arrested along with 13 other people, including her husband, Mauricio Barillas, and their three children, Nora Patricia, 11, Mauricio Gerardo, 5, José, 2, all Salvadoran refugees living in Honduras. A witness to the arrest, an agricultural specialist from the Netherlands, sent a written statement about the case to the U.N. Working Group on Enforced or Involuntary Disappearances.[17] Some reports indicate that the Barillas' children were turned over to Salvadoran authorities by Honduran officials.[18]

On March 3, 1988, the Honduran Permanent Mission in Geneva informed the United Nations that Gómez had been turned over to Salvadoran authorities May 1, 1981, according to a report printed in the San Pedro Sula daily *Tiempo* of May 25, 1981. At the same time, CODEH, one of the groups that brought the case before the U.N. Working Group on Enforced or Involuntary Disappearances, reported that, according to *Tiempo*, only the Barillas children and Mauricio Barillas' mother-in-law Ursula María Navarro, were turned over to Salvadoran police at the border checkpoint "El Amatillo." The newspaper reported that Mauricio Barillas and his wife had not been turned over to Salvadoran authorities but were being held in a detention center unknown to the press.[19]

The detention of Gómez de Barillas, as well as the detention of other Salvadorans, provoked diverse reactions in Honduras. The press reported dozens of protests by public school students in May 1981 demanding the release of the nine Salvadorans, including Gómez de Barillas.[20]

Repeated requests for information about Gómez de Barillas and demands for her release by international human rights organizations were

---

[17] U.N. Working Group on Forced and Involuntary Disappearances, *Report on Enforced and Involuntary Disappearances in Honduras* (Geneva, 1993). (Hereinafter "U.N. Working Group, *Report*").

[18] A communiqué sent October 1, 1981 by Amnesty International to the U.N. Working Group on Enforced and Involuntary Disappearances. *Ibid.*

[19] *Ibid.*

[20] *Tiempo,* May 29, 1981, p. 23.

consistently denied.[21]

The fate of Nora Trinidad Gómez de Barillas and her husband, Mauricio Barillas, is still unknown; they have not been found either dead or alive.

3. Tomás Nativí Gálvez (1981)

Tomás Nativí Gálvez was a professor and a union leader. Politically, he was also one of the founders of the People's Revolutionary Union (URP). Shortly after midnight on June 11, 1981, Nativí was disappeared by six hooded men from the house of his wife, Bertha Oliva, located in the El Hogar neighborhood, Block I, number 3, Tegucigalpa. At the time, Nativí was with Fidel Martínez, an agronomist and co-founder of the URP who also disappeared that night. Nativí was 33 years old when he disappeared, and had been married only four months. His wife was pregnant at the time; their child was born after Nativí's disappearance.[22]

Nativí had been detained many times before his disappearance. In March 1979, he was arrested along with other union members who were on strike at the Bemis Handal textile factory in San Pedro Sula. On March 6, 1979, in the midst of the strike, there was a fire at the factory and Nativí was arrested and falsely accused of setting the blaze. The union leaders accused the security forces of setting the fire at the factory during an assault. Four union members were killed and several injured in the police action. Nativí was released in December 1979.[23]

Nativí was arrested once again on August 15, 1980, by DNI agents. His arrest occurred after URP militants had occupied the offices of the Organization of American States (OAS) in Tegucigalpa. Nativí was accused of knowing the location of a weapons depository used by subversive groups.[24] He was released pending trial on September 7, as a result of an amnesty granted by the

---

[21] *Tiempo*, July 4, 1981, p. 28.

[22] CODEH, *List of the Disappeared: 1979-1988,* Tegucigalpa, Honduras. (Hereinafter "CODEH, *List*").

[23] *Tiempo*, September 8, 1980.

[24] *Tiempo*, September 8, 1980.

Constituent Assembly.[25] He was, nevertheless, arrested again on the same day. Amnesty International organized a campaign calling for his release.[26] Nativí was kept incommunicado and stated that he was mistreated.[27] He was released shortly after the second arrest.[28]

Tomás Nativí had also been temporarily disappeared before. On December 23, 1980, at approximately 10:00 a.m., Nativí was making a telephone call from the Hondutel [telephone company], in downtown Tegucigalpa. While speaking by phone to his wife, Nativí was detained by DNI agents. At the time, he was not involved in any illegal activity and there was no warrant for his arrest. During his detention, which was denied by the security forces, he was subjected to brutal torture. He was left semi-conscious in the early morning hours of December 25 at the five-kilometer mark on the highway leading to the department of Olancho. He had been beaten severely, but managed to ask for help from a passing taxi driver. The taxi driver brought him to his sister's house in the Buenos Aires neighborhood and he later received medical attention. His liver and kidneys were damaged, several ribs were broken, he had permanently lost all feeling in his left hand, and his hearing was impaired due to blows to his head. He was still receiving treatment for his injuries when he disappeared several months later.[29]

Nativí was arrested again on June 11, 1981, in the El Hogar neighborhood, Block 1, No. 5 in Tegucigalpa by DNI agents. Nativí's wife, Bertha Oliva Guifarro, three months pregnant at the time, witnessed the events. In her account, Oliva stated:

> I had gone to my room. It was about 1:30 a.m. when we heard two

---

[25] On August 14, 1980, *Tiempo* published the names of people who were benefitted by the amnesty decree. Tomás Nativí was among those mentioned who were released pending trial.

[26] Amnesty International, *Disappearances in Honduras: A Wall of Silence and Indifference* (London, 1992), p. 16. (hereinafter, "Amnesty, *Disappearances*").

[27] *Tiempo*, September 8, 1980.

[28] *Tiempo*, September 9, 1980.

[29] Statement from Bertha Oliva Guifarro de Nativí to the National Commissioner for the Protection of Human Rights, December 24, 1993.

distinct sounds, like when a gun with a silencer is fired. Something fell over. Thinking back about it now, it was probably Fidel [Martínez]'s body, collapsing from the shots. We could smell the gunpowder from the shots. One of them ordered, "take care of the other one." They began to pound on the door of our room. They yelled that if we didn't open the door they would start shooting. Tomás decided we had to open the door, telling me that maybe this way we could save my life. When I opened the door they grabbed me, put guns to my head and said if I didn't leave they'd kill me. Tomás came out with his hands over his head. When he lowered them they hit him on the back of his neck and took him away. He only had on pants and socks; he wasn't wearing a shirt. Later, I tried to give him a shirt to put on but one of the six men stopped me, the one who didn't have a hood on. This one talked with a Nicaraguan accent. I tried to resist and, at one point, tried to pull the hood off of one of the men. They hit me and left me unconscious. When I came to I was on my bed and one of the men—this one had a Honduran accent and was wearing a lot of cologne—tied my feet and hands. Before they could cover my eyes I saw them taking away Fidel's body wrapped in a curtain. His eyes were open, but he looked dead. Later, I found a piece of human bone, it guess it was from him. They asked for Gloria and she came out of the bathroom. They also tied her up.[30]

Oliva stated that she could identify Alexander Hernández, whom she later met, as one of the men who participated in the kidnapping. She also gave her eyewitness account of the detention of Tomás Nativí and Fidel Martínez to several journalists, who published the details of the case.[31]

Two people who were part of Battalion 3-16 during this time have stated that there was a specialized unit in charge of kidnapping people suspected of belonging to left-wing movements or involved in arms trafficking. They explained the methodology used, which usually involved six men.[32] Because of

---

[30] *Ibid.*

[31] *Tiempo,* June 13, 1981, p. 3.

[32] Q: "How many were there, for example? A: There were six kidnappers and the squadron leader, this is where Lt. Flores Murillo fit in." (Florencio Caballero, testimony given to Americas Watch [now Human Rights Watch/Americas], 1987, p. 4). "The

his political activity, Nativí was a typical target of this kind of action. According to witness accounts, he was kidnapped by six men.[33]

A few days later, on June 16, the FUSEP issued a press release denying any participation in the events.[34] At the same time a public letter to the provisional president and commander of the Armed Forces, Division Gen. Policarpo Paz García, printed in a local paper, demanded the release of the victims and respect for their physical and moral integrity.[35]

According to a declassified cable from the U.S. Central Intelligence Agency (CIA), then-Lt. Col. Erick Sánchez told the Official Commission for Human Rights Investigations in Honduras that "Chino Lau" had been involved in the disappearances of two Honduran left-wing militants.[36] The same cable stated that Lau had been a commander in Somoza's National Guard (in Nicaragua) and later became part of a counter-intelligence unit of the "Nicaraguan Democratic Force" (FDN), widely known as the *contras*.[37] Later, "he was placed in the Honduran Army CI [counter-intelligence] section because of his demonstrated ability to work effectively against the Sandinista intelligence

---

groups were divided, that is, in groups of six to eight people" (José Valle, testimony given to Americas Watch, Canada, March 1987, p. 34).

[33] CODEH, *List.*

[34] The FUSEP press release stated in part: "We see most of these comments as biased attempts intended to implicate the DNI in this action. We are forced, in the name of truth, to publicly declare that at no time and under no circumstances were Mssrs. Fidel Martínez and Tomás Nativí Gálvez detained. Furthermore, an investigation of Gálvez has been ordered to clear up any suspicions about those mentioned. In order to prevent such rash and unfounded declarations, FUSEP reserves the right to proceed legally against anyone who falsely and wrongfully tries continually to disparage the institution. *Tiempo,* June 16, 1981, p. 5.

[35] *Tiempo,* July 1, 1981, p. 13.

[36] Document declassified by the U.S. Government, TOR: 050222Z, March 1985, p. 001.

[37] *Editor's Note*: the FDN was the armed organization of Nicaraguans fighting to overthrow the Sandinista government from Honduras.

services."[38] The presence of this former Nicaraguan National Guard officer in the Honduran military intelligence service was corroborated by statements of a former member of Battalion 3-16.[39]

Gen. Walter López stated to the Commissioner that during his time as Commander of the Armed Forces he learned about Chino Lau's presence in Honduras and his actions against Honduran citizens. Unfortunately, Lau had a great deal of international support and managed to evade his captors, leaving Honduras for Guatemala.[40]

The press reported on June 18, 1981, that two bodies, whose characteristics matched those of the kidnapped activists, had been left outside of the village of Yaguasire, close to Tegucigalpa, three days earlier by unknown individuals. Area residents said that the bodies were dumped in an empty lot by unknown individuals driving a yellow truck.[41]

Oliva, in her testimony for this report, stated that she went to the area where the bodies had reportedly been dumped. After arriving in Yaguasire she talked with a woman who told her where the bodies had been found. Oliva said the woman's description of the cadavers matched the features of her husband

---

[38] *Ibid.*

[39] Q: You said that you had heard that "contra" activities could have been carried out in Honduran territory, that the "contras" had kidnapped and assassinated people. Could you expand on this statement. A: I only know, from Chávez Hernández, Flores Murillo and the others, that a group of contras were active in El Paraíso, that they were part of their intelligence service and worked simultaneously with the (Honduran) intelligence service, that is, the 3-16 in Danlí. They collaborated with the 3-16 in Danlí. I was never in Danlí, that's why I never knew any contras. I didn't have any contacts. I only knew about a contra safe house, which had earlier been the military headquarters in La Florencia. It was one block from the Monimbó house where Reyes Baca was captured. That's where Chino Ulloa or Ochoa, I don't remember his name but he was of Asian descent, could be found. He had been a major in the Somoza Army and had been in command for some time, I guess." (Testimony of Florencio Caballero to Inter-American Court of Human Rights, public hearing, October 6, 1987, transcribed in Spanish by the Asociación Centroamericana de Familiares de Detenidos-Desaparecidos-ACAFADE, p. 72 [herafter "IACHR Testimony of Florencio Caballero"]; *Our translation.*)

[40] Testimony of Gen. Walter López before the National Commissioner for the Protection of Human Rights, Tegucigalpa, December 23, 1993.

[41] *Tiempo,* June 18, 1981.

and those of Martínez. As far as she could make out from the versions of the villagers, dogs belonging to the landowner uncovered black plastic bags which contained the bodies. The landowner informed the local authorities and a white car arrived and removed the bodies to an unknown location. Oliva checked with all the local morgues without results. Later, she went to the police station in Loarque, where they had information about the cadavers. When she arrived, the officer in charge removed his name badge from his uniform and told her she should check with the morgue. When Oliva told him that she had just come from the morgue he told her in a threatening tone—revealing that he knew what was happening—that she should keep her mouth shut.

In his statement before the Inter-American Court of Human Rights, an ex-member of Battalion 3-16 explained that when they decided to kill a detainee, she or he was turned over to another group who carried out the execution and then disposed of the body, usually at night and using a yellow pickup.[42]

At the time of the disappearance, Gen. Gustavo Adolfo Alvarez Martínez was the Commander-in-Chief of the Armed Forces, Daniel Balí was Police Commissioner and Juan López Grijalba was head of the G-2.

In Resolution No. 4787, issued July 29, 1987, the Inter-American Commission of Human Rights found that all of the evidence presented in the case was accurate.

The fate of Tomás Nativí and Fidel Martínez remains unknown.

---

[42] Q: If an execution was ordered, what was the process? A: After the interrogation they were transferred in a yellow Toyota van with tinted windows. They were taken to Támara or sometimes to Pío Flores' house. Ramón Peña Paz already had the order, so that they could turn them over to . . . . Q: Who was Ramón Peña Paz? A: He was responsible for the four executions. ("IACHR Testimony of Florencio Caballero, p.174; *Our translation.*)

Q: And when a person who had been kidnapped was in an interrogation center, such as the house used by kidnapping teams, what happened then with the person? How was the person sent to death? Did a death squad come and take them away or what happened to the person? A: The person was generally taken away in a Toyota "Hi Ace" yellow van with tinted windows. The car was driven by Barahona, who, as I said, was the chauffeur for Miguel Azcona's family. (Caballero, Testimony given to Americas Watch [now Human Rights Watch/Americas], p. 24).

4. José Eduardo Becerra Lanza (1982)

José Eduardo Becerra Lanza was a medical student at the National Autonomous University of Honduras (Universidad Nacional Autónoma de Honduras-UNAH). Becerra Lanza, 24, was the son of Gertrudis Lanza Gonzales and Roberto Becerra Lanza. At the time of his detention he was the general secretary of the Honduran Federation of University Students (Federación de Estudiantes Universitarios de Honduras-FEUH) and a member of the University Reform Front (Frente de Reforma Universitaria-FRU). He was disappeared on August 1, 1982, by DNI agents.

As a university leader and member of the FRU, Becerra Lanza participated in anti-government demonstrations demanding the release of students who had been detained and accused of subversion.[43] He had apparently been followed by DNI agents in the days leading up to his detention, according to statements made after the arrest of another student leader, Guillermo Ayes. Ayes was detained by the DNI, tortured, and then released. During the torture, Ayes was forced to give the names of the most active student leaders with whom he worked and he mentioned Becerra Lanza. Ayes himself told Becerra Lanza that the agents had asked about him and he recommended that the student leader leave the country.[44] Ayes later left Honduras for Mexico.

At about 10:00 p.m. on August 1, 1982, Becerra Lanza was with two of his fellow medical school students at a bar, known as the "Bar de los Solteros" (The Bachelors' Bar) in downtown Tegucigalpa. His two friends, Flavio and Oscar, were detained during a police round-up of young men for obligatory military service. Becerra Lanza was not arrested in this raid, but several minutes later DNI agents entered the bar and arrested him. From the vehicle in which they were being held, Becerra Lanza's two friends could see the agents, who arrived in a jeep, enter the bar.[45] A waitress at the bar named Zoila told Becerra Lanza's parents that their son had been detained by DNI agents. The events took place near the Regis pharmacy in downtown Tegucigalpa. Flavio and Oscar were brought to a fire station and released the

---

[43] *Tiempo,* September 17, 1981.

[44] Interview with the parents of José Eduardo Becerra Lanza, December 22, 1993. This testimony was also presented by María Getrudis Lanza de Becerra in a *habeas corpus* petition filed before the Supreme Court on August 11, 1982.

[45] *Ibid.*

following day, August 2, at 6:00 a.m. Becerra Lanza was never seen again. Despite the fact that they were separated, Flavio and Oscar assumed their friend had been taken to DNI headquarters, given the presence of DNI agents at the bar after they were detained.

The day after the kidnapping, the students occupied the UNAH medical school to demand Becerra Lanza's release.[46] In the days and years following Becerra Lanza's detention, legal actions were initiated to demand his release. These actions failed to produce any results. María Gertrudis Lanza, Becerra Lanza's mother, filed an unsuccessful petition for a writ of *habeas corpus* before the Supreme Court. In April 1984, Gertrudis Lanza filed another petition for a writ of *habeas corpus* after receiving information that her son, along with 14 other people who had disappeared, was being held in a clandestine jail in the basement of the First Infantry Battalion barracks near Tegucigalpa. The petition was also unsuccessful.[47]

At the same time, an officer in the Armed Forces denied that Becerra Lanza had been detained and suggested that he probably had left the country using a pseudonym.[48]

Becerra Lanza's parents received information from two sources claiming to have seen their son. According to these sources, he was first held in the DNI, then at the First Infantry Battalion and later at a clandestine detention center in Colonia 21 in Tegucigalpa. According to another source, two weeks after he had been arrested, Becerra Lanza was seen in a DNI cell by another detainee. He was apparently at the point of death, suffering from convulsions as a result of torture.[49]

Relatives of some of the disappeared filed criminal charges against Gen. Gustavo Alvarez Martínez and other high-ranking officers, accusing them of

---

[46] *Tiempo,* August 2, 1982.

[47] *See* Honduran Supreme Court records, August 3, 1982; August 21, 1982; August 27, 1982; October 7, 1982; November 8, 1982; November 24, 1982; June 21, 1983; June 24, 1983; July 4, 1983; October 10, 1983; April 5, 1984; and April 9, 1984.

[48] *"DNI Chief Asks Human Rights Commission for Proof of Existence of Political Prisoners:"* Maj. Juan Blas Salazar asserted that there are no subversives in the DNI's jails and that if any person with ties to subversion has disappeared he or she may be in Nicaragua or another communist country. *Tiempo,* March 29, 1983.

[49] Amnesty, *Disappearances.*

assassination, torture, and abuse of authority in several cases, including that of Becerra Lanza. The case was dismissed in January 1986 by the First Criminal Court in the state of Francisco Morazán. The judge did not subpoena any of the accused and declared key evidence inadmissible, including testimony from a former colonel who implicated Gen. Alvarez (who never appeared before any judicial authority in connection with these cases).[50]

The family's lawyer met with the highest ranking officers of the Armed Forces. There he was shown a report about Becerra Lanza, which stated that he was a communist agitator who had received training outside of Honduras. According to his mother, Becerra Lanza had been outside of Honduras only once to attend a meeting of student representatives and leaders in Nicaragua.[51]

The papal nuncio, Monsignor Cordero Lanza, served as mediator when students took over the Chamber of Commerce in 1982 to demand Becerra Lanza's release. According to testimony from Becerra Lanza's father, the Dean of the Foreign Service Corps told him that his son had not been released and that he had better get a good lawyer if he wanted to save his life since Becerra Lanza was being held at the First Infantry Battalion's barracks.[52]

In 1983, Becerra Lanza's parents were informed that their son's body was in the morgue and that they should come to identify it. When they arrived at the morgue it was heavily guarded by soldiers. They looked at several corpses, but could not identify their son. Despite the lack of identification, the lieutenant in charge said that one of the bodies was that of Becerra Lanza.[53]

In 1986, a member of the Nicaraguan contras, who had worked in

---

[50] *Ibid.* p. 7. In January 1986, the *El Heraldo* newspaper reported "the First Court of Appeals upheld the ruling on the decision issued by Judge Francisco Bocanegra Deras of the First Criminal Court. The military officers charged were: Gen. Gustavo Alvarez Martínez, Ret. Gen. Daniel Balí Castillo, Col. Juan López Grijalba, Maj. Juan Blas Salázar, Alexánder Hernández and Marco Hernández. They were accused of attempted homicide, homicide, application of torture and other prohibited forms of mistreatment, abuse of authority, and disobedience against Rolando Vindel, Jorge Eurake, José Eduardo (Becerra) Lanza, Reynaldo Díaz, Manfredo Velásquez and others. The courts dismissed the charges against all the military officers."

[51] Interview with parents of José Eduardo Becerra Lanza, December 22, 1993.

[52] *Ibid.*

[53] *Ibid.*

Tegucigalpa, admitted in a press interview to having participated in the assassination of José Eduardo Becerra Lanza and Félix Martínez. He explained in detail how the two had been executed. In his statement he indicated that Captain Alexander Hernández, a member of an anti-communist network, handed the two men over to him with clear instructions that they were to be executed. Hernández specified that Becerra Lanza should disappear. Becerra Lanza was killed and his body was buried somewhere between Tegucigalpa and Choluteca. The contra stated that Captain Hernández had told him the orders came directly from Gen. Alvarez Martínez.[54] The statements were corroborated by the testimony of José Barrera Martínez, who claims to have been a member of the Armed Forces' Battalion 3-16. Barrera claimed that Carlos Peralta handed Félix

---

[54] "One evening in the summer of 1982, Miguel received a call from Alexander Hernández, a Honduran army captain who was chief of the *Dirección de Investigaciones Especiales*—known by the acronym DIES—a clandestine anti-communist intelligence network. Hernández told Miguel there were 'two packages to be picked up.'

The contras were told to meet a Honduran military jeep on a freeway near Tegucigalpa. There a Honduran soldier handed over two young men, Eduardo Lanza and Félix Martínez. The Hondurans referred to the two men only as 'the skinny one' and 'the bigger one.' Lanza was emaciated after forty days of detention and torture by the Honduran authorities.

'Our orders were that Eduardo Lanza was to vanish, to never appear again,' Miguel says. 'As for Félix Martínez, he was to be found dead, and to have died in such a brutal way that no communist who saw him would want to be in his skin.'

Hernández told Miguel the orders came directly from the Honduran commander-in-chief, General Gustavo Alvarez Martínez.

The contras drove south from Tegucigalpa toward Choluteca, where they stopped to dig a single grave on an isolated hillside. 'Don't kill me,' Lanza begged Miguel. 'I'll go to work for you people.'

'—and who the fuck are you? (*Y vos quien puta sos?)*', Miguel responded.

Lanza told Miguel he was a leader of the student federation at the medical school in Tegucigalpa. 'My name is Eduardo Lanza,' he said. 'Give me a pencil and a piece of paper so I can write a note to my mother.'

Lanza was made to lie down in the grave. One of the contras was handed a knife and instructed to kill him. 'But our man did it badly, as if he was afraid, and the kid screamed,' Miguel recalls. 'There were some houses at the edge of the hill. So four or five bullets were fired into his head using a pistol with a silencer. Then lime was shoveled over him. You know, so there wouldn't be a bad smell.' Linda Drucker, "A Contra's Story," *The Progressive*, August 1986, pp. 25-26. *Tiempo* published a report on the information contained in Drucker's article, August 18, 1986.

Martínez over to the Nicaraguan contras.[55]

The fate of José Eduardo Becerra Lanza remains unknown. His body has not been found.

5. Milton Danilo Jiménez Puerto (1982)

Milton Jiménez was a 20-year-old law student at the National Autonomous University of Honduras and an activist in the Revolutionary University Force (*Fuerza Universitaria Revolucionaria*-FUR when he was temporarily detained-disappeared in April 1982. Today, Jiménez is a practicing lawyer in Honduras.[56] Jiménez's case illustrates the circumstances of the arrest, detention, and the torture suffered by those detained, and evidences the existence of clandestine jails. It also reveals the subordinate role of the judicial branch.

A native of the north coast, Milton Jiménez had rented a house in the Miraflores neighborhood with his sister. Also living in the house were Rafael Rivera Torres, a lawyer and then-assistant attorney general, his two daughters, Gilda and Suyapa, and two students, Adán Guillermo López Lone and his brother Edwin. The six young people were all friends and university students.

The detention occurred on April 27, 1982. Very early in the morning a group of armed men dressed in civilian clothes burst into the house where the students were sleeping. Jiménez's account of what happened follows:

> Rivera Torres, the lawyer, strongly objected to the attempt to detain us without any legal authority and the individuals retreated. A larger group of about 20 men returned about a half hour later and forcibly arrested all of us, including Rivera Torres. The one who was apparently in charge of the operation was armed and carried a walkie-talkie. He said, 'we are only carrying out orders.'[57]

---

[55] Sworn affidavit of José Barrera Martínez declaration before Salvador Godínez Viera, Mexico City Public Notary No. 42, July 2, 1987.

[56] The National Commissioner for the Protection of Human Rights received testimony from Milton Jiménez on December 22, 1993, at 3:00 p.m.

[57] In testimony before the Inter-American Court of Human Rights, Miltón Jiménez stated:

> The house where we were detained was in a residential neighborhood. One of

As their neighbors and family members looked on, the group of six students and the assistant attorney general were put into two Toyota double-cabin pickups, one green and the other yellow, without license plates. They were all taken to the police precinct in El Manchén. Rivera Torres was released about two hours later. The six students were kept incummunicado in a cell until that night when they were transferred in vehicles, bound and blindfolded, to an unidenitified location.[58]

Jiménez, his sister, the two daughters of the assistant Attorney General and the López Lone brothers were held for four days. In his testimony before the Inter-American Court of Human Rights, Jiménez said:

> That same night the torture began ... they began to torture the tallest person—not me—to the verge of death. I know this because I could hear them, they had to give the victim artificial respiration because they had put the *capucha* on 15 times without stopping. Later, they began beating me, but they didn't use the capucha on me. They put me in front of a firing squad and pretended to fire. They told us very clearly that they were going to kill us.[59]

---

our neighbors had been a Supreme Court justice, labor minister, vice rector at the university and dean of the law school. In front of us lived Liberal Party representative and attorney, Carlos Rivas García. Both these people—the former Court Justice and the representative—made them see that they couldn't arrest us without a warrant and that the assistant attorney general had judicial immunity, that he couldn't be arrested under any circumstances. This didn't stop them from arresting us. What's more, they arrested [Rivera Torres] in his pajamas.

Testimony of Milton Jiménez before the Inter-American Court of Human Rights, Public Audience, Oct. 1 1987 (hereafter IACHR Testimony of Milton Jiménez).

[58] In his testimony before the Commissioner, Jiménez stated that based on his personal investigation, he believes the clandestine detention center was the country home of Col. Amílcar Zelaya, which the peasants in the area knew as "the DNI house."

[59] Jiménez stated that "The capucha is a rubber hood that the security forces use ... they hit a person and knock the wind out of him and then they put the hood over the person's head until he's about to suffocate..."

During his testimony, Jiménez also talked about the conditions in the clandestine detention center, which he described as "inhuman, with constant physical tortures."

> We were blindfolded the entire time and weren't given anything to eat. While we were being tortured we were interrogated continuously about university politics because a new rector was going to be chosen in a few months. They asked us who were the student leaders, they never accused us of being terrorists or subversives. On one occasion, when they took me to the bathroom, I could see through my blindfold a person wrapped in newspapers lying on the floor. As a result of the torture, this person was reduced to a bloody mass that could only groan in pain.

On the fourth day the students were taken, blindfolded, to a different section of the detention center. They were asked to forgive their captors and forget what had happened "in order to avoid problems for the armed forces." Jiménez could see through his blindfold that the group was being addressed by a uniformed military officer.[60]

After this, four of the students were released and returned to their home, while Jiménez and Adán López Lone, who was also a FUR leader, were transferred back to the jail at El Manchén. On May 7, 1982, they were tried for the crimes of "antisocial and totalitarian activities against the democratic and representative government of the State of Honduras" and sentenced by Judge Wilfredo Madrid of the First Criminal Court to serve prison terms.[61] The

---

[60] Testimony given to the Commissioner, December 22, 1993. Jiménez added that they were asked if they could recognize any of the people who had detained them. Everyone in the group said they did not recognize their captors.

[61] In his testimony to the Inter-American Court of Human Rights, Jiménez stated:

> When I asked (Judge Wilfredo Madrid) why he had rendered a jail sentence for this crime, when he, more than anyone else, knew that the case had no merit he answered me as follows: "Look, this is the least harm I can do to you. My goal is for you go free on bail because they are asking me to sentence you for a much more serious crime, for which you could not get out on bail."

IACHR Testimony of Milton Jiménez.

accusation was presented by the commander of the First Detectives Squadron and chief of the Criminal Investigations Section of the DNI.[62]

After six days the two students were released on bail. The judicial process lasted approximately 18 months and was eventually dismissed by the First Criminal Court in November 1983. This decision was affirmed by the Court of Appeals one month later.[63]

6. Germán Pérez Alemán (1982)

Pérez Alemán was a union leader and was married. He was disappeared on August 18, 1982. Pérez Alemán was the treasurer of the Union of Public Employees of Roads and Airport and Terminal Maintenance (Sindicato de Empleados Públicos de Caminos, Mantenimento de Aeropuertos y Terminales-SEPCAMAT).

Six heavily armed men abducted Pérez Alemán at about 4:00 p.m near the Columbus monument on the European Economic Community Boulevard. He attempted to resist, but was beaten (causing head injuries) and forced into a car.[64] Pérez Alemán's fellow union leaders publicly denounced the kidnapping based on eyewitness accounts of what had happened.[65]

Given the notoriety of the detention, which occurred in broad daylight on a busy street, the car into which Pérez Alemán was forced was followed by a highway safety patrol car (No. 12) of the Department of Communication, Public Works and Transportation (Secretaría de Communicaciones, Obras Públicas y Transporte-SECOPT). The patrol car, occupied by Second Sgt. Juan Bautista Aguilar and Cpl. Nicolás Aguilar Carrasco, caught up with the kidnappers.

According to testimonies given at a later time, one of the kidnappers was Lt. Segundo Flores Murillo. Flores Murillo got out of the car and identified himself as a G-2 agent, thus halting pursuit by SECOPT.

In relation to this case, Florencio Caballero gave the following

---

[62] The head of the DNI at this time was Maj. Juan Blas Salazar.

[63] The case was presented May 6, 1982, in the First Criminal Court of Francisco Morazán and dismissed several months later.

[64] CODEH, List.

[65] La Tribuna, August 28, 1982.

testimony before the Inter-American Court of Human Rights:

> Q: Do you remember an example of the regular police interfering in an
> action?
> A: Yes, in the case of Germán Pérez Alemán and the case of
> Andrónico Espinal. In the case of Germán Pérez Alemán, he was
> kidnapped near the Toncontín Airport in Tegucigalpa. He tried to resist
> and in the struggle some of the kidnappers lost their fake beards and
> wigs. Everyone witnessed this kidnapping. We were chased by a
> SECOPT patrol car.
> Q: What is SECOPT please?
> A: The Department of Communications, Public Works and
> Transportation (Secretaría de Comunicaciones, Obras Públicas y
> Transporte). It was the police force that patrols the roads and also takes
> care of transportation problems on the highways. They followed us and
> near the Tiloarque neighborhood and Vincent Cáceres Central Institute
> they caught up to us since the car we were driving was small and didn't
> have much speed and they were driving a Ford. Lt. Flores Murillo
> identified himself to them and told them if the journalists asked any
> questions to say that they didn't catch us. If they didn't, they would
> have to pay the consequences. Germán Pérez Alemán was then taken
> to Támara.[66]

Pérez Alemán's mother was told by SECOPT Minister José Azcona that
the union leader had been detained because of his numerous visits to El
Salvador.[67] The family explained that he made the trips in order to collect
payments on his Salvadoran father's life insurance policy. The trips, however,
made him a suspect in the eyes of the security forces. This disappearance may
well have been a "mistake" in the security forces' evaluation of the activities of
the victim. The characteristics the security forces considered suspect—a union
leader travelling frequently to El Salvador—were present in this case. However,
the purpose behind Pérez Alemán's trips was apparently not to make contact
with Salvadoran guerrillas but to take care of family matters. In his testimony
before the Inter-American Court, Florencio Caballero confirmed that this case

---

[66] IACHR Testimony of Florencio Caballero, p. 171. *Editor's Note*: According to
Caballero, Battalion 3-16 held prisoners in clandestine detention in Támara.

[67] U.N. Working Group, *Report*.

constituted a mistake on the part of security forces carrying out kidnappings and disappearances.[68]

There are also accounts of the torture to which Pérez Alemán may have been subjected during his detention.[69] CODEH reported the case (like many others) to the U.N. Working Group on Enforced or Involuntary Disappearances, but this international pressure was unsuccessful. On May 29, 1983, the Honduran Permanent Mission in Geneva informed the U.N. Working Group that, according to information supplied by the Honduran Armed Forces, the DNI was carrying out an investigation of the case. The Honduran government again informed the U.N. Working Group on August 31, 1983, that an investigation was being conducted. The investigations produced no results. There was apparently no further communication.[70]

Pérez Alemán's fate remains unknown. His body has not been found.

7. Inés Consuelo Murillo Schwaderer (1983)

Murillo Schwaderer was a lawyer, political activist, and advisor to labor and peasant organizations at the time of her disappearance on March 13, 1983. The DNI admitted to detaining her on May 31, 1983—some 78 days after the fact. Murillo's case is an example of a temporary disappearance and reveals

---

[68]   Q: Do you know of any case or person, who because of that mentality, was detained or kidnapped in error? That is, that you yourselves became convinced it was a mistake, that the man or woman was not involved?

          A: The case of Germán Pérez Alemán. He was not acting with any leftist group, and I believe that he wasn't guilty and did not deserve what they did to him. Although no one deserved to be judged. That is what the judicial authorities are for, to judge him. Then, that is one case.

IACHR Testimony of Florencio Caballero, p. 203.

[69] "As an example of the methods used by Battalion 3-16, Caballero said he saw other soldiers tie an inner tube around Pérez Alemán's face until he fainted." Terri Shaw and Herbert H. Denton, "Honduran Death Squad Alleged," *Washington Post,* May 2, 1987.

[70] U.N. Working Group, *Report.*

much about the treatment of detainees, the clandestine centers where they are detained and the forms of torture used. Murillo was not only able to identify her captors as agents of the armed forces, but could positively identify one individual.

Murillo was detained in the city of Choloma at approximately 6:30 p.m. on March 13, along with José González Trejo, a Salvadoran shoe repairman. Murillo was leaving the house of a doctor friend of Flores Trejo. The two were detained by a group of men, claiming to be agents of the Immigration Bureau, who arrived in a pickup truck that was backed up by another vehicle. The two victims tried to resist, but they were beaten and eventually forced into the pickup. Once in the truck they were blindfolded and bound.[71]

Murillo was not committing any crime, nor were there any outstanding warrants for her arrest. According to her testimony, at the time of her arrest she was involved in political organizing in relation to her work with peasants. Murillo had been a student leader and her work involved advising peasant organizations.[72]

Because she feared reprisals against her family, Murillo hid her true identity when she was first captured. Her kidnappers did not ask her for identification documents when she was captured because they sought to force her to admit she was Salvadoran and a member of the Salvadoran guerrilla movement, the FMLN. Murillo used a false name for more than a week after being detained. On the tenth day of her detention she told the kidnappers her real name.[73] Murillo's detention and her description of what happened were confirmed by the testimony of an ex-member of the Honduran Armed Forces.[74]

---

[71] Testimony of Inés Consuelo Murillo before the Inter-American Court of Human Rights, Public Hearing, October 5, 1987 (hereafter "IACHR Testimony of Inés Consuelo Murillo). pp. 7-8.

[72] *Ibid.*, 8-9.

[73] *Ibid.*, pp. 12-13.

[74]   Q: Did you review Inés Consuelo Murillo's file?
        A: Yes. It contained information about her. First when she was kidnapped. In the first interrogation the name she gave. She said she was from Ocotepeque and all that. I don't remember the names of the relatives that those documents had, but about 10-14 days later Inés told us her real name and everyone knew she was Inés Consuelo,

Years later, Gen. Gustavo Alvarez Martínez said that if she had been detained it was because she was "a communist."[75]

Murillo was transferred to a clandestine detention center in the Bella Vista neighborhood in San Pedro Sula immediately after being detained. She was able to identify the site after her release.[76] After spending 37 days in the first detention center, Murillo was transferred to a military installation near Tegucigalpa. While she was there she came into contact with other people who had been kidnapped.[77]

During her detention, Murillo was subjected to various forms of degrading treatment and torture.[78] Other sources have confirmed Murillo's testimony.[79]

It appears that the torture to which Murillo was subjected was

---

daughter of who, father and mother, her profession and all, we all knew. We knew, our bosses knew, even Alvarez Martínez knew.

IACHR Testimony of Florencio Caballero, p. 209.

[75] "Honduran Denies Rights Charges," *Washington Post*, May 3, 1987.

[76] "It was in the Bella Vista neighborhood, very close to the first street in San Pedro Sula, at the very end of the street. I even thought we were going to climb the "El Merendón" mountain, which is at the outer limits of the city. It was above the city's first street and to the left, when we got there they honked the horn. A heavy metal door was opened and we drove in. We were then thrown into a basement pit." IACHR Testimony of Inés Consuelo Murillo, p. 10.

[77] *Ibid.*, p. 15.

[78] "I was tied up and beaten. I was left naked most of the time and was given almost nothing to eat. We were fed as a reward or as a confidence. The officer's orders were to give us a half glass of water a day. I was subjected to electroshocks, hung, subjected to suffocation attempts, threatened with weapons and having my eyes burned; for example, they burned my legs, made cuts in my skins with needles, made me lose my sense of time and space, drugged, and sexually abused me." *Ibid.*, p. 11.

[79] Q: Did you see what they did to Inés Consuelo?
A: Inés Consuelo was kept naked and they threw water on her every 10 minutes all night. Every night she was there. IACHR Testimony of Florencio Caballero, p. 173.

controlled by a doctor.[80] Her cell was never cleaned nor was she permitted to clean it herself. She described being hit, receiving electric shocks, repeatedly being drenched with ice water and tormented. The tortures were aimed at forcing her to render false statements regarding subversive activities.[81] Murillo testified that she remembered the visit of someone named "Mr. Mike," apparently an American. Before his visit, her cell was cleaned and she was allowed to bathe. The visitor could tell, however, that she had been tortured.[82] The presence of Americans during Murillo's interrogations and/or their visits to see her is supported by other testimonies.[83]

During her detention Murillo was able to recognize Sub-lieutenant

---

[80] A: There was a doctor in the special squadron. Unfortunately, I don't know his name, but I know his last name: Dr. Cruz, who works or worked in the San Felipe Hospital, in the Thorax Institute. He had access, to even see them. He looked at Inés, at Flores. He examined many, many detainees.
Q: Did you ever see the doctor?
A: Yes, he even treated me on several occasions.
Q: Did he have very long hair?
A: No, he had very short hair. There isn't anyone here who looks like him. Short hair, about 34 or 35 years old, about 5 feet 8 inches tall, rugged in build, dark-skinned, mustache; he drove a white sedan. *Ibid.*, p. 193.

[81] Charlotte Montgomery, "Death squad survivor feels sympathy for torturers," *The Globe and Mail,* Canada, October 20, 1988.

[82] "Murillo added that when 'Mr. Mike' came to visit the detention center, she was allowed to wash and her cell was cleaned. But, she said, 'he should have known what torture I suffered. It was obvious.' "Shaw and Denton, "Honduran Death Squad Alleged," *Washington Post*, May 2, 1987.

[83] Q: Did the foreign advisors know about the detention centers and this whole situation? A: Yes. There was an advisor who used the pseudonym "Mr. Mike," I don't know his real name. He was living in the U.S. embassy, and had full access to us. He was there for (Inés) Consuelo Murillo's and Duarte Salgado's interrogation. He led the interrogation. At times he would write down his questions so the questioner could ask them. IACHR Testimony of Florencio Caballero, p. 173.

Marco Tulio Regalado Hernández of her captors.[84]

Finally, on May 31, Murillo's detention was officially acknowledged and she was transferred to the DNI in Tegucigalpa. The DNI, through Maj. Juan Blas Salazar Meza, assumed responsibility for her detention, although military intelligence had kidnapped, interrogated, and tortured her. According to some testimonies, there existed an unofficial policy by which the DNI agreed to assume responsibility for detentions when circumstances required they be made public. The objective of this policy was to maintain the existence and actions of the military intelligence unit secret.[85]

After Murillo's detention was made public she was transferred to an ordinary prison where she remained for thirteen months until her release on July 5, 1984. Eventually, Murillo was forced to leave the country.[86]

8. Gustavo Adolfo Morales Fúnez (1984)

Morales, an economist, worked for the National Childrens' Foundation (Patronato Nacional de la Infancia-PANI). He had been president of the National Agrarian Institute Employees' Union (Sindicato de Trabajadores del Instituto Nacional Agrario-SITRAINA). Morales was married and the father of three

---

[84] "I heard names, real names because I heard people correcting each other. For example, 'my name isn't Portillo it's Giovani.' One officer one time—I already knew his name, 60 days having passed—began to torture me very unnecessarily and I said to him, 'Regalado Hernández, never forget what you have done now.'"
Q: Who was this officer you mentioned?
A: Regalado Hernández. Marco Tulio Regalado Hernández. He is the younger brother of the current commander in chief of the Armed Forces." IACHR Testimony of Inés Consuelo Murillo, p. 18. Murillo's identification of Regalado Hernández is ratified on p. 32.

[85] "Juán Blas at first, I think that when she was in San Pedro, Blas Salazar already knew that she was detained but he never had her in the DNI. He knew that she was detained because they said to him, 'look, Blas, Alexánder told him one day when he arrived at INDUMIL, if anything happens with Inés, we'll give her to you.'
Blas Salazar was in charge the whole time of the people that were going to be taken to court. And he said, yes, I had her, but she was undocumented, with a false name. Faces don't lie. in the newspapers Inés Consuelo appeared and everyone knew her." IACHR Testimony of Florencio Caballero, p. 209.

[86] Montgomery, "Death Squad survivor," *The Globe and Mail,* October 20, 1988.

children. His political activism and opposition to the government were well known. Morales was disappeared on the morning of March 18, 1984, while he was on his way to the television studios of Channel 5, where he was to supervise the national lottery.[87]

This is one of the few cases in which an eyewitness to a kidnapping could be identified and interviewed. Then-Supreme Court Justice Luis Mendoza Fugón[88] was walking to his office one Sunday when he witnessed Morales's detention. It was early in the morning when Mendoza reached the intersection of Los Próceres Avenue and what is now Ramón Ernesto Cruz street. Mendoza saw a blue van intercept an old jeep that was heading north. Several men armed with machine guns and pistols got out of the van. A light-colored pickup pulled up behind the jeep to cover Morales's vehicle. The kidnappers struggled to get the person driving the jeep into the van. A shot was fired, apparently only to frighten, since no one was injured.

Despite his struggle, the driver of the jeep was finally forced into the blue van, which drove off heading east, in the direction of the 21 de Octubre neighborhood.[89]

The action was also witnessed by a FUSEP agent who was guarding the Foreign Ministry, but who did nothing to stop the kidnapping. Luis Mendoza urged the agent to do something since the jeep was still running, with its keys inside. There were also other military personnel nearby, guarding the U.S. Embassy. When they were approached by Mendoza they responded evasively, indicating that had not heard or seen anything. Although Mendoza reported what he had seen to the press, he was never called to give an official statement to any authority until requested to do so by the National Commissioner for the Protection of Human Rights.[90]

Morales's kidnappers acted with complete impunity. They had no fear that they would be stopped or attacked by members of the public security forces. They carried out their "operation" in broad daylight, in a busy downtown section

---

[87] CODEH, *List*; *See also* Amnesty, *Disappearances*.

[88] Supreme Court Justice from January 1982 to May 1985.

[89] Testimony of former Supreme Court Justice Luis Mendoza Fugón to the National Commissioner for the Protection of Human Rights, Tegucigalpa, December 22, 1993.

[90] *Ibid.*

of Tegucigalpa, near public offices and used several vehicles and numerous weapons during the detention.

Morales's jeep was later seen parked at DNI headquarters. The National Childrens' Foundation received an anonymous telephone call informing them that Morales's car could be retrieved from DNI headquarters and that additional information on Morales could be obtained by calling a certain telephone number. The number corresponded to the DNI offices. The DNI, for its part, denied any involvement in Morales's detention.[91]

Numerous petitions for writs of *habeas corpus* were presented in the days following Morales's detention, but none of them proved successful.[92] Morales's case has been brought before the U.N. Working Group on Enforced or Involuntary Disappearances (case No. 007666). On repeated occasions, the Honduran government denied responsibility in the case to the Working Group. On April 25, 1984, the Honduran government submitted information on the case to the United Nations. The information included an official report from the Honduran Supreme Court stating that Morales had not been arrested. Yet, information from the Honduran Armed Forces, provided April 30, 1984, stated that Morales had not been detained. The Honduran Government also forwarded to the U.N. on that day a copy of the denial of the petition for a writ of *habeas corpus* which stated that Morales was not being held by the military intelligence unit (G-2) or the DNI.[93]

At the time of Morales's disappearance, Maj. Juan Blas Salazar was DNI chief and Col. Luis A. Discua Elvir was the Commander of Battalion 3-16.

The fate of Gustavo Adolfo Morales Fúnez remains unknown.

9. José Eduardo López (1984)

López, a 38-year-old journalist, had been the past president of the regional branch of the Committee for the Defense of Human Rights in Honduras (CODEH) in Cortés. He was an active member of the Communist Party of Honduras and had also been a sergeant in the Honduran Army. López was known for writing articles criticizing the political and economic conditions in the

---

[91] *See also* Amnesty, *Disappearances*, p. 28.

[92] Amnesty International, *Honduras: Civilian Authority-Military Power: Human Rights Violations in the 1980s.* (London: February 1988), p. 50.

[93] U.N. Working Group, *Report.*

country.[94]

López had previously been detained by the security forces. In 1981, he was detained and tortured for five days. In 1984, he was forced to return to Honduras after trying unsuccessfully to obtain asylum in Canada. In April 1984, he began receiving repeated threats to his life. In a statement to CODEH, López indicated that if anything happened to him the security forces would be responsible.

Human rights activists link the harassment and eventual disappearance of López to suspicious individuals involved in the CODEH section in Cortés who were passing information to the security forces.

López was detained on December 24, 1984, in San Pedro Sula. His captors appear to have been government agents, presumably from the DNI. Another detainee claimed to have seen López in the DNI jail cells in San Pedro Sula.[95] After being detained a second time, however, the witness retracted the previous statement. The commander of the DNI in San Pedro Sula denied that López was in detention there.

An unsuccessful petition for a writ of *habeas corpus* was presented to the Court of Appeals in San Pedro Sula. López's case was also presented to the U.N. Working Group on Enforced or Involuntary Disappearances. The last submission of the Honduran government to the Working Group, dated April 19, 1988, stated that López had never been detained in Honduras. As evidence they used the judicial denial of the petition for writ of *habeas corpus*.[96] The fate of José Eduardo López is still unknown.

10. Corina Cruz Pineda (1986)

Cruz was 17 years old when she was detained, along with her mother and two sisters, on October 7, 1986, in San Antonio, Intibucá, by Lt. Vaquero of the Fifth Infantry Battalion. Though she was released the same day, Cruz was rearrested the following day in San Antonio and detained in that town for two days. October 10, 1986, she was transferred to Marcala, the site of the Fifth Battalion's headquarters. The basis for López's detention was her supposed

---

[94] CODEH, *List.*

[95] *Ibid.*

[96] U.N. Working Group, *Report.*

collaboration with Salvadoran guerrillas.[97]

A petition for a writ of *habeas corpus* was filed October 16 on her behalf. Military authorities accepted responsibility for her detention, but stated that she had been released. Col. Armando Rivera Gómez, Sub-Commander of the battalion, told the judge that according to information from the G-2 intelligence unit, López had been detained due to her suspected involvement with the Salvadoran guerrillas, and was released October 10, after being questioned. The judge visited the battalion's holding cells and did not find any evidence of civilian prisoners. No evidence was presented to establish that Cruz had been released. Neither was it explained why, unlike the rest of her family, Corina Cruz remained disappeared.[98]

The acknowledgment of Cruz's detention, mostly likely because of the existence of numerous eyewitnesses, makes clear that she was in the custody of public authorities. Those authorities are thereby responsible for determining her whereabouts and assuring her physical integrity.

11. Eliazar Paguagua Mayorga (1987)

A Nicaraguan, Paguagua was detained by the contras on June 19, 1987. His detention was denounced before the U.N. Working Group on Enforced or Involuntary Disappearances.[99]

Paguagua was detained along with seven other young Nicaraguans, all of whom were completing their military service. The young men were kidnapped by contra forces and brought to Honduras where the contras had set up their base. The other detainees were: Domingo José Escobar Sánchez, Manuel Antonio González Sánchez, José Antonio Hernández Pernudy, Juan José López Venegas, Richard Lugo, Melvin Humberto Morán, and Franklin Sánchez Jiménez. All eight were detained on July 19, 1987, in Cano de la Cruz, in the Cerro Milambe district, Department of Jinotega, Nicaragua.[100]

---

[97] CODEH, *List.*

[98] *Ibid.*

[99] U.N. Working Group, *Report.*

[100] Cases number 007678, 007734, 007627, 007631, 007638, 007641, 007668 and 007704 presented to the U.N. Working Group on Enforced or Involuntary Disappearances. U.N. Working Group, *Report.*

There were many cases like this, in which non-Honduran citizens were captured in Nicaragua during confrontations between the contras and the Sandinista forces. The Commissioner received the written statement of María Mercedes Rivas Obregón, originally given to the International Center for the Legal Protection of Human Rights (Interights), who was disappeared September 27, 1984, by the contras. She was detained along with Elman Luis Cortéz Siesa, Guillermo Ríos Martínez, Blandón Zeas, and Ana Julia Cortéz. According to this version, at least Elman Cortéz, Guillermo Ríos, and Ana Julia Cortéz were presumably killed by contras. They continue to be listed as "disappeared," because their deaths have never been confirmed. Rivas Obregón was able to escape to Nicaragua in 1985 and give her testimony to Interights. Two other women who were kidnapped in Nicaragua and brought to Honduras, Teresa González Talavera and Maritza Cubillo Molina, were also interviewed by Interights.

González Talavera was kidnapped May 3, 1986, and was able to return to Nicaragua on September 13, 1990. Cubillo Molina was detained November 4, 1984, and returned to Nicaragua in February 1991.[101] Both women were taken to military camps in Honduras where they were tortured, sexually abused, and made to perform forced labor.

These Nicaraguan citizens, or in some cases, citizens of other nations, were brought into Honduran territory and later disappeared. The fact that they were foreign nationals with no relatives in Honduras rendered the search for them difficult. Further, the autonomy and impunity enjoyed by the contras during these years undermined any legal control over their actions by the authorities. There are also some complaints involving people who were disappeared after being assaulted *in* Honduras by contra forces.[102] A few cases concerning the disappearance of foreign nationals have surfaced, but there are probably many more for which documentation simply does not exist.

It should be noted that international law prohibits the taking of hostages,

---

[101] Notarized Affidavit of María Mercedes Rivas Obregón, Before Alba Delia Cespedes, Public Notary, February 11, 1986.

[102] In this respect, the Commissioner received information on the cases of Nicaraguans Roberto Elvis Cabrera, 26, and William Thomas Santamaría, 27, from COFADEH. Cabrera and Santamaría disappeared February 25, 1981, while they were driving a blue Mercedes Benz 220 (Nicaraguan license plant No. KY430) on their way to San Francisco, California. CODEH indicated that the two men were assaulted by a band of contras that attacked cars in later brought to Guatemala. (CODEH, *List.*)

as well as homicide, or acts of cruelty or torture, directed against prisoners or civilians. Common Article 3 of the four Geneva Conventions of 1949, which applies to non-international armed conflicts (such as that taking place in Nicaragua during those years) prohibits these practices.[103]

It is also worth noting that these crimes, having been committed in Honduras, are also subject to sanctions provided for in the Honduran Criminal Code.

12. Roger Samuel González Zelaya (1988)

González was a 24-year-old student and an employee of the Honduran Forestry Development Corporation (Corporación Hondureña de Desarrollo Forestal-CODEHFOR). He had been a leader of the Federation of Secondary

---

[103] Article 3. In the case of an armed conflict not of an international character occurring in the territory of one of the High Contracting Parties, each Party to the conflict shall be bound to apply, as a minimum, the following provisions:

    (1)   Persons taking no active part in the hostilities, including members of the armed forces who have laid down their arms and those placed *hors de combat* by sickness, wounds, detention, or any other cause, shall in all circumstances be treated humanely, without any adverse distinction founded on race, colour, religion or faith, sex, birth or wealth, or any other similar criteria. To this end, the following acts are and shall remain prohibited at any time and in any place whatsoever with respect to the above-mentioned persons:

        (a) violence to life and person, in particular murder of all kinds, mutilation, cruel treatment and torture;

        (b) taking of hostages;

        (c) outrage upon personal dignity, in particular humiliating and degrading treatment;

        (d) the passing of sentences and the carrying out of executions without previous judgement pronounced by a regularly constituted court, affording all the judicial guarantees which are recognized as indispensable by civilized peoples.

    (2)   The wounded and sick shall be collected and cared for.

An impartial humanitarian body, such as the International Committee of the Red Cross, may offer its services to the Parties to the conflict. The Parties to the conflict should further endeavor to bring into force, by means of special agreements, all or part of the other provisions of the present Convention. The application of the preceding provisions shall not affect the legal status of the Parties to the conflict.

School Students (Federación de Estudiantes de Segunda Enseñanza-FESE).

González was disappeared around noon on April 19, 1988, as he was walking through Tegucigalpa's Central Park. He was kidnapped by three people, at least one of whom was identified as a DNI agent. An eyewitness to González's detention provided this account:

> It was Tuesday, April 19 about 12:25 p.m. and I was on a bus on the Santa Fe-Miraflores route. When the bus passed by the Central Park, I saw Roger Samuel González, whom I knew personally as a friend. He was walking on the side of the park where the bus stops are located. He was wearing a pair of blue jeans, a khaki-colored shirt and brown shoes .... He was carrying a leather briefcase and two backpacks. He had a beige-colored sweater tied to the briefcase. A National Investigations Directorate (DNI) agent was walking in front of Roger. I knew him (the DNI agent) because he would follow the democratic student leaders. He was a strapping man, about 30 years old, with curly hair and a slight mustache. Behind Roger there was another man, also a DNI agent. He was thin, with straight hair and approximately 23 years old. About ten paces behind him was a young woman. She was tall, attractive and had short hair. She was well-dressed and always carried a black pocketbook. I recognized the woman because she had followed me on April 14. The bus I was on did not stop at the park, so I couldn't warn Roger about the danger he was in. I was one of the people who saw Roger before he disappeared on that date—April 19. Since then, he has not returned home, to his school or to his work.[104]

Five petitions for writs of *habeas corpus* were filed to discover González's whereabouts. In response to these constitutional actions, the DNI, the FUSEP, and the First Infantry Battalion denied having González in their custody. In at least one case, the judge in charge was denied access to one of the jails mentioned in the *habeas* petition.

At first, Col. Manuel Enrique Suárez Benavides, the official spokesperson of the Armed Forces, recognized that González had been detained by the FUSEP. Later, however, the spokesperson for the FUSEP, Maj. Manuel Antonio Urbina, denied this, stating that FUSEP had been looking for González in connection with a protest in front of the U.S. Embassy. In his statement given in support of a Honduran seeking asylum in the United States, a former

---

[104] Anonymous sworn notarized affidavit provided by CODEH.

policeman who had collaborated with Battalion 3-16, Fausto Ramón Reyes Caballero, stated that he had seen González alive in Battalion 3-16 headquarters after his disappearance.[105] Significantly, the information provided by the FUSEP spokesperson—that González was being sought in connection with a protest at the U.S. Embassy—coincided with Reyes Caballero's statement that González had been detained by Battalion 3-16 for that same protest.[106]

In a public statement to the press, the commander-in-chief of the Armed Forces maintained that Roger González was probably living underground outside the country. He did not, however, offer any evidence to support this allegation. There has been no official comment offered, nor any evidence that questions the statements of the witnesses to the detention or Reyes Caballero's statement

---

[105] Just now, August 1, I was in San Pedro Sula, at Battalion 316. I was in the back in the 105th Infantry Brigade, in a building that was cream-colored which used to be the military hospital of the old Third Infantry Battalion. I went into the interrogation roomsand I saw Mr. Roger Gonzalez, who was in the interrogation room, and his eyes were bandaged, kind of a tape, adhesive tape on his eyes . . . . Deposition of Fausto Ramon Reyes Caballero, *In re: Application for Asylum of Ines Elizabeth Castro Escobar*, No. A28-574-289 (U.S. Department of Justice, Immigration and Naturalizaton Service) (December 23, 1988).

[106] "A: And all of this has been as a result of a narcotics trafficker, Ramon Mata Ballesteros. . . .
Q: How is the detention of Roger Gonzalez related to Mr. Mata Ballesteros?
A: Because Mr. Roger Gonzalez was connected with a protest, because the Honduran government had allowed Ramon Mata Ballesteros, a fugitive from one of the main prisons in Colombia, he had come into the country and gone out freely, and could live in Honduras without being bothered by any authority. After a year of being in Honduras, he was extradited from the United States to come here.
Q: Was there a protest in connection with his extradition?
A: Yes, of the students.
Q: And was Roger Gonzalez arrested in connection with being part of a demonstration?
A; Correct. The protest that these people were saying was that the Honduran government had him for a whole year and they had never sent him to the United States.
A: Was Mr. Gonzalez arrested in connection with this demonstration?
A: Correct. At the beginning the government said that they had him, but then afterwards they said they didn't have him. In other words, Roger Gonzalez had been followed before this by Battalion 316. He was one of the student directors.
Q: How do you know that it was Roger Gonzalez in the interrogation room?
A: Because my companions of Battalion 316 told me so.
Ibid., pp. 19-21.

regarding the unit where González was detained.

At the time of González's detention, Lt. Col. Luis Alonso Villatoro Villeda was head of Battalion 3-16 and Juan Blas Salazar was the DNI director.

13. Dionisio Portillo (1989)

Portillo was a Honduran who worked with refugees as an employee of Catholic Relief Services, a U.S.-based development organization. Portillo's disappearance was reported to the U.N. Working Group on Enforced or Involuntary Disappearances.[107]

Portillo was arrested February 3, 1989, as he travelled in the direction of San Marcos de Ocotepeque, Department of Ocotepeque. Portillo was travelling from the Mesa Grande refugee camp in a vehicle belonging to the U.N. High Commissioner for Refugees (UNHCR), when he was detained.[108] Portillo had worked as a carpenter in Mesa Grande.

José María Vaca, a UNHCR employee, was driving the vehicle from which Portillo was detained. Col. Moraya told Bishop Luis Alfonso Santos, extra-officially, that Portillo had been detained in the Infantry Battalion in Santa Rosa de Copán. Portillo's detention, however, was never officially recognized.[109]

Portillo's relatives stated that they feared for his life, since he had been detained by military authorities for three days in 1987 and been subjected to torture. They also indicated that Honduran authorities tended to consider anyone who worked with or visited Salvadoran refugees to be a guerrilla.[110]

A petition for a writ of *habeas corpus* was presented to the court in Santa Rosa de Copán, on February 10. The petition named Col. Ricardo Luque Portillo, commander of the Seventh Infantry Battalion based in Cucuyagua, Copán, as the party responsible.[111]

---

[107] *See* U.N. Working Group, *Report.*

[108] *Tiempo,* February 7, 1989.

[109] U.N. Working Group, *Report.*

[110] *Tiempo,* February 7, 1989.

[111] *Tiempo,* February 11, 1989.

14. Juan Humberto Sánchez

Juan Humberto Sánchez, a 26-year-old Honduran, was kidnapped July 11, 1992. According to reports, Sánchez was detained July 9 and held for two days by troops from the Tenth Infantry Battalion in Marcala, La Paz. On the night of the same day that he was released—July 11—Sánchez was detained by a group of fifteen armed men whom his stepfather, Juan José Vijil, identified as soldiers.[112]

According to his mother, on the night of the kidnapping, 15 soldiers arrived at the Sánchez's house. She said that three of the soldiers climbed onto the roof and began tearing it apart, seven soldiers surrounded the house, and another five burst inside. These men ordered the lights turned off and required everyone to lie face down on the ground. The light reflecting from the kidnappers' flashlights allowed Vijil to identify the weapons, boots, and hats as those used by the Territorial Forces Battalion, which is part of the Tenth Infantry Battalion. The soldiers bound Juan Humberto Sánchez and drove off, threatening the family if they did not keep quiet.[113] In statements to the press, Sánchez's mother identified Sub Lieutenant Angel Belisario Hernández as the person who gave the order to capture her son. Sánchez's parents were pressured to change their original version of what had happened.

Juan Humberto Sánchez's remains were discovered near Río Negro, Santo Domingo, several days after he had disappeared. According to press reports, he had been shot in the forehead and there were signs that he had been tortured.[114]

This case, despite the fact that it happened in 1992, is very similar to the cases registered in the 1980s.

In this example, as with many others presented in this chapter, we found that the Honduran authorities confused the national interests of Honduras with those of the United States administration of that time. This attitude led to an unnecessary tolerance that permitted the presence and illegal activities of the so-called Nicaraguan resistance, or contras. For Honduras, these years were the worst in terms of registered disappearances and violations of human rights.

---

[112] *Tiempo*, August 11, 1992.

[113] *Tiempo*, August 11, 1992.

[114] *Ibid.*

IV

TESTIMONIES

Perhaps one of the most direct ways to express the human aspect of disappearances is through direct testimony. The following are the testimony of two individuals who participated in disappearances in Honduras.[1]

Public Hearing: Testimony of Florencio Caballero
(IACtHR, Official Transcript of the Public Hearing at the
Seat of the Court on October 6, 1987, Original: Spanish.)[2]

. . .

PRESIDENT: . . .Will the Secretary please call the next witness.

SECRETARY: Florencio Caballero.

PRESIDENT: Will Mr. Caballero please state his name, his nationality, current place of domicile and the number of his document of identification.

MR. CABALLERO: I am Florencio Caballero. I was born in Naranjito, Department of Santa Barbara, Honduras, on February 26, 1958. I am currently living in Canada. My passport number is 20342.

. . .

PRESIDENT: Will the Secretary please instruct the witness.

SECRETARY: Witnesses shall be limited to answering the question asked of them clearly and precisely, to those facts or circumstances that they know, without expressing personal opinions. The witness is instructed that, in accord

---

[1] In the original Spanish version, the testimony of attorney René Velásquez Díaz was presented. We have substituted the testimony of Florencio Caballero for the English version, because of the remarks he makes concerning U.S. involvement.

[2] Translation by Thomas Buergenthal, Robert Norris, Dinah Shelton, authors of *Protecting Human Rights in the Americas: Selected Problems*, (N.P. Engel: Kehl, Strasbourg, Arlington, 1990.)

with Article 39.2 of the Rules, States cannot try persons who appear before the Court because of their testimony. But the Court may request the States to take the measures permitted by their legislation against whomever the Court determines has violated their oath.

. . .

Do you swear, or solemnly affirm, with all honor and conscience, that you shall tell the truth, the whole truth and nothing but the truth?

MR. CABALLERO: I do.

PRESIDENT: Will the President of the Commission indicate the name of the person who shall examine the witness and proceed.

DR. RUSSOMANO: Thank you, Your Honor. The witness, Florencio Caballero, on the first question, will be examined by Dr. Juan Méndez.

PRESIDENT: You may proceed.

. . .

DR. MENDEZ: What is 316?

MR. CABALLERO: It is an intelligence battalion of the Armed Forces.

DR. MENDEZ: In what year did you become a member of Battalion 316?

MR. CABALLERO: Toward the end of 1979 and the beginning of 1980, I was selected to attend an interrogation course in the United States.

. . .

DR. MENDEZ: Then, from 1979 on you were already a member of Battalion 316?

MR. CABALLERO: Yes, I was already a member.

DR. MENDEZ: At that time with the rank of Corporal.

MR. CABALLERO: Yes, after I took the interrogation course. . . they promoted me to First Inspector.

DR. MENDEZ: What rank is First Inspector?

MR. CABALLERO: Like a Sergeant in the Infantry.

. . .

DR. MENDEZ: When were you made First Inspector?

MR. CABALLERO: In 1981.

DR. MENDEZ: Can you give us a little description of Battalion 316, for example, when it was organized?

MR. CABALLERO: I do not know when this battalion was organized because it was already organized when I became a member.

. . .

DR. MENDEZ: Do you know who organized it?

MR. CABALLERO: It was organized formally when former General Adolfo Alvarez Martínez became Chief of the Armed Forces.

. . .

DR. MENDEZ: Was it a secret unit?

MR. CABALLERO: It was secret.

. . .

DR. MENDEZ: What was the purpose of Battalion 316?

MR. CABALLERO: To combat subversion and arms traffic, more than anything else.

DR. MENDEZ: By what means? What is the complete name of Battalion 316?

MR. CABALLERO: When we were members, we knew it as the Death Squadron.

DR. MENDEZ: Then the purpose is to combat arms traffic and subversion through intelligence activities. What else?

MR. CABALLERO: First information was obtained through outside agents, civilian personnel. The information was processed, establishing surveillance, following and in the majority of cases tapping telephone lines. When this information was obtained, after a month or two, if the case was very strong, he was kidnapped in 10 or 15 days. If there was time, sometimes after a month or two, it was sent to the operations section.

DR. MENDEZ: When you say kidnapping, do you mean that an irregular arrest was made, without a warrant issued by a competent judge?

MR. CABALLERO: The courts did not know about the kidnappings, that was illegal.

DR. MENDEZ: . . .Who gave the orders to Battalion 316 within the chain of command of the Armed Forces of Honduras?

MR. CABALLERO: The Head of Intelligence of the Chief of Staff, G-2.

. . .

DR MENDEZ: The Head of Intelligence, then, depends upon the Commander in Chief of the Armed Forces.

MR. CABALLERO: Yes. As I said before, the founder was General Alvarez.

DR. MENDEZ: . . .Who was your superior at the time you became a member? And who replaced him?

MR. CABALLERO: The Head of 316 was Major Alexánder Hernández. Under him, was Captain Fernández Chávez.

. . .

DR. MENDEZ: What was the structure of the Battalion?

MR. CABALLERO: It had four sections. The Section One was in charge of personnel.

DR. MENDEZ: Who was the head of Section One?

AGENT OF HONDURAS: Objection, Your Honor. Are we here to investigate the formation, creation, of 316 or the violations of human rights by that Battalion?

PRESIDENT: The information about that organ is an important piece of evidence. The objection is overruled.

DR. MENDEZ: I repeat. Who was the head of the First Section?

MR. CABALLERO: The head of the personnel section was Lt. Hueso. Second Section. The Intelligence and Counterintelligence Section within the Squadron, that is 316, was headed by Lt. Reyes.

DR. MENDEZ: In what year?

MR. CABALLERO: In 1982.

DR. MENDEZ: You have described two sections, please mention the other two and give the name of the section and the names of those in charge.

MR. CABALLERO: Section Three, Operations and Analysis, was commanded by Captain Ciro Pablo Velásquez, known by the pseudonym of Urquía. Section Four, Supplies, was commanded by Lt. Gravis.

DR. MENDEZ: Returning to Section Three, what did Operations and Analysis do?

MR. CABALLERO: Operations and Analysis was in charge of the processing of information which was transmitted to the kidnapping group, under the command of Lt. Flores Murillo, which was subordinate to the Operations

Section.

DR. MENDEZ: How many groups did the Operations Section have?

MR. CABALLERO: Only the kidnapping group, which included the interrogation group.

DR. MENDEZ: Did Battalion 316 operate only in Tegucigalpa?

MR. CABALLERO: No, as I recall, also in Danlí, Choluteca, Santa Rosa de Copán, San Pedro Sula, Colón.

. . .

DR. MENDEZ: What was the physical location of Battalion 316?

MR. CABALLERO: Its principal headquarters was in Tegucigalpa and its headquarters was what used to be the Morazán Athletic Club, in the 21 de Octubre neighborhood.

. . .

DR. MENDEZ: Did they use other centers?

MR. CABALLERO: Yes, they had secret jails in a building owned by the military in INDUMIL, Military Industries, that is, in Las Tapias, located near the Armored Cavalry Regiment.

DR. MENDEZ: And that served as a detention center?

MR. CABALLERO: That was a clandestine jail and was also our headquarters. We of the kidnapping and interrogation groups slept there.

DR. MENDEZ: What other sites did they use?

MR. CABALLERO: There was the house owned by Colonel Amílcar Zelaya, a country house in Támara, Francisco Morazán, near the Río de Hombre. It was a very large house, where the number of kidnapping victims sometimes reached 30, 20, 15. There was also the house of Captain Pío Flores and there were other safe houses for the contacts of surveillance and following and those who gathered information, . . .

DR. MENDEZ: What members of the Battalion were quartered at the place you mentioned near the Río del Hombre, in Támara?

MR. CABALLERO: Four men from 316 who executed the kidnap [victims] slept there.

DR. MENDEZ: Was there a particular group within the Battalion that specialized in executions?

MR. CABALLERO: They were only in charge of executing at the command of Juan Ramón Peña Paz, pseudonym Mata.

. . .

DR. MENDEZ: In those places where they kept prisoners, was there any judicial control? Did any judge appear from time to time to inspect the locales?

MR. CABALLERO: Never. No judge ever observed that, no one knew.

. . .

DR. MENDEZ: Did you ever observe any inspection by any high-ranking officer of the Anned Forces?

MR. CABALLERO: No. Except for the visits from Colonel López and General Alvarez Martínez.

DR. MENDEZ: Did you actually see them?

MR. CABALLERO: At INDUMIL I did.

DR. MENDEZ: Who decided which prisoner to take and to which of these places?

MR. CABALLERO: Major Alexánder Hernández made that decision, depending on the case, if it was a special case he went directly to INDUMIL, otherwise, to

Támara . . .

DR. MENDEZ: Among the members of the Battalion, did you know one another's identity?

MR. CABALLERO: In some cases, but generally not, because they used pseudonyms.

. . .

DR. MENDEZ: Did you have the cooperation of other units or military or police facilities?

MR. CABALLERO: The Public Security Forces (Fuerza de Seguridad Pública), the DNI cooperated.

DR. MENDEZ: What type of support?

MR. CABALLERO: The Public Security Force, when we operated, we first informed the Cobra Squadron what was going on.

DR. MENDEZ: What other type of support did you receive?

MR. CABALLERO: Most of the time from 1982 to 1983, they loaned us the cells in El Manchén.

DR. MENDEZ: What is El Manchén?

MR. CABALLERO: The cells of El Manchén is a squadron of the Public Security Force, where they took common criminals, delinquents, in Tegucigalpa, in El Manchén neighborhood, that why it had that name. We used the second floor for the disappeared.

DR. MENDEZ: Was that with the knowledge of those in charge of that locale?

MR. CABALLERO: The case of Melba Cáceres de Mondragón is an example.

DR. MENDEZ: Who is Melba Cáceres?

MR. CABALLERO: Melba Cáceres de Mondragón was a Nicaraguan kidnapped in Choluteca, in San Marcos de Colón and was taken there.

. . .

DR. MENDEZ: I want you to describe a typical operation of the Battalion. Who determined who was going to be investigated and eventually taken prisoner, if they decided to take him prisoner?

MR. CABALLERO: Alexánder Hernández gave the order to investigate, watch and follow a certain person, when information was received from the sources of information.

DR. MENDEZ: Who carried out that surveillance and observation?

MR. CABALLERO: A group commanded by Lt. Mario Quiñónez, pseudonym Quintero.

. . .

DR. MENDEZ: After that surveillance and observation, at some point was a decision made to drop the case or make an arrest? Who made that decision?

MR. CABALLERO: Alexánder Hernández. In some cases the investigation was ended because they sometimes discovered safe houses of the "contras" they had thought to be subversives . . . and they were left alone. When the investigation was carried out, it was confirmed by telephone and those who investigated in the streets it was confirmed that he was working for the left or in arms traffic, then Alexánder would say: Flores Murillo, you may move in.

DR. MENDEZ: Then the order was given to the group of Flores Murillo to detain the person?

MR. CABALLERO: Yes, through Captain Ciro Pablo Velásquez.

DR. MENDEZ: Was that carried out by personnel in uniforms or civilian clothes?

MR. CABALLERO: Personnel in civilian clothes, with masks, disguises such as wigs, beards and moustaches. On occasion one would dress as a woman.

DR. MENDEZ: Were they armed?

MR. CABALLERO: With UZI machine guns, sometimes with a 45 caliber pistol. They mostly used 38s.

DR. MENDEZ: What type of vehicles did they use?

MR. CABALLERO: The vehicles were the property of the 316, Toyotas. There were 4 simple, double-cabin pick-ups.

DR. MENDEZ: Were they vehicles without markings of the Armed Forces, police, or of any kind?

MR. CABALLERO: They were unmarked. There were two with darkened windows, and the others were not. They used stolen license plates, sometimes those from abandoned cars. Even cars that had been owned by subversives.

. . .

DR. MENDEZ: . . . What methods did they use? Did they mistreat the prisoners in those places?

MR. CABALLERO: Yes. There was a torture group and an interrogation group, they were separate groups, but they were always chosen from the kidnapping and interrogation group.

. . .

DR. MENDEZ: Who were the torture group?

MR. CABALLERO: There were four. Agent Gerónimo Venegas, Sergeant Mauricio Zelaya, Lt. Flores Murillo, and Colindres, I do not remember his name.

. . .

DR. MENDEZ: What methods, what type of torture did they normally use?

MR. CABALLERO: Electric shock.

DR. MENDEZ: How? With some instrument?

MR. CABALLERO: With two wires with the tips exposed, they plugged them into the socket and used them on the genitals, the navel, the ribs, and parts of the back.
     They also used the barrel of water. They tied the hands and feet behind them would put them repeatedly head first into a barrel of water.
     There was also the hood, a method of torture used by the DNI, but the one used by the DNI was a big cover, made of rubber, from a tire tube, which was used to cover the mouth and nose.
     There were tortures such as keeping them nude; drenching them with very cold water from the refrigerator when it was cold. They did not give them food.

DR. MENDEZ: Tell me, who made the final decision, once the interrogation was over?

. . .

MR. CABALLERO: In 1982, Alexánder decided not to let anyone go. I believe there were some exceptions in the period 1982 to 1983. Alexánder Hernández made the decisions.

DR. MENDEZ: Did he have to consult with his superiors, or was it basically his decision?

MR. CABALLERO: He had full authority, but sometimes he would meet with Colonel López Grijalba and General Alvarez Martínez to consider the case.

. . .

DR. MENDEZ: If execution was ordered, what was the procedure?

MR. CABALLERO: After interrogating him, he was taken in a small yellow panel truck, a Toyota, with darkened glass. He was sent to Támara, or sometimes to the house of Pío Flores. Ramón Peña Paz would already have orders to turn him over to any of the assassins.

DR. MENDEZ: If a decision was made to kill the prisoner, what was done with the body?

MR. CABALLERO: First they would do it, according to what I learned later from Reyes, this Mr. Mata, and Peña Paz. Sometimes I had the opportunity to talk to him when he visited in INDUMIL . . . He said first they used firearms, then they stopped using firearms and began to use knives and machetes.

DR. MENDEZ: You said that if the prisoner agreed to talk, then the interrogation group would interrogate him, that is when you took part.

MR. CABALLERO: Yes, because the torturers were one group and the interrogators were another.

DR. MENDEZ: If you were interrogating a prisoner and he did not want to talk, who made the decision to turn him over to the torturers?

MR. CABALLERO: Lt. Flores Murillo was always present at the interrogations, in addition to other officers who were sometimes present.

DR. MENDEZ: Then, he supervised the interrogation?

MR. CABALLERO: He was the one who said, well, he does not want to cooperate, get out of here, take off. You leave and let someone else take over.

DR. MENDEZ: Did you also participate in kidnappings?

MR. CABALLERO: Yes, I was in the kidnapping of Mr. Duarte Salgado. Also in the kidnapping of Félix Martínez, and that of Germán Pérez Alemán.

DR. MENDEZ: Now I want to ask you some questions about the cases being investigated in this international proceeding. Do you know anything about Mr. Angel Manfredo Velásquez?

MR. CABALLERO: Yes. I did not know him, nor did I participate in his kidnapping. But Flores Murillo told me how he had been executed.

DR. MENDEZ: Did he also tell about the kidnapping? Do you remember when the Velásquez kidnapping occurred?

MR. CABALLERO: I do not remember. I believe it was in 1981.

DR. MENDEZ: But, you do remember when Mr. Flores Murillo told you these things, or was it over a series of conversations?

MR. CABALLERO: In a series of many conversations, because I was with him all the time. He told me about the kidnapping, near the Palace and Lido movie theaters, in Tegucigalpa. Sergeant José Isaías Vilorio was in charge of that kidnapping.

. . .

DR. MENDEZ: What was his role in Battalion 316?

MR. CABALLERO: He was in charge of the files, in the personnel section, but he also took part in the operations. When the Manfredo Velásquez operation took place, the 316 was not very well organized. At that time, they used office personnel in the kidnappings. At that time, José Isaias Vilorio was in personnel, now - I do not know if I am mistaken - he is still in personnel, but in DNI. There was a man named Ezequiel, another named Titanio, those are pseudonyms, and Lt. Murillo. After the kidnapping, going toward the Social Security, from the Palace and Lido theaters, down towards Merrián's hole, as we call it, because Merrián never finished it.

DR. MENDEZ: Who is Merrián?

MR. CABALLERO: He was the mayor of Tegucigalpa. Then, right there, Ezequiel's gun went off, wounding Manfredo in the leg.

DR. MENDEZ: Why did it go off, was there a struggle?

MR. CABALLERO: Yes, there was. He was resisting inside the vehicle. He was taken to INDUMIL and there he was tortured and held a long time. Afterwards, he was turned over to the executioners.
DR. MENDEZ: Did they tell you anything about the execution? How he was disposed of?

MR. CABALLERO: Yes. Flores Murillo said Alvarez gave the orders, to be sure they would never discover his body, they took him from Tegucigalpa, after killing him with a knife and machete, to Progreso de Lloro, where parts of his body were buried in different places. I do not know where they are.

. . .

PRESIDENT: I ask the Agent of the Honorable Government of Honduras to identify the person who will cross-examine.

AGENT: Yes, Your Honor. Attorney Juan Arnoldo Hernández will cross-examine.

PRESIDENT: You may proceed.

ATTORNEY HERNANDEZ: May it please the Court.
Mr. Caballero, at the beginning of your testimony, you said that you had left (the country) with an identity card. Where did you get it and how did you get a Honduran passport?

MR. CABALLERO: I obtained the Honduran passport in the month of March, 1985, in Tegucigalpa. I kept the passport with me, but I did not use it in the customs of El Salvador or Honduras at Amatillo. In the first place, because I did not have to, and secondly, for security reasons, I used my identity card.

ATTORNEY HERNANDEZ: What is your current status in Canada?

DR. MENDEZ: Objection, Your Honor. The question is irrelevant.

PRESIDENT: No, I believe the question is relevant. You may proceed.

MR. CABALLERO: I am classified as a refugee.

ATTORNEY HERNANDEZ: Not as a political exilee. What is your current status with the Armed Forces of Honduras?

MR. CABALLERO: Now they call me an enemy of the State. I do not consider myself an enemy of the State because I state the truth and publish something that may not be convenient for the nation of Honduras.

ATTORNEY HERNANDEZ: That is with regard to the State. What is your status with the Armed Forces?

MR. CABALLERO: I am an ex-member of the Armed Forces, with no criminal record.

. . .

ATTORNEY HERNANDEZ: In your testimony you stated that you became a member of Battalion 316 in 1979.

MR. CABALLERO: At the end of 1979

ATTORNEY HERNANDEZ: Later, you said that it was organized when General Alvarez Martínez became Chief of the Armed Forces. In what year did General Alvarez Martínez become Chief of the Armed Forces?

MR. CABALLERO: In 1982. In 1981, there was a small group which was a part of the intelligence branch of the Chief of Staff. The 316 was organized by General Alvarez Martínez.

ATTORNEY HERNANDEZ: You say that Alvarez Martínez became Chief of the Armed Forces in what year?

MR. CABELLERO: I do not remember exactly in what year he came to the Armed Forces?

ATTORNEY HERNANDEZ: I want you to repeat what you said. Because a witness must testify to a fact that occurred.

DR. MENDEZ: But he said he does not remember.

ATTORNEY HERNANDEZ: Your Honor, I ask you to order the witness to look at me when I am asking him a question and when he is answering. With all due respect, Your Honor.

PRESIDENT: I believe the witness may only be ordered to answer the question.
ATTORNEY HERNANDEZ: Excuse me, Your Honor, but he could be receiving signals or something from the opposing counsel. That is why I ask you to order him to look at me when I am asking him a question.

PRESIDENT: I believe the witness rather should look at the Court. I cannot require the witness to move in a certain manner. So, I believe the witness is warned that he must tell the truth. He is under oath. That is the warning I repeat to the witness.

ATTORNEY HERNANDEZ: Thank you, Your Honor. Did you say in what year Alvarez Martínez had become Chief of the Armed Forces?

MR. CABALLERO: I do not remember the date.

ATTORNEY HERNANDEZ: At first you *did* say it.

MR. CABALLERO: I said 1982, approximately, I do not remember the date.

ATTORNEY HERNANDEZ: You say the Battalion has existed since 1979. That is enough for me. Thank you. What do you mean by clandestine jails?

MR. CABALLERO: Those we had in the 316, because they were not visited by any judge, or any other judicial official. It was restricted by the military, for example, in INDUMIL no one else entered where we were. Even officers of the Armed Forces did not come in, unless they were members of 316 and had access to the interrogation and kidnapping section.

ATTORNEY HERNANDEZ: Do you remember, or can you tell us, how many kidnappings you participated in? Numbers, not names, will be sufficient.

MR. CABALLERO: Well, but I am always going to mention the names.

ATTORNEY HERNANDEZ: No, you are going to answer what I ask you, Sergeant.

PRESIDENT: Excuse me, but I believe in a question like that the witness may give the names because it does not change the answer.

ATTORNEY HERNANDEZ: That is all right then, we agree.

MR. CABALLERO: I took part in the case of Gerrnán Pérez Alemán, the case of Efraín Duarte Salgado, the case of Félix Martínez, and also in the case of Melba Cáceres Mondragón.

. . .

ATTORNEY HERNANDEZ: That is enough. As a sergeant of the army, that is, a low rank, how did you have so much access to information that is only for high-ranking officers?

MR. CABALLERO: I think we knew more than anyone how it was organized and the rules of order and discipline. I had access to the information because I was an interrogator and also kidnapper. I also had access, as well, to the main sections located in the 21 de Octubre neighborhood.

. . .

ATTORNEY HERNANDEZ: When a military order is given, I understand it must be obeyed. You say that your superior was Lt. Flores Murillo. How did you manage not to carry out the orders he gave you, when he said to make a person disappear?

DR. MENDEZ: Objection, Your Honor. The witness did not say he received such orders.

PRESIDENT: The objection is sustained.

ATTORNEY HERNANDEZ: . . . Such ugly, terrible things the Battalion did, were you forced to carry them out?

MR. CABALLERO: Yes, because if I deserted, they would kill me. If I asked to leave the Armed Forces, and at the time they were saying, you are not going to leave, and I opposed, they would kill me. Then I was forced to, because I was only obligated to two years military service, and I had more than that.

. . .

ATTORNEY HERNANDEZ: Were you an eyewitness of the torture of the prisoners?

MR. CABALLERO: Yes, I was an eyewitness.

ATTORNEY HERNANDEZ: How did you stand that, if it was contrary to your training?

MR. CABALLERO: I could not oppose. I was a subordinate of Lt. Flores Murillo, and I do not know whether you know anything about the Army, but one must obey orders. I could not oppose, if I did, I would be accused of whatever they accused him.

ATTORNEY HERNANDEZ: You said that those in charge of making the prisoners disappear used pseudonyms. How do you know those were pseudonyms?

MR. CABALLERO: Because all the members of 316 - from the very day they became members - were told by Alexánder Hernández or the chief of personnel, told them, well, change your name and use the first part of your name, but change it for security reasons. Everyone, without exception, used a pseudonym.

ATTORNEY HERNANDEZ: Thank you. When a person was captured by that Battalion 316, was it because there were good reasons to believe the State of Honduras was in danger because of the activity of that person, or did they give orders haphazardly to grab a person and take him?

MR. CABALLERO: No, there was an investigation, and if he was not arrested, he was kidnapped.

ATTORNEY HERNANDEZ: But it was because it had been proven that he was an active participant in some subversive movement.

MR. CABALLERO: Yes, but in some cases a person engaged in subversive activities was kidnapped and may have been with someone who had nothing to do with it, and that person also died innocently.

ATTORNEY HERNANDEZ: Were you aware of your responsibility in taking part in those events?

MR. CABALLERO: I knew that the ones responsible for that were the higher ranking officers, such as Generals, Colonels, Lieutenants, Captains. I had nothing to do with it because I was ordered. I was going to obey an order. I was not afraid.

. . .

ATTORNEY HERNANDEZ: Thank you. That is all, Your Honor.

. . .

PRESIDENT: Judge Espinal.

JUDGE ESPINAL: Thank you, Your Honor.
Tell me, if one of your companions participated in the death, or could have participated in the disappearance of a person, was there any possibility of him being charged with a crime or not?

MR. CABALLERO: I do not believe so because the Armed Forces was never going to surrender anyone, at that time, when it was under the command of General Alvarez Martínez, was never going to allow the surrender of anyone who would compromise the Armed Forces.

JUDGE ESPINAL: That is a question. Are they members of the Armed Forces, are they in the hierarchy of the Armed Forces?

MR. CABALLERO: They are under the command of the Armed Forces, but the four executioners I spoke of received a salary through the Armed Forces. But I am not sure they were on the payroll of the Armed Forces, I do not think so, because those four were - according to what I learned in conversations with Flores Murillo and Peña Paz - prisoners with long sentences from the Central Penitentiary who were forced to work with them.

JUDGE ESPINAL: You just said that some of those officers, four of them in particular, were paid directly by the Armed Forces, but, who paid you?

MR. CABALLERO: Lieutenant Gravis of the Payroll Section which is within the Fourth Section of Battalion 316 - what is now Battalion 316 - but it is under the Chief of Intelligence of the General Staff of the Armed Forces.

. . .

JUDGE ESPINAL: Sir, there is another thing that bothers me. As you have heard and read, like everyone else, you make a distinction between an interrogator and a torturer.

MR. CABALLERO: Yes. I do distinguish. But one is an accomplice by observing and not telling about it.

JUDGE ESPINAL: Who is the accomplice?

MR. CABALLERO: From the moment I watch and do not report a torture, or do not report everything that is happening, I am an accomplice. Moreover, I was a member. But I never tortured, because, in the first place, it is not convenient for the interrogator to torture. Those are the rules we are taught, that an interrogator cannot torture. . ..

JUDGE ESPINAL: Excuse me, in some reports I have seen that the interrogator and torturer are one and the same, was that the case in your Squadron or could it be that way in other divisions?

MR. CABALLERO: It could be that way elsewhere, although in some cases those responsibilities were assumed. For example, Lt. Regalado Hernández - I do not know if it is Hernández - Marco Tulio Regalado, attended the interrogation course with me and he was a torturer in San Pedro Sula.

JUDGE ESPINAL: What did that interrogation course consist of, did they use only words or some means of coercion to get them to talk?

MR. CABALLERO: We were taught to eliminate torture, but Alvarez Martínez said that was not effective, that they should continue torturing and that the person who was going to interrogate should not torture, because we were taught not to torture, but to take note of all the questions and nothing more, that someone else should torture. In practice, in our second training, we had to use psychological methods.

JUDGE ESPINAL: If a person is exposed to these and other means of physical violence, didn't the unit in which you worked take some precaution by providing some medical assistance to revive the victim and continue with the torture?

MR. CABALLERO: Yes. The special Squadron had a doctor. Unfortunately, I do not know his name, but I do know his surname. Dr. Cruz, who works or worked at the San Felipe Hospital, in the Thorax Institute. He had access, as well, to watch. He watched Inés, he watched Mr. Flores. He saw many, many prisoners.

. . .

PRESIDENT: Judge Nikken.

. . .

JUDGE NIKKEN: . . . What was done with persons after their execution? Where did they hide the bodies? Were there secret cemeteries? What was the situation?

MR. CABALLERO: I suspect, but I do not know, that persons may be buried in the house of Amílcar Martínez in Támara, because many were assassinated. Then, according to conversations I had with Peña Paz and Matamoros - a pseudonym - who went crazy after three months of so much killing. They had him with us in INDUMIL - he told us that after they assassinated some, they buried them and poured a layer of cement, over which they might build a toilet, a bath or a house or whatever, but they always covered it with cement, building walls, so they would never be found.
When they saw that so many were arriving, I do not know where they decided to bury them. In some cases they left them in places where people would find them and their families would pick them up. That was the case of Félix Martínez, as I recall.

. . .

JUDGE NIKKEN: Were you trained in interrogation?

MR. CABALLERO: I was trained, I suppose, I cannot be sure, in the United States, but I cannot be sure of the place . . .

JUDGE NIKKEN: Why can't you be sure?

MR. CABALLERO: Because I traveled from Tegucigalpa, in a private Air Force plane, to where there was a house in the country, like an academy or something, which had no other houses around. It was only for training. It had a dirt landing strip. When we arrived there, we did not leave. When the course was over, they took us back to Tegucigalpa. We even had a small reception in the Hotel La Ronda, with just the four instructors and the four members who were: Lt. Montañola, Lt. Flores Murillo, Lt. . . .. Ramón Mejía, no, it was not Ramón Mejía, I do not remember the other name, and myself. We were chatting with the instructors who brought us back.

JUDGE NIKKEN: What nationality were the instructors?

MR. CABALLERO: North American.

JUDGE NIKKEN: Was the course in Spanish or in English?

MR. CABALLERO: No, they had interpreters.

JUDGE NIKKEN: . . . You said there were psychological techniques. What were those psychological techniques?

MR. CABALLERO: There are twelve methods, but I cannot give you all of them, because I do not remember.
I remember, for example, deprivation of sleep. First, investigate his attitudes since childhood, if possible, to find out what his weak points are, and according to the weak points, attack him. Locking up in a cell, where we even have to know the colors that offend him, the odors he doesn't like, the food he doesn't like. The hours he likes to sleep. And one does just the opposite, that is, what he doesn't like.
Secondly, the good and the bad, they call it. One instructor assumes the role of the good guy, the other the bad guy, the other is the torturer, the one who hits him or is going to make an impression on him.
Thirdly, they might place rats on him, or any sickening animal, or if he likes food, they might show it to him without giving him any.
They also use blackmail. There is always the wife or someone he loves most, or one of three or four children, or his mother. But it must be someone he most loves. We never brought anyone like that, but we would tell we were, that we were going to grab that person, when we were not sure who was the person he loved most.

. . .

JUDGE NIKKEN: According to your instructors, none of those methods constituted torture?

MR. CABALLERO: No, but we never completely carried out what they taught us because there were always the tortures. The kidnappings, disappearances, calmed down a lot when Alvarez Martínez left the command of the Armed Forces and when Alexánder Hernández left the 316, because - there were two, sometimes three, operations a day - and Colonel Padilla said only one a month and after a good investigation. Then the number came down.

JUDGE NIKKEN: What was the foreign role in these kidnappings? . . .

MR. CABALLERO: In the vehicles used to detect clandestine radios, for example, foreigners from the United States were in those cars. There was participation in instruction, in La Venta and also in the 21 de Octubre neighborhood. Chilean, Argentinian and American instructors.

JUDGE NIKKEN: Do you have personal knowledge of that?

MR. CABALLERO: Yes, because I was trained by them. They were my instructors. I recall that one of them, the head of the interrogation instructors, Cerella, that would be his pseudonym, his real name, but we called him Mister Bill. After a number of months, back in 1982. I don't remember if it was July or what month, he died. They said he died in Beirut when they put a bomb in the American Embassy in Beirut.

JUDGE NIKKEN: Did the foreign advisers know of the detention sites and what was going on?

MR. CABALLERO: Yes. There was an adviser by the pseudonym of Mister Mike. I do not know his name, who was living in the American Embassy. He had access to us. He witnessed the interrogation of Duarte Salgado and Consuelo Murillo. He was directing it, and in some cases submitted written questions to the interrogator.

. . .

JUDGE BUERGENTHAL: You mentioned American, Chilean, and Argentinian instructors. Were the Argentinian and Chileans in Houston?

MR. CABALLERO: No. They were in Tegucigalpa, in La Venta, Francisco Morazán, near the city of Talanga. Approximately 30 minutes from Tegucigalpa. That place is called CIP, Centro de Instrucción Policial (Police Training Center).

It is a branch of the Public Security Force, but there is an annex where the special forces are, where they trained personnel to assault houses. When there was a kidnapping and ransom was demanded, they were specially for that purpose and in case of an anti-subversive operation. They could not work against insurgence.

. . .

JUDGE BUERGENTHAL: The disappeared persons were looked for, I understand, by civilian judges. Did you ever see a civilian judge looking for a disappeared person?

MR. CABALLERO: I was aware that the relatives brought writs of habeas corpus, that the Commission of Human Rights demanded that those persons be recognized, that it was before the courts. But they did not care. They never investigated, they never visited the jails. And they were not going to be able to.

JUDGE BUERGENTHAL: You never saw a civilian judge ask that a disappeared person be recognized?

MR. CABALLERO: No.

JUDGE BUERGENTHAL: What was your attitude, and I imagine that of your colleagues, when they talked about judges who were trying to carry out writs of habeas corpus?

. . .

MR. CABALLERO: What I can tell you now sounds absurd, but the truth is that they laughed at what was being said outside.

JUDGE BUERGENTHAL: Why?

MR. CABALLERO: They said, they are fools, why are they asking about this person when this person is never coming back?

JUDGE BUERGENTHAL: Why not?

MR. CABALLERO: They were almost sure he was going to die, because the cases in which they were set free were exceptional, most were not. Then everyone said, no, this one is not coming out, so why are they fighting, why do they ask?

. . .

JUDGE PIZA: What criteria did they use to start surveillance or the investigation of a person?

MR. CABALLERO: First, the information they received. Sometimes the intelligence and counterintelligence services had a little information, but most of the time the sources of information were Alexánder Hernández' men and women in the street. They supplied some information and it was processed by the command of Lt. Quiñónez.

JUDGE PIZA: No, but what kind of information? For example, if 316 was informed that he was a communist or had strange ideas or ran around with strange people. What type of information?

MR. CABALLERO: In Honduras, the simple fact that more than three single men lived in the same house, they came under suspicion. They came under suspicion because they met at night, and a lot of things could awaken suspicion they were subversives. The sources took this information to Alexánder Hernández. Alexánder Hernández would say: Good, Quiñónez, come here, prepare your people for surveillance and following, investigate this case as soon as possible. Then it would be investigated.
For example, a car would arrive at certain time at a house. They would arrive, they would look at the license plates, they had access to that information, to find out who the car belonged to. Then, if that person had any contact with a person already known to be leftist, they would say, logically, he is also a leftist. They reported to Alexánder Hernández and he would say, well, go ahead.

JUDGE PIZA: Do you know of any person, who because of that procedure, was detained and kidnapped in error? That is, whether you yourselves became convinced it was a mistake, that the man or woman was not involved?

MR. CABALLERO: The case of Germán Pérez Alemán, who was not acting with any leftist group, whom I do not believe was guilty and did not deserve what they did to him. Although no one deserved to be judged. That is what the judicial authorities are for, to judge him. Then, that is one case. Another case, a girl who was captured in a house of the San Francisco neighborhood, who was with some who were guilty. She did not know anything, she did not even know what was in each room of the house. I do not know what happened to her.

. . .

JUDGE PIZA: You mentioned the case of Angel Manfredo Velásquez. You said insofar as Mr. Godinez Cruz you did not know anything but you had seen the list.

MR. CABALLERO: His name was on the list, but I do not know anything else.

JUDGE PIZA: What list?

MR. CABALLERO: In the files of 316 - what is now 316 - is a complete list of all the disappeared so that if a person disappears and it was not done by 316, they would look for him.

. . .

JUDGE PIZA: Was that a list of those kidnapped or those who were to be kidnapped?

MR. CABALLERO: Those who had been kidnapped.

JUDGE PIZA: That was the list where you saw the name of Saúl Godínez?

MR. CABALLERO: That is correct.

JUDGE PIZA: In that list or in any other, did you see anything related to Francisco Fairén Garbi?

MR. CABALLERO: Francisco Fairén, a Costa Rican, was also in the same list.

JUDGE PIZA: He was on the list?

MR. CABALLERO: On the same list.

JUDGE PIZA: The list of 316? On the list of those kidnapped, the list of persons to be kidnapped, the list of suspects or what?

MR. CABALLERO: On the list of those kidnapped. That is, that was a list of those executed, kidnapped, and even of those who had been released. But all who had been in the hands of 316 were on that list. They kept that list because there was also a Kardex, a file, where logically in alphabetical order, one went to look for the name of each person. To not have to go the file, they looked on the list and if he was they would to say, well, let's look for him, he is in the file, this person was here.

JUDGE PIZA: Then you affirm that you saw the name of Francisco Fairén? You swear under oath that you saw it?

MR. CABALLERO: Yes, I am telling the truth and nothing but the truth.

. . .

Volume 1576

-74,346

—SEVENTY FOUR THOUSAND, THREE HUNDRED FOURTY SIX—

In Mexico City, on the second day of the month of July of the year nineteen hundred and eighty six, before me, Salvador Godínez Viera, Esquire, Notary Number 42 of the Federal District, appeared Mr. José Barrera Martínez to make the following:

Declarations

First:

That he belonged to the Armed Forces of Honduras from nineteen hundred seventy two until September of nineteeen hundred eighty six, in which month he deserted the special military unit called Battalion Three-Sixteen.

Second:

That the Battalion Three-Sixteen, is beneath the Armed Forces General Staff (*Estado Mayor Conjunto*), and since its formation in nineteen hundred and eighty two, it is the military unit responsible for the kidnapping, torture, and murder of more than one hundred Honduran citizens, executed for threatening the security of the State.

Third:

That prior to Battalion Three-Sixteen, there existed two paramilitary groups called: the Group of Ten and the Group of Fourteen. The declarant joined the Group of Fourteen in the month of April of nineteen hundred eighty two. The Group of Ten is the closest predecessor of Battalion Three-Sixteen and existed for a few months.

Fourth:

that he did not belong to the Group of Ten and became aware of the same through former companions of his who had belonged to the Group of

Fourteen and who still belong to the Three-Sixteen of Tegucigalpa; among those are: Carlos Peralta, Transit Sergeant Maggin, Police Sergeant Person, and Banegas. This last individual, ex-agent of the DNI (Dirección Nacional de Investigaciones—National Investigations Directorate), in Olancho, pseudonym "Alvarado;" These individuals told him that the locale of the Group of Ten was below the Troops's Club of the Casamata barracks, the commander was Major Alexander Hernández, and, among other things, that the Ten were responsible for the bodies found in the clandestine cemeteries of la Montañita and other outlying areas of Tegucigalpa.

Fifth:

He joined the Group of Fourteen under the following circumstances: during the years nineteen hundred seventy nine, nineteen hundred eighty and the beginning of nineteen hundred eighty one, he worked in the Public Security Force (Fuerza de Seguridad Pública-FUSEP) in the Department of Olancho. Previously, he had requested his discharge from the FUSEP because he had personal problems with Major Trejo Rosas, the officer who prevented his ascension to the rank of Sub-lieutenant in the reserves (*de complemento*) by erasing him from the attendance list of a course to be given in Panama. Living in the city of Juticalpa, in the Las Flores neighborhood and living in the house of Esperanza, widow of Guifarro, he was approached by a brother-in-law of this widow by the name of Bruno Arnulfo Guifarro; Guifarro had the rank of Sergeant and he proposed to the declarant that he work in a special group of the Armed Forces of Honduras in which they would afford him a good salary, a personal weapon, civilian clothes, and the possibility of promotion.

Sixth:

Declarant adds that between the years nineteen hundred seventy two and nineteen hundred seventy seven, he belonged to the Seventh Infantry Battalion "Dragons," based in Cucuyagua, in the Department of Copán. In this unit, he reached the rank of Second Sergeant, was assigned to the Fourth section of the Battalion, and took the following military courses: Communications, eighty, eighty one and one hundred twenty millimeter mortar; Basic Army classes; Advanced Army classes; parachuting (forty two promotion). Finally in nineteen hundred seventy seven, he was offered to take the course for Special and Nighttime Operations Troops (Tropas Especiales y Operaciones Nocturnas—TESON), from which he did not graduate. In nineteen hundred seventy seven, he requested his discharge from the Armed Forces and he became a Second Sergeant in the Police; he was assigned to the General barracks of the FUSEP in Casamata, where he remained for a period of two years.

Seventh:

In April of nineteen hundred eighty one, the declarant travelled to the city of Tegucigalpa to have an interview in the offices of the Armed Forces General Staff. Sergeant Guifarro introduced him in the first instance to Sergeant Peña, in charge of personnel within the Group of Fourteen, and then to the then Major Adolfo Díaz who accepted the declarant's entry into the Group of Fourteen.

Eighth:

Adolfo Díaz was the only officer within the group. It was called fourteen, because there were fourteen members in the group. The work consisted of eliminating those individuals that caused problems for the Armed Forces of Honduras and who were incorrigible communists.

Nineth:

The members of the group received 500 lempiras as monthly salary, they always carried photos of the persons to eliminate and they operated in groups of three. Among the persons murdered the declarant recalls the attorney Cabrera, killed in Juticalpa, Olancho, and the attorney Salinas, killed near the Central Park in Tegucigalpa by Sergeant Peña, Sergeant Arnulfo Guifarro, and Agent Padilla.

Tenth:

The Group of Fourteen was dissolved when the Honduran press denounced the existence of a "Death Squad." This situation was provoked by a member of the group, Agent Ostilio Peralta Dormes, who was detained in a drunken state in the Department of Olancho and it was discovered that he was carrying photos of persons that the group would later eliminate.

Eleventh:

After this incident, Major Adolfo Díaz ordered the elimination of Peralta Dormes, who was killed with a thirty-eighty revolver and a forty-five pistol in the Municipality of San Francisco de la Paz, in the Department of Olancho. His killers were Agents Elio Person, Saúl Najano, and the declarant.

Twelfth:

The members of the Group of Fourteen were sent to different posts. The declarant was sent to work in the Transit Section in the city of San Pedro Sula; later he was designated Transit Delegate in the city of La Lima. In that city he married the Supervisor of Nursing in the Hospital of the Tela Railroad Company, Mrs. María Suyapa Machado Funez.

Thirteenth:

Working as Transit Delegate in the city of La Lima, the declarant met Sub-Lieutenant Ramón Mejía, former classmate in the TESON course, and told him of his interest in obtaining different work because he was having a series of economic problems. Mejía made an appointment for him to go to the offices of the now already established Battalion Three-Sixteen in San Pedro Sula, where he would have an interview with "Attorney Rony" and "Engineer William."

Fourteenth:

In November of nineteen hundred and eighty two, he presented himself to the offices of the Battalion Three-Sixteen, in San Pedro Sula, located on the first floor shared by the North Military School and the One hundred and fifth brigade. Attorney Rony turned out to be sub-Lieutenant Marco Tulio Regalado Lara who was a friend of the declarant's when he was a sergeant in the Third Infantry Battalion; "Engineer William," was Captain Vicente Rafael Canales Núñez, whom the declarant knew as the officer in charge of internal security at the Casamata barracks. After speaking with both officers he was sent to perform duties of watching and following suspected subversives and he was given the pseudonym of Carlos Alfredo Membreño.

Fifteenth:

In the middle of the year nineteen hundred and eighty three, with more than thirty members of the Three-Sixteen nationally, the declarant attended in Lepaterique, Francisco Morazán, various counterinsurgency courses taught by eight American advisors and four Argentines. They were instructed in combat maneuvers, Pursuit in A, B, C, torture, explosives, interrogation and interchange of packages with the enemy. Later, he attended other courses given by Americans in San Pedro Sula; explosives and others on electronic warfare, this last course consisting principally in the implementation of techniques of wiretapping telephones.

Sixteenth:

That from the beginning and during the entire time that he belonged to the Battalion Three-Sixteen, the declarant realized that the payment of personnel, the maintenance of clandestine prisons, and, in general, the very existence of the Three-Sixteen, was due to the financing and participation of the American Central Intelligence Agency (CIA). That this intelligence agency coordinated with the Armed Forces General Staff and the Battalion Three-Sixteen through the American Raymond, nicknamed "Papi."

Seventeenth:

Raymond "Papi" periodically visited the locales of the Battalion Three-Sixteen, in San Pedro Sula and, further, they sent him weekly reports by plane from Tegucigalpa in a large, yellow envelope. The envelope had the word "Papi," or rather "for Papi," and the personnel of Three-Sixteen in the Ramón Villeda Morales airport would transport it.

Eighteenth:

The Personnel assigned to the airport was transported in a vehicle belonging to the unit everyday at seven in the morning. The last person to be picked up was Sonia at the bus stop at Cofradía; this woman worked with computers and lived in the hacienda belonging to Col. Inocente Borjas Santos (pseudonym Sr. Márquez). This last individual was until the end of nineteen hundred and eighty six National Commander of the Battalion Three-Sixteen. The other members of the personnel assigned to the Ramón Villeda Morales airport were: Hernán Escobar (pseudonym Sabillón) and one last individual named Humberto Cantarero who was called "Tacotales."

Nineteenth:

During the four years in which he remained in the Battalion Three-Sixteen, the declarant recognizes as officials of thereof the following: Maj. Alexander Hernández (pseudonym Mr. Diez); Maj. Oscar Ramón Hernández Chávez (pseudonym Attorney Pastrana and former commander of the Three-Sixteen in San Pedro Sula); Cpt. Rafael Canales Núñez (pseudonym Engineer William and until the end of nineteen hundred eighty four commander of the three sixteen in San Pedro Sula); Lt. Noel Corrales (pseudonym Juan de Dios Peña and sub-commander of the Three-Sixteen in San Pedro Sula); sub-lieutenant Marco Tulio Regalado Lara (pseudonym Attorney Rony) who was until nineteen hundred and eighty four sub-commander of the Three-Sixteen in San Pedro Sula and currently assigned to Tegucigalpa, serving as torturer and interrogator; sub-lieutenant Ramón Mejía (pseudonym Attorney Mercado) until the end of nineteen hundred eighty four, he remained in Tegucigalpa and currently is the Chief of Operations of the Three-Sixteen in San Pedro Sula. Ramón Mejía, together with Regalado Lara, is one of the officers most involved in torture, interrogation and murder. Other officers that the declarant was able to know in this period were: Sub-lieutenant Mario Asdrubal Quiñones (pseudonym Attorney Quintero) the current chief of surveillance and following/pursuit of the Three-Sixteen in San Pedro Sula, having been for many years commander of the robbery section of the National Investigations Directorate of Tegucigalpa; Captain Billy Joya Améndola (pseudonym Attorney Arrazola) founder of the Battalion Three-Sixteen, coordinator between Tegucigalpa and San Pedro Sula, who ordered the capture and execution of innumerable persons; Lieutenant Rusch (pseudonym Ruschelino), national commander for explosives; Police Sub-lieutenant Montiño (pseudonym Berríos) in charge of dogs at the national level; Captain Avelar (pseudonym Villarreal) located at the same level as Captain in the hierarchy of the Three-Sixteen; Lt. Rivera (pseudonym Attorney Javier) technician with the CIA of Puerto Rican nationality; Lieutentant Colonel Luis Alonso Villatoro who is the current commander of the Three-Sixteen at the national level and who was 'S dash one' (S-1) of the Seventh Infantry Battalion. The subcommander of the Three-Sixteen, a the national level a major in the Army whose name I can not remember and who uses the pseudonym Mr. Urquía, also known as Ronald. The sub-commanders in the Three-Sixteen devote themselves principally to counterintelligence.

Twentieth:

The declarant adds various names of officers involved in the Three-Sixteen, whose level in the hierarchy and pseudonyms he cannot recall. Among other: Sub-lieutenant Nazar (from Comayagua); Maj. (ret.) Padilla, who lives in the Mayangie neighborhood of Tegucigalpa; Lt. Col. Fuentes Delgado (ex-regional commander of the FUSEP in San Pedro Sula); Infantry Maj. Paz (ex-officer of the Seventh Infanty Battalion); Sub-lieutenant Altamirano Najarro who is "TESON" and carries out bank robberies to inculpate subversives; and Police Lt. Salinas.

Twenty first:

That the ties of the Three-Sixteen with other military and governmental divisions are quite extensive. In this regard, the declarant notes, for example, that since nineteen hundred eighty two, all the commanders of the National Investigations Directorate (DNI) in San Pedro Sula have participated in or have been complicit in the actions that the Three-Sixteen executes. This unit has its own offices to interrogate and torture in the downstairs part of the National Investigations Directorate (DNI) and in some battalions like the Third Infantry located in Naco. Other ties include individuals like the Immigration Inspector Izaguirre (who works for the unit), collaborators and informers within the unions like Mr. Rafael Valle of SITRATERCO, collaborators within the universities like Attorney José María Kury (Director of the Regional University Center of the North), doctors that work for the Three-Sixteen like Dr. Kuncar of the Honduran Institute of Social Security and the dentist Francisca Pagge. In sum, the Battalion Three-Sixteen is above any of the military brigades or the sixteen battalions of the Army, which is where its name comes from.

Twenty second:

That all officers that the declarant has mentioned he has done with actual knowledge since in the majority of the cases, the declarant has been a subordinate of the same in the course of fourteen years of belonging to the Armed Forces of Honduras. With regard to the personnel of troops of the Three-Sixteen at the national level, the declarant can locate more than fifty of them, by their names, pseudonyms, military rank and the functions they exercise in the unit.

Twenty third:

The declarant knows of the existence of clandestine jails, called within the Three Sixteen "warehouses," among those that he mentions are: in the Guamalito neighborhood of the city of San Pedro Sula there is a two story house with dark oval shaped windows, located on the corner of Eighth Avenue and Tenth street northeast number fifty eight. In the same city but in the Ideal neighborhood there is another house located across from one side of the Mormon church. The declarant estimates that many of the disappeared and killed by the Three-Sixteen passed through these houses and he calculates that, in total, the kidnapped and killed in that city numbered more than one hundred.

Twenty fourth:

The declarant knows of the existence of the following clandestine cemeteries: in El Zamorano, near the place where they killed Father Arsenault, there is a turn off, the only one towards the east and approximately some three hundred kilometers inward. There is another cemetery in San Pedro Sula, near the Channel Two (television) guard station; this is guarded by armed personnel that live in a humble laborer's house, some meters ahead of that house they perform the burials. In the San Alejo sector, in Tela, upon crossing the railroad line there is a place where they leave African palm wastes, there they have buried various persons. In the city of Santa Bárbara, by the makeshift turn off to go to the Normal School (Escuela Normal) and some three blocks from there are buried some eight persons. In the Municipality of Salamá, Olancho, Sergeants Padilla and Matamoros, executioners of the Three-Sixteen in Tegucigalpa, buried six persons in just one place well known because there they killed Mr. Aníbal Cano, they placed three cadavers on each side of the cross. The drivers of the Three-Sixteen ("Mute" Panigua, Bustillo and Cano Lobo) are those who know most about the clandestine cemeteries because they transported the cadavers.

Twenty fifth:

That the agents from San Pedro Sula that participated the most in captures, tortures, and executions are: Sgt. Nuñez, who is from Santa Cruz Yojoa and whose pseudonym is Chifay; Víctor López (pseudonym Enrique

Maradiaga); Sgt. Manuel González who uses the nickname Porcio and the pseudonym of Arnulfo Paz González; Sgt. (from the Cobra Unit) Efraín Domínguez, who uses the pseudonym Huete Deras; Manuel Robles (pseudonym "La Mole"); Mayro Antúnez Pagoada, from Santa Bárbara and who nickname is "Mirón Socadito") In the city of Tegucigalpa: Matamoros, who is the executioner since the Group of Fourteen, who lives in the Los Profesores neighborhood (across from the Martell supermarket) and who has as the special characteristic of a patch of grey hair that is very noticeable; Sgt. Peña Paz; Transit Sergeant Maggin; Padilla who has a very large scar on his face, Second Sgt. Servellón; Carlos Peralta, who turned Félix Martínez over to the Nicarguan contras.

Twenty Sixth:

The declarant wants to mention some of the cases of disappearance and murder committed by the Three-Sixteen.

Herminio Deras Case: among the killers of Deras were Marco Tulio Regalado Lara, the officer who was reprimanded for not being able to kidnap the victim alive, having killed him in the street. Another of the killers was Luis Hernández, who is retired from the Three-Sixteen and lives in the Barandillas neighborhood of San Pedro Sula (Fourth Street and Fourth Avenue).

Case of Mr. Ricardo García: This man was tortured to the point of destroying his testicles and afterwards was killed by order of Cpt. Canales Nuñez. The executioners were Arnulfo Paz González and the declarant; for the work performed each one of them was given three hundred lempiras as travelling expenses that they spent enjoying themselves in the *Juniana* Fair of San Pedro Sula.

Cristóbal Pérez Case: Initially, the declarant and Arnulfo Paz González were ordered to kill Cristóbal Pérez, but later, from Tegucigalpa, came the order that officers should kill this labor leader. The executioners were, Sub-lieutenant Ramón Mejía, and the motorist of this action an individual with the last name Bustillo. The day after the killing, the declarant was warned by officers of the Three-Sixteen of San Pedro Sula not to comment for any reason what he knew and was given two hundred lempiras. By the way the officers spoke to the declarant, he thought they would eliminate him for knowing too much.

Attorney Salvador Díaz del Valle: This man was killed by the officer Billy Joya, accompanied by Sub-lieutenant Mejía. Mejía recounted this to the declarant in confidence. Díaz del Valle was captured, a month before his death, along with a cousin of the declarant named Antonio Barrera Vázquez. Due to this fact, the declarant was very interested in this case.

Disappearance of Mr. Adonay Morataya: In November of nineteen hundred and eighty five, in the village of Arenales, in the jurisdiction of San Pedro Sula, the declarant participated in the capture of this man. Sub-lieutenant Mejía was in charge of interrogating him. It is very probable that Moratay was eliminated.

Murder of Mr. Jorge Alberto Cubas Carrillo: This man had personal problems with Cpt. Canales Nuñez, who ordered his execution in December of nineteen hundred eighty three. Canales Nuñez gave the declarant six hundred lempiras as travelling money for carrying out this work. The act occurred in Juticalpa, Olancho, in the "La Ultima Copa" (The Last Glass) bar and the victim received just one shot from a nine millimeter Browning. The declarant indicates that he returned to Tegucigalpa very nervous that day because he had been recognized by a woman named Alejandrina López (sister of "Pikirike", a famous soccer player from Juticalpa). He also stated that he was assigned to participate in the cases in the Department of Olancho because the Three-Sixteen knew that he had worked in that place for a long time.

Juan Hernández Domínguez case: The detention order of this man was given by Cpt. Billy Joya Améndola, in the month of August of nineteen hundred and eighty five. Hernández Domínguez resisted capture and attempted to flee. Faced with this situation, the declarant thrust a bayonet (*yatagán*) (those that the contras used) which penetrated deeply in his stomach. The declarant received orders to take the wounded man to the Hospital of the School of Tegucigalpa, where he finally died.

Disappearance of Rolando Vindel: Those who kidnapped Vindel were members of the G-2, and they turned him over to the Three-Sixteen, after having been interrogated and tortured. The declarant transported Vindel from the First Infantry Battalion to the headquarters of the Three-Sixteen in Tegucigalpa, located in the 21st of October neighborhood. On this occasion the declarant was accompanied by Cpt. Aveler, who told Lt. Silvan and Sub-lieutenant Urbina (of the G-2) "You guys are brave; I'll take them to the Three-Sixteen." The lieutenants answered, "Thank you, my captain, those are risks of the job." The declarant indicates that by chance he found himself in those days in Tegucigalpa and there being personnel to carry out this transfer, they looked to him.

Murder of Eduardo López: Mario Asdrubal Quiñones captured and interrogated López in the National Investigations Directorate (DNI) of San Pedro Sula, but López had to be transferred to the house in the Guamalito neighborhood since he was recognized by another prisoner in the Directorate's offices. In the house in Guamalito, the declarant interrogated López over five days, at the end of which he was executed by Manuel Robles (alias "La Mole") and by Maj. Antúnez Pagoada ("Mirón Socadito"); the motorist on that occasion was Cristóbal Lainez ("El Loco Hogman"). When these men returned at two in the morning, Pagoada's shirt was bloodied, which prompted the declarant to ask if the detainee had resisted, to which they responded no and that he had stained the shirt dragging López's body.

Murder of José Villanueva: Sgt. Ramos (pseudonym Polanco) on one occasion confided: "I don't like the mission I'm going on tomorrow." The next day, Villanueva appeared dead, prompting the declarant, in a joking tone, to tell Polanco, "good job they did with Villanueva!" He responded "it wasn't me; Colón killed him, I just drove the motorcycle."

Hermes Aguilar Case: The declarant gathered information and watched Aguilar, who days earlier was captured by elements of the G-2, from the Fourth Infantry Battalion. By radio, the men from the Fourth Battalion communicated with the Three-Sixteen, and the detainee was brought to the National Investigations Directorate (DNI) in La Ceiba. Aguilar did not want to cooperate, and thus the order to eliminate him was given. Those in charge of the execution were Sub-lieutenant Ramón Mejía and Mayro Antúnez Pagoada ("Mirón Socadito").

Twenty Seventh:

The declarant deserted Battalion three sixteen for fear of being killed because he was frequently reprimanded for maintaining friendships with persons considered by the officers as "Marxists." As confidence in him diminished, the declarant considered that he could be killed for possessing a lot of information. That is what happened to Juan Constantino García Gómez (pseudonym Colón Garay) ex-member of the Three-Sixteen in San Pedro Sula and who was killed by Sub-lieutenant Mario Asdrubal Quiñónez and by Jaime Raudales ("Quico").

Another factor in his leaving the Three-Sixteen was the rejection he felt in the last months for the work he performed.

Twenty eighth:

That the month after leaving the Three-Sixteen, he was captured in his house (located in the Planeta neighborhood, number eighteen hundred nineteen and eighteen hundred twenty, duplex) by agents of the National Investigations Directorate (DNI), among them Canales, Fiallos and Domínguez. He was told that the reason for his arrest was for having deserted, however, in his questioning, he was asked about arms, bank robberies and was even accused of being a leftist. He remained forty-eight days in the National Investigations Directorate (DNI) in San Pedro Sula and he was tortured by Agent Domínguez, Fiallos and Ortega. He was freed only because of the pressure exercised by friends who belong to the Christian Democratic Party, others who are journalists and also because of the demands of his family. After being freed, he went to live in his parents' house in the Perpetuo Socorro neighborhood (next to the Satélite neighborhood). After about five days of staying there he began to notice the presence of motorcyclists and vehicles from the Three-Sixteen; under these circumstances he decided to change his residence and looked for ways of leaving Honduras, because he was certain that they were going to kill him.

—-THAT THE PRIOR STATEMENTS ARE MADE BY THE DECLARANT FOR WHATEVER LEGAL EFFECT THEY MAY HAVE— —-GENERALITIES—-

— Under Protest to speak the truth and remaining warned of the penalties to which one is subject when declaring falsely, the declarant stated that: he was born on the twenty second of October of nineteen hundred fifty eight, is unmarried, an office worker, with residence in San Angel Street, San Gerónimo Avenue, number fifty seven, C.U.E., four, Alvaro Obregón delegation, Postal Code 01060, originally from San Pedro Sula, Cortés Department, Honduran nationality, with Federal Contributors Registry number "BAMJ fifty eight, ten, twenty two."—

-In the condition of non-immigrant (D) in the country, as the FMT document, number zero six-hundred sixty seven thousand, five hundred and six, issued the first day of April of nineteen hundred eighty six by the Secretary of Government.—

Identifying himself with Honduran passport number two hundred seventy nine thousand, two hundred eighty one, issued the first of April of nineteen hundred eighty seven by the Secretary of Foreign Relations of Honduras.—-

—-I, the Notary Certify: The knowledge and identity of the declarant, who in my judgment had the legal capacity to authorize this instrument, of which I read him this copy, explaining to him its legal consequences and value, of which he indicated his consent and which he signed the second day of July of nineteen hundred eighty seven.—I certify.—

—AUTHORIZING IMMEDIATELY AND DEFINITIVELY WITH MY SIGNATURE AND SEAL.—- I CERTIFY——

Making known that I assure myself of the identity of the declarant, with the document related in the section of generalities. I certify.

JOSE BARRERA MARTINEZ—SEAL.-SALVADOR GODINEZ VIERA.— SEAL.-THE SEAL OF AUTHORIZATION.——

THIS IS THE FIRST TESTIMONY THAT I PERFORM FOR MR. JOSE BARRERA MARTINEZ, AS INTERESTED PARTY.- IT CONTAINS SIXTEEN PAGES, DULY COLLATED—-MEXICO, FEDERAL DISTRICT, ON THE SECOND OF JULY OF NINETEEN HUNDRED EIGHTY SEVEN.—I CERTIFY

[Notary Seal and Signature of Salvador Godinez Viera]

V

THE INTERNATIONAL CONTEXT

An objective study of disappearances in Honduras requires special attention to the context in which these violations occurred. It would be impossible to understand disappearances in Honduras without addressing the international context that surrounded, and to a large degree conditioned our nation during this dark period of its history.

First, the region's history reveals that the period during which the greatest number and most systematic disappearances occurred in Honduras corresponds to the years in which armed conflict in Honduras's neighboring countries was at its peak. The years immediately following the ascension to power of the Sandinistas in July 1979 were years of intense conflict in Nicaragua. Similarly, the period from 1980-1983 saw a marked rise in the level of official and rebel violence in El Salvador and Guatemala.

Second, our region, and in particular our country, experienced significant effects from the policies adopted by the United States in response to the regional crisis noted above, particularly its policies concerning El Salvador and Nicaragua.

The documentation to which we had access in elaborating this report allows us to conclude that U.S. policy towards Central America during the 1980s was characterized by the search for a military solution to the region's crisis. According to official analysts and documents, this policy meant supporting the military and security structures of our countries in order to resolve what was seen as a threat to the United States' national security and strategic interests in the region.

Unfortunately, this U.S. policy was carried out in an illegal and covert manner. The policy not only constituted a violation of the fundamental principles of international law, such as respect for sovereignty and non-intervention in the internal affairs of other countries, but also signified a transgression of the United States' own laws. This was more than amply documented by the results of the Iran-Contra scandal.

Even worse is the discovery that the cost for our country was not only the renunciation of the defense of our national interest, but also the sacrifice of the lives of hundreds of our fellow citizens, as well as citizens of El Salvador, Nicaragua, Guatemala, Costa Rica, Panama, etc. (*See* the list of disappeared in Chapter II).

Finally, it is ironic that the period of greatest "militarization" of

Honduran society (1982-1984) occurred precisely during the period of return to the rule of law. In these years, the country was ruled by democratically elected governments and official bodies functioned as stipulated in the Constitution of the Republic, at least formally.

The Use of Honduran Territory as a Base for Military Actions Against Neighboring Countries

The victory of the Sandinistas in July 1979, after a bloody struggle, resulted in a great flow of refugees opposed to the new government in Managua to Honduras. Even in this early period of Sandinista rule, there was evidence of efforts—mainly by former Nicaraguan National Guardsmen—to organize armed anti-Sandinista groups:

> Reported ex-GN [National Guard, identification erased] description of attempts to recruit counter-revolutionary force among GN refugees in Honduras and his request USG [United States Government] intercede with new Nicaraguan government to allow them to return home.

> Other information reaching me seems to confirm recruitment efforts.[1]

> One of the most effective steps we could take would be to encourage vigorously the resettlement of former National Guardsmen, whose presence in Honduras is a source of Nicaraguan fear and suspicion. The Honduran government considers the presence of about 1,500 former Nicaraguan National Guard ... to be a burden. The economically strapped Honduran government cannot offer jobs to these refugees, who in frustration might conceivably provide fertile

---

[1] Cable from the American Embassy in Tegucigalpa to the Secretary of State, "Subj: National Guard Refugees in Honduras," July 30, 1979, signed by Mari-Luci Jaramillo. [NSA 1007]

grounds for recruitment as mercenaries.[2]

Beginning in early 1980, the Sandinista Government accused the United States, and particularly the CIA of promoting the organization of armed anti-Sandinista groups with bases in Honduras.[3] Throughout 1980, the escalation of supply operations and periodic incursions, as well as the discovery of the use of Honduran territory for the shipment of arms destined for Central American rebel groups, converged and increased internal tension, putting Honduras on an irreversible path towards involvement in the regional conflict.

Beginning with the transition effected by the 1980 presidential elections in the U.S., the Reagan administration began a campaign that accused the Soviet-Cuban-Nicaraguan axis of promoting regional destabilization. Washington denounced political and military support of rebel groups in El Salvador and Guatemala. The Reagan administration involved Honduras in this process not only as a point for the shipment of arms, but also as a target for internal subversion. Only 10 days after becoming Secretary of State, Alexander Haig met in Washington with the Honduran Foreign Minister Elvir Sierra. A cable from the State Department informing the embassy in Tegucigalpa about the meeting states:

> Secretary Haig said he wanted to inform Elvir about certain changes in U.S. policy toward Central America which he could expect in the years ahead. ... He said that we now have absolutely firm evidence of massive Cuban intervention in El Salvador via Nicaragua. He expressed appreciation of Honduran efforts to rapidly mobilize and

---

[2] Cable from the American Embassy in Tegucigalpa, "Subj: Nicaraguan Refugees in Honduras: a Cause of GRN Suspicion," signed by Mari-Luci Jaramillo. November 26, 1979. [NSA 1103]

[3] A cable from the American Embassy in Managua noted:
FSLN daily Barricada, Radio Sandino and Sandinista TV have carried a series of commentaries over last week denouncing alleged CIA efforts to destabilize revolutionary process in Nicaragua.... Feb. 28 Barricada also carried a Prensa Latina item datelined Moscow (quoting Novosti) which "reported" that the CIA is training 5,000 ex-GN in Honduras for the counter-revolution.
Cable from the American Embassy in Managua, "Subject: FSLN Denounces CIA Maneuvers Against Nicaragua," signed by O'Donnell, March 1, 1980. [NSA 1118]

combat such Cuban intervention via Honduras. ... Elvir replied that
Honduras shared our concern ... He said that the Honduran
authorities had recently discovered a very large quantity of arms
clandestinely transitting Honduras to El Salvador. ... Noting that the
time was important, Elvir said Honduras was ready to cooperate in
any action program which the U.S. might undertake to deal with this
problem.[4]

The cooperative attitude of the Honduran minister is confirmed by a
revealing secret memorandum from State Department Deputy Secretary of
State Thomas Enders, dated May 6, 1981, which states:

Tensions between Honduras and Nicaragua recently have erupted
into firefights along their border. Border incidents in the past months
resulted from armed incursions into Nicaragua by ex-Somocista
guardsmen, and from cattle-rustling activities in Honduras by groups
of Nicaraguans. ... Nicaragua's nervousness is stimulated by the
raids by Honduran-based exiles who receive support from certain
GOH sources.[5]

During this time, actions of armed Honduran groups intensified. In
March 1981, in one of the actions with the greatest repercussion, a
subversive group occupied the Chamber of Commerce of San Pedro Sula
where they took civilian hostages and then hijacked a SAHSA airplane.
    In 1981, U.S. policy towards Nicaragua sought to neutralize the
threat in Central America to its national interests, within the limits imposed
by domestic legislation that prohibited direct involvement of Americans in an
open confrontation with the Sandinista regime. The Reagan administration
thus implemented a covert plan utilizing "intermediaries" from third countries
to achieve its objectives. On March 9, 1981, Reagan issued a presidential
finding authorizing the CIA to carry out "covert activities" directed against

---

[4] Cable from the State Department to the American Embassy in Tegucigalpa,
"Subject: Memorandum of Secretary Haig's Conversation with Honduran Foreign
Minister Elvir," February 3, 1981. [NSA 1266]

[5] Confidential Department of State memorandum from Thomas Enders to the Deputy
Secretary, "Subject: Background for your May 8, 10:45 am meeting with Honduran
Foreign Minister Cesar Elvir Sierra," May 6, 1981. [NSA 1266]

Nicaragua. More than 19 million dollars were authorized to finance such operations.[6] On November 23 of the same year, Reagan issued an executive order known as "National Security Decision Directive 17" through which he authorized a consignment of more than $19 million for the CIA to promote a strong opposition to the Sandinistas and organize a paramilitary force "working with foreign governments." The Intelligence Committees of the U.S. Congress were informed that the CIA would create a paramilitary force of some 500 men used only to block the flow of arms from Nicaragua to the Salvadoran rebels and attack some Cuban military installations in Nicaragua.[7]

The Argentines in Honduras

The period of military rule in Argentina (1976-1983) was characterized by the implementation of a bloody anti-subversive campaign known as the "dirty war." Though it succeeded in totally dismantling both urban and rural guerrilla groups, the tactics used constituted systematic and massive violations of human rights. To carry out this campaign with total impunity, a clandestine structure was established—inserted in the heart of the militarily controlled security forces—and operationally divided into "work groups" (*grupos de tarea*). These work groups carried out kidnappings, clandestine detention, torture, disappearances and the extrajudicial execution of persons considered to be "subversives." The result was a toll of between 20,000 and 30,000 victims, including some 9,000 disappearances registered by the National Commission on Disappearances.[8]

The doctrine employed by the Argentine military considered the anti-subversive fight to be an ideological war between "western and Christian civilization" and "atheistic communism," whose theater of operations

---

[6] *The Chronology: The Documented Day-by-Day Account of the Secret Military Assistance to Iran and the Contras,* (National Security Archives, Washington, D.C.: 1987). *See also The Washington Post,* May 8, 1983.

[7] *The Chronology,* p. 10; *The Washington Post,* January 1, 1983; Annex A, World Court Documents for *Military and Paramilitary Activities in and Against Nicaragua* (Nicaragua. v. U.S.) 1986 I.C.J. 14 (Merits: Judgment of 27 June 1986).

[8] *Nunca Mas, Informe de la Comisión Nacional Sobre la Desaparición de Personas,* [Never Again: Report of the National Commission on the Disappearance of Persons] (Buenos Aires: 1984).

exceeded national boundaries. Based on this, the concept of "ideological borders" was introduced, which justified the direct intervention in external conflicts in order to halt the advance of international communism. The Argentine authors of *Malvinas: La Trama Secreta* (Malvinas: the Secret Plan) describe the following:

> Argentina had attempted, without success, to stop the overthrow of the Nicaraguan dictator Anastasio Somoza, supplying him up to the final moments with weapons and money. The Argentine government then sent advisors—experts in "counterinsurgency"—to Honduras and Guatemala, and [General and later President] Galtieri even extended offers of assistance to Somocistas in exile who were engaged in defeating the new regime of the Sandinista Liberation Front. This peculiar external use of military force was conceived in 1979 by the General Staff (*Estado Mayor General*) of the Army, based on the hypothesis that Argentina could "occupy the vacant spaces in the continental struggle against communism" that, according to the military analysis, the Carter administration, with its emphasis on human rights, was leaving open.[9]

Information available from various sources shows that the Argentine military presence in Honduras was established in 1980, in an effort by the military junta send experts in anti-subversive warfare to assist security forces.

Scott Anderson and John Lee Anderson, in their book *Inside the League,* write:

> By 1980, Argentine advisors were already operating in Honduras, training Honduran police units in "suspect interrogation techniques." The junta in Buenos Aires had sent the consultants there to help develop an internal security apparatus similar to their own; this mission directly benefitted an old friend, Colonel Gustavo Alvarez Martínez.[10]

---

[9] O.R. Cardoso, R. Kirschbaum and E. van der Kooy, *Malvinas: La Trama Secreta,* (Ed. Sudamericana-Planeta: Buenos Aires: 1986), p. 27.

[10] Scott Anderson and John Lee Anderson, *Inside the League,* (Dodd, Mead & Co.: New York, 1986), p. 224.

Further on, the authors add that in 1991 Alvarez established within the FUSEP, with Argentine assistance, a Unit of Special Operations (*Comando de Operaciones Especiales, COE*). In addition to being an elite counter-insurgent force, "the COE was converted into the command center of Alvarez's 'dirty war'."[11] On this topic, a December 1982 report by Americas Watch [now Human Rights Watch/Americas], entitled *Human Rights in Honduras: Signs of the "Argentine Method,"* states:

> These [Argentine] advisors remain unidentified, and both the Honduran and the Argentine governments have denied their presence in Honduras. ... The participation of Argentine agents in disappearances is not yet completely proven, but human rights observers cannot help noticing the striking similarities between the pattern now evolving in Honduras and the 15,000 to 20,000 disappearances conducted by the Argentine armed forces between 1976 and 1980. Those similarities include the use of heavily armed plainclothesmen who do not identify themselves, but clearly exercise official authority. They conduct their operations in broad daylight, stay for long periods in residences and places of work, stalk their targets in public, and yet are never stopped or interfered with by regular police forces. Other similarities include the use of unmarked cars, and secret or clandestine detention centers.[12]

---

[11] Christopher Dickey refers in his book to "a bright young captain named Alex Hernandez in 'Special Operations,' a squad that [Alvarez] personally organized on the Argentine model to take care of suspected subversives." Christopher Dickey, *With the Contras: A Reporter in the Wilds of Nicaragua,* (Simon & Schuster: New York, 1985), p. 116.

[12] Americas Watch [now Human Rights Watch/Americas], *Human Rights in Honduras: Signs of the "Argentine Method,"* (Human Rights Watch: New York, December 1982), pp. 11-12. According to Ephron, the anonymous source cited in *Inside the League:* "We got people, killed them, put their bodies aboard helicopters, and threw them into the Río Sumpul [the river dividing part of Honduras and El Salvador and an area of intense fighting between the Salvadoran army and Salvadoran guerrillas] to make it look like the Salvadorans did it. Before dumping them, we would remove all ID and put Salvadoran coins in their pockets...." This particular disposal method echoes that employed in Argentina. Investigators for the new civilian Argentine government have discovered that hundreds of Argentina's "disappeared" were stripped of identification and then thrown from military aircraft over the South Atlantic during the "dirty war." *Inside*

Beginning in 1981, the new policies of the Reagan administration in Central America, the acquiescence of Honduran civilian and military authorities, and the international anti-subversive crusade of the Argentine military junta, converged to formalize a second objective for the Argentine military advisors in Honduras: the training and channelling of resources to anti-Sandinista paramilitary groups based in Honduran territory.

Though this alliance was broken in April 1982 due to American support for the British government during the Malvinas (Falklands) War, various testimonies and reports show that Argentine advisors remained after that date.[13]

In late 1982, a member of the group of Argentine advisors in Central America was kidnapped in Costa Rica. A short while later, in a video-tape released to the press, he declared that he was Hector Francés of the 601st Intelligence Battalion of the Argentine army. Francés described the system of coordination between the Argentines, Hondurans, Nicaraguans, and North Americans in Honduras, and revealed the names of the principal protagonists:

> The Argentine side is under military commanders like Davico, possibly the head of the G2 of the Army General Staff. . . . The 601st battalion is commanded by Arismendi. Under these men is the Argentine general staff in Honduras, composed of José Oyas (known as Villegas), head of military logistics, and Col. Osvaldo Riveiro, operational and political commander. This staff is related to a Honduran general staff composed of ... Alvarez and Alexander, the commander of the FUSEP.[14]

---

the League, p. 226. According to Dickey, "The Hondurans were long used to corruption but not to brutality. ... Alvarez was changing that. People began to talk of the 'Argentine method.'" Dickey, *With the Contras*, p. 116.

[13] "Only a handful of Argentines remained with the FDN by year's end, among them Col. Carmelo Gigante, who was awarded a Honduran army medal in February." Alfonso Chardy and Juan O. Tamayo, "CIA Calls Shots Against Nicaragua," *The Miami Herald*, April 17, 1983.

[14] Excerpts, "Hector Francés Tape," December 6, 1982, p. 3.

About the Argentine safe houses in Tegucigalpa, Francés stated:

The information that we processed contains repeated references, by diverse sources, regarding the identity of the Argentine military advisors in Honduras. The following is a list of names that has been compiled during the elaboration of this report:

- Gen. Alberto Alfredo Valín or Mario Valín[15]

One was in Brisas de la Granja, where two to four people lived; one in Lomas de Guijarro, with five people, including Villegas (Oyas), two Argentines and a Nicaraguan. ... The political leadership, under the supervision of Colonel Riveiro (alias "Balita"), pays for a house in the Florencia neighborhood. *Ibid.*, p. 5.

[15] Mentioned by Roberto Bardini, "La Red Mercenaria del Proceso," *Caras y Caretas,* Buenos Aires, (date unknown); William Baltodano Herrera in comments to the press in Nicaragua; and Dieter Eich and Carlos Rincón, *The Contras: Interviews with Anti-Sandinistas,* (Synthesis Publications: San Francisco), pp. 22-23. In *Malvinas, La Trama Secreta,* the authors state that General Galtieri, before becoming president, travelled twice to the United States in 1981, finalizing, among other things, the terms for Argentine cooperation in Central America. During his November 1981 trip, at a reception at the Argentine Embassy for Secretary of Defense Caspar Weinberger, National Security Advisor [Richard] Allen, Thomas Enders, Vernon Walters, General Edward Meyer, and others, Galtieri stood up and gave a toast:

"Argentina and the United States will march together in the ideological war that is being released throughout the world," he confidently asserted. He added that "in the exterior, Argentina has an overwhelming role to play in the world ..." These words had the desired effect, because for the Americans, they were a ratification of the Argentine intervention in Central America. For Galtieri it was nothing but the consummation of a project that had been meticulously executed. Part of this consisted in the inclusion of *Alberto Valín*—who had already served as an advisor to Somoza's National Guard during the Nicaraguan civil war—in his committee of generals, as well as Mario Menéndez, an officer who had gained his reputation by participating in Operation Independent Tucumán during the repression of the leftist guerrillas active in that province of Argentina.

- Col. Mario Davico or Davido[16]
- Col. Osvaldo Ribeiro or Riveiro, alias "Balita"[17]
- Col. José Hoyas or Oyas, alias Santiago Villegas[18]

---

[16] Mentioned as Capitán Davido in *The Contras: Interviews with Anti-Sandinistas*, p. 23.
Mentioned in the testimony of Hector Francés.
Mentioned in Roberto Bardini, "La Red Mercenaria del Proceso," *Caras y Caretas*, (Buenos Aires, date unknown), p. 23.

[17] Mentioned in Christopher Dickey, *With the Contras*, p. 115. The author states that Ribeiro's identity was confirmed by various sources, such as Edgar Chamorro, a former spokesman for the contras in Tegucigalpa, on August 9, 1984; by José Francisco Cardenal, on August 11, 1984; by CIA sources in October and November 1984; and by military sources in Argentina interviewed by Martin E. Anderson, *Washington Post* correspondent in Argentina. Anderson tried to interview Ribeiro, but he refused. According to Dickey, "Ribeiro and the Argentines had set themselves up at the Honduran Maya Hotel ... They liked the Monte Carlo Casino there, the steak house downstairs, the bar and the disco full of young fawn-eyed and willing women every Friday night." (p. 126); Mentioned by William Baltodano Herrera to the press in Nicaragua; Jorge Ramírez Zelaya, *The Contras*, p. 31;   Jonathan Marshall, Peter Dale Scott and Anne Jane Hunter, *The Iran Contra Connection. Secret Teams and Covert Operations in the Reagan Era,* (South End Press: Boston, 1987), p. 130; and testimony of Hector Francés.

[18] Dickey, *With the Contras*, p. 119: "The Argentine called Villegas met Chicano Cardenal in the lobby of the hotel at the Miami airport one afternoon in August [1981] . . . Villegas, who was now second-in-command to Ribeiro, laid out the plan. Support for the fight against the Sandinistas was going to be 'tripartite', Villegas said. The United States was going to give the money. Argentina was going to provide the training. Honduras was going to provide the base of operations." *Also see* "Bestias-Honduras-CIA ... Todo al Desnudo," *Barricada,* August 6, 1983. Three photos of Villegas were published with the article;   Testimony of Hector Francés, December 6, 1982; Roberto Baldini, "La Red Mercenaria del Proceso," and "Assesores Argentinos en Honduras," *Humor,* (Buenos Aires: 1983).

- Hector Francés or Hector Ricardo Francés Garcia or Estanislao Valdez[19]
- Col. Jorge O'Higgins[20]
- Col. Jorge de la Vega[21]
- Emilio Jasón[22]
- Col. Carmelo Gigante or Carmilio Grande[23]
- Juan Carlos Galasso or Galeso[24]

---

[19] *See,* transcription of his filmed testimony, December 6, 1982; "Argentino Secuestrado aquí está en Prisión de Managua" *República,* San José, Costa Rica, November 19, 1982; Suzanne Garment, "Hector is Missing and it Would Seem Nicaragua Has Him," *Wall Street Journal,* April 15, 1983; Horacio Verbitsky, *La Posguerra Sucia,* (Legasa: Buenos Aires), p. 128. The author states: "Francés García, whose real name may have been Estanislao Valdés, was one of the instructors of the 601st Battalion."

[20] Bardini, "La Red Mercenaria del Proceso," pp. 25-26: "The Argentine colonels Jorge O'Higgins, Jorge de la Vega, and Carmilio Gigante supply training to the Honduran military and counter-revolutionary Somocistas and participated in the kidnapping and assassination of trade unionists and university students. ... According to what could be confirmed, O'Higgins was the military attaché of the Argentine Embassy in Tegucigalpa; De la Vega, a permanent advisor of the Honduran army; and Gigante led paramilitary groups."

[21] Bardini, "La Red Mercenaria," pp. 25-26.

[22] Bardini, "La Red Mercenaria," p. 22.

[23] Bardini, "La Red Mercenaria," pp. 22, 25-26; Alfonso Chardy and Juan O. Tamayo, "CIA Calls Shots Against Nicaragua," *The Miami Herald,* April 17, 1983 (indicating that Col. Carmelo Gigante, who received a medal from the Honduran Armed Forces, was one of only a handful of Argentines who remained at the end of the year).

[24] Testimony of Héctor Francés, December 6, 1982; and Verbitsky, *La Posguerra Sucia*: "[Francés] travelled to Panama, where another Argentine agent gave him 100,000 dollars, and in the company of a third colleague they brought it to Honduras, in order to pay salaries and emergency expenses for the safe houses and offices. Safe houses that the Argentine advisors maintained in

- Juan Martin Ciga or Ciga Correa, alias Mariano Santamaría[25]
- Cesar Carro[26]
- Leandro Sánchez Reisse[27]

United States Policy in Honduras

With the formal exit of the Argentines as advisors and trainers of the anti-Sandinista armed groups, the presence of agents of the United States government to fill the vacuum became more necessary and evident.

On July 28, 1983, President Reagan signed National Security Decision Directive (NSDD) 100, which allowed for the strengthening of the presence and military assistance of the United States in Central America. This secret document reveals the determination of the United States to pressure the Nicaraguan government through the use of force, and the consequent "militarization" of its policies towards other countries in the region, including Honduras. Thus, decisions that directly affected Honduras were generally made without consultation with, or the consensus of the Honduran authorities. Some of the relevant sections of NSDD 100 state:

> Adequate U.S. support must also be provided to the democratic resistance forces within Nicaragua in an effort to ensure that Nicaragua ceases to be a Soviet/Cuban base...
> The democratic states of Central America must be assisted to the maximum degree possible in defending themselves against externally

---

various parts of Tegucigalpa." The man who gave him the money was Juan Carlos Gallardo.

[25] Testimony of Héctor Francés; Verbitsky, *La Posguerra Sucia,* pp. 127-131, mentions that Ciga Correa was detained for larceny in Mar del Plata, Argentina, with a false identification in the name of Army Maj. Mariano Santamaría.

[26] Bardini, "La Red Mercenaria," indicates, "A Honduran insurgent group mentioned officer César Carro, about whom there is no certainty whether he belongs to the army or the police."

[27] *Somos,* Buenos Aires, February 25, 1987, pp. 20-22.

supported subversion or hostile neighbors. U.S. military activities in
the region must be significantly increased to demonstrate our
willingness to defend our allies and to deter further Cuban and
Soviet bloc intervention.

To this end, the following measures are directed:

... Exercise AHUAS TARA II should begin on or about August 1,
1983. While the specific duration and scope of the exercise will be
determined by the situation, plans should be made for the exercise to
continue for four to six months.[28]

United States Assistance, Human Rights
Reporting and Covert Operations[29]

Throughout the first half of the 1980s, the United States Government
provided substantial economic and military aid to Honduras. Beginning in
1981, each year the amount of both military and total aid to Honduras
increased. In 1981, aid totalled $45.3 million; in 1982, the figure more than
doubled, totalling $111.9 million. By 1985, this figure reached $291.4
million—more than six times the figure of just four years earlier.[30]

During this same period, despite the significant increases in foreign
assistance to Honduras, the State Department failed to recognize and respond
to credible reports of human rights violations in Honduras, particularly the
increasingly common phenomenon of disappearances. The Annual Country

---

[28] National Security Decision Directive 100, "Enhanced U.S. Military
Activity and Assistance for the Central American Region," July 28, 1983.

[29] The following section is the Editor's synopsis of the text and documents
included in the original Honduran version in the subsections entitled "United
States Assistance to Honduras and Human Rights in the Most Critical Years,"
and "The Iran-Contra Scandal and Events in Which Honduran Civilian and
Military Officials are Implicated."

[30] The original Honduran version of this document contains the precise
figures for economic, military and total aid for the years 1980 to 1985. These
figures are included in the Appendix of this version.

Reports of the State Department in this period tended to downplay reports of
human rights violations supplied by non-governmental organizations. These
State Department Reports also included the Honduran Government's response
to the charges of disappearance, thus lending credibility to the official
denials.

At the same time that the State Department publicly minimized the
sordid human rights record of the Honduran Government, high level executive branch officials were engaging in covert operations designed to assist the
contras by diverting funds from arms sales to Iran. What became known later
as the Iran-Contra scandal is documented by excerpts from the stipulated facts
recognized by the government and the defense in the federal prosecution of
Lt. Col. Oliver North that follow. The relationship between this aid to
Honduras and the covert operations documented below is also noted in these
excerpts.[31]

> In early July 1984, a CIA officer reported to headquarters
> that Honduras was taking the position that it would continue
> to support the Resistance following the cut-off of U.S. aid,
> but that Resistance operations would have to be covert to
> avoid political embarrassment to Honduras. (Point 42. p.
> 16)

> In mid-November 1984, a CIA officer reported to CIA head-
> quarters about assistance provided to the Resistance by
> Guatemala and Honduras. Honduras had permitted the
> Resistance to operate from within its borders, had repaired
> Resistance aircraft at no cost, had allowed government
> aircraft to bring in aircraft parts, had permitted the Resistan-
> ce to borrow ammunition when Resistance stocks were low,
> and had provided the Resistance with false end-user certifi-
> cates for the purchase of weapons. (Point 44, p. 16)

> According to [a November 1984 CIA] analysis, Honduras
> had facilitated the purchase of ammunition and hand grena-

---

[31] The excerpts provided here are significantly more abbreviated than those
included in the original Honduran version of this report. The full text of the
excerpts included there appears in the Appendix to this version.

des and had donated 10,000 pounds of military equipment
and two C-47 aircraft. (Point 45, pp. 16-17)

In late February 1985, President Reagan sent [a letter] to
President Suazo through the U.S. Ambassador in Honduras.
The letter urged that Honduras do all in its power to support
"those who struggle for freedom and democracy." (Point
54, p. 22)

In March, when Vice President Bush met with President
Suazo, Bush told Suazo that President Reagan had directed
expedited delivery of U.S. military items to Honduras. Vice
President Bush also informed Suazo that President Reagan
had directed that currently withheld economic assistance for
Honduras should be released; and that the United States
would provide from its own stocks critical security assistance items that had been ordered by the Honduran armed
forces. (Point 58, p. 23)

On April 25, 1985, McFarlane informed President Reagan
that military support for the Resistance from Honduras was
in jeopardy as a consequence of the House vote refusing to
provide new funds to the Resistance. (Point 62, p. 25-26)

On April 26, 1985, U.S. Ambassador Negroponte notified
McFarlane that President Suazo had called Negroponte
immediately after Suazo's telephone conversation with
President Reagan to say that he was satisfied with the U.S.
government commitment to continue support for the Resis-
tance. President Suazo told Ambassador Negroponte that he
(Suazo) had assured President Reagan of his full support . .
. (Point 63, p. 26)

In early May 1986, President Reagan wrote to Presidents
Azcona and Duarte thanking them for their support for the
Resistance and announcing that the U.S. was disbursing the
economic support funds (ESF) that Honduras sought. (Point
92, p. 36-37)

In May 1986, President Azcona indicated to President Reagan that Honduras's continued support for the Resistance depended upon significant increases in U.S. military aid to the Honduran armed forces and the Resistance. President Azcona noted that his armed forces wanted weapons and ammunition for use by the Resistance to be transferred to the Honduran armed forces to assure the military success of the Resistance. (Point 95, p. 38)

VI

PRELIMINARY CONCLUSIONS

The forced disappearance of persons, a practice which shook Honduras during the 1980s, extended into the first years of the 1990s. The practice was both systematic and widespread, particularly from 1982 to 1984, during which years the number of persons disappeared increased dramatically. Yet disappearance was not the only grave human rights violation which our country experienced in this period. Extrajudicial executions, arbitrary detentions, torture, and the lack of due process also characterized these years of intolerance. Perhaps more troublesome than the violations themselves was the authorities' tolerance of these crimes and the impunity with which they were committed.

These years were also characterized by the generalization of violence in the Central American isthmus, especially in the countries that border Honduras. Official violence in Honduras—though beyond acceptable limits and undeniably deserving of condemnation—did not reach the levels experienced in other countries in the region either in magnitude or duration.

Political and judicial authorities tolerated, either by action or omission, the practice of forced disappearance in this period. Evidence gathered to date establishes the responsibility of members and units of the Armed Forces of Honduras for these disappearances. Similarly, the responsibility and participation of Nicaraguan contras in many disappearances, particularly those of foreign nationals, has been established.

Nonetheless, exhaustive and impartial judicial investigations of these crimes have not been undertaken, thus denying the right of the families of the disappeared to know the truth. As a result of this lack of investigation, those directly responsible for disappearances have still not been sanctioned. Neither has the Honduran Government recognized the status of the disappeared and their families as victims, nor has it compensated them for the damage they have suffered. These failures of the government contrast sharply with the official condemnation of the state of Honduras by both the Inter-American Commission and Court of Human Rights for these practices.[1]

Despite the official failures noted above, during these dark years,

---

[1] *See, e.g.,* Inter-American Court of Human Rights, *Velázquez-Rodríguez*, Judgment of July 29, 1988, Series C, no. 4.

there were certain moral reserves in Honduras that deserve mention. Fortunately, indolence was not the only reaction to violations of human rights. There were Hondurans who, faced with what was happening, spoke out. In contrast to the media in other countries in the region that turned away and pretended not to see when confronted with violence, media owners and journalists in Honduras played an important role in exposing the truth. There were others who raised their voices in protest over what was happening, including some of our bishops, priests, and members of the Catholic church; and some politicians, as well as the Bar Association. There were also many members of the Armed Forces who recognized that the defense of the nation and the rule of law were not compatible with violations of the right to be free from *ex post facto* laws and democracy. In recent years, the Armed Forces of Honduras have given all of America a lesson of democratic loyalty that Honduran citizens should value.

Special mention must be afforded the human rights groups, especially CODEH and COFADEH, the Vicariates of Solidarity of El Progreso, Tocoa, Yoro, and Copán, the Unitary Federation of Workers of Honduras (Federación Unitaria de Trabajadores de Honduras-FUTH), and the Union of Workers of the National Electrical Energy Company (Sindicato de Trabajadores de la Empresa Nacional de Energía Eléctrica-STENEE), among others. These groups, often misunderstood by the authorities, called attention to the principles and values which—like the defense of human life—Hondurans must never forget.

It is the presence of this moral reserve that permits us to envision a different future for our country. Even in the most difficult conditions, there were Honduran men and women that knew how to stand up for the nation's morality and dared to raise their voices in protest and indignation against acts of inhumanity.

I. Who Were the Victims of Disappearances?

As a general rule, the victims were persons arbitrarily considered "dangerous" by those who claimed to protect the security of the State of Honduras. To be a likely target, it was enough that someone was a student leader (or sometimes simply a student), a union leader or member, a peasant leader or a sympathizer of an opposition party or political group considered leftist. People who were believed to support or empathize with the Salvadoran guerillas or the Sandinista government were also detained. Some disappearances may be due to differences that victims may have had with their kidnappers, who could also make use of their limitless power to resolve personal disputes.

Based on the information obtained in the process of preparing this report, a list of 179 cases of disappearance in Honduras between 1980 and 1992 (*see* Chapter II) has been compiled.

Based on analysis of these cases of disappearance, we have discerned two general types of disappearance. The first type was more selective and was directed at those individuals considered dangerous. This type of disappearance was planned and executed by specialized units, like the Battalion 3-16. The second group of disappearances arose from the routine action of military and police forces. These detentions, most likely based on simple suspicion, were then followed by tragically disproportionate reaction and excesses by those who effectuated them out.

In the case of other human rights violations such as extrajudicial executions, the victims fit in the same pattern as those who suffered disappearance.

II. What Human Rights are Violated by Disappearances?

Forced disappearance as practiced in Honduras violates individual rights guaranteed in international law, as well as norms of Honduran criminal law.

Among the rights violated we find:

a. Violation of the Right to Life

Disappeared persons were arbitrarily executed by the groups who abducted them. Others died as a result of abusive treatment during their detention. This constitutes a violation of the Universal Declaration of Human Rights (Article 3); of the International Covenant on Civil and Political Rights (Article 6); of the American Declaration of the Rights and Duties of Man (Article 1); of the American Convention on Human Rights (Article 4). These acts also constitute clear violations of the internal norms of Honduras, specifically Article 65 of the Constitution of the Republic, as well as the section entitled "Crimes Against Life and Bodily Integrity" (*Delitos contra la vida y la integridad corporal*), contained in the Second Book, Special Part, Title I of the Penal Code in force.

b. Violation of the Right to Freedom and Personal Security

Persons subjected to kidnapping and arbitrary detention suffer a violation of the right to freedom and personal security. This constitutes a violation of the Universal Declaration of Human Rights (Article 3); of the International Covenant on Civil and Political Rights (Article 9); of the American Declaration of the Rights and Duties of Man (Articles 1, 8 and 25); and of the American Convention on Human Rights (Article 7). These acts also constitute clear violations of the internal norms of Honduras, contained in Article 69 of the Constitution of the Republic, and codified as "Crimes Against Liberty and Security" (*Delitos contra la libertad y la seguridad*) in the Second Book, Special Part, Title VI, Chapter I of the Penal Code in force.

c. Violation of the Right to Physical Integrity and the Right to be Free from Torture and Cruel, Inhuman and Degrading Punishment

Disappearances and subsequent detentions were accompanied in all cases by mistreatment and the use of torture to extract information. Detention without access to anyone outside, and the recognition that one has been disappeared and thus reduced to a state of complete exposure to one's kidnappers is itself an act of psychological torture. To this, various forms of physical abuse, which were the norm for disappeared persons, would be added. This constitutes a violation of the Universal Declaration of Human Rights (Article 5); of the International Covenant on Civil and Political Rights (Article 1); of the American Declaration of the Rights and Duties of Man (Article 5). These acts also constitute clear violations of the internal norms of Honduras, specifically of Article 68 of the Constitution of the Republic, as well as the norms codified as "Crimes against life and bodily integrity" (*Delitos contra la vida y la integridad corporal*) in the Penal Code in force, in its second book, special part.

d. Violation of the Right to an Impartial Trial and the Right to Recognition as a Person Before the Law

Kidnapping, prolonged illegal detention, and "investigation" through torture to establish detainees' presumed guilt preceeded the decision regarding the life of persons who were disappeared. The "sentence" would then be issued by a person without preparation or authority to render verdicts. In this way, those detained were denied their right to defend themselves or to have anyone defend them before an impartial judge. The self-appointed judges, juries, and executioners violated the right to an impartial trial and the right to be recognized as a person before the law.

This constitutes a violation of the Universal Declaration of Human Rights (Article 8); of the International Covenant on Civil and Political Rights (Articles 9 and 10); of the American Declaration of the Rights and Duties of Man (Article 26); and of the American Convention on Human Rights (Article 8). These acts also constituted clear violations of internal norms of Honduras, which are codified as crimes against liberty, such as the illegal assumption of authority contained in Title VI, Chapter I and Title IX, Chapter IV of the Penal Code, respectively.

e. Violation of the Duty to Respect International Human Rights Treaties

Article 1 of the American Convention establishes the duty of States Parties to abide by the Convention and to respect the rights and freedoms which it recognizes, without any form of discrimination.

f. Violation of the Right to the Truth

New developments in international human rights law confirm the existence of a right to know the truth. The work of various commissions charged with the investigation of human rights violations have rendered this right to be evident.[2]

The Inter-American Court established this right, when it sustained that "The second obligation of the States Parties is to 'ensure' the free and full exercise of the rights recognized by the Convention to every person subject to its jurisdiction . . . . As a consequence of this obligation, the States

---

[2] See CONADEP, *Nunca Más: Informe de la Comisión Nacional Sobre la Desaparición Forzada de Personas,* [Never Again: Report of the National Commission on the Forced Disappearances of Persons] (Buenos Aires: 1989); *Informe de la Comisión Nacional de Verdad y Reconciliación,* [Report of the National Commission on Truth and Reconciliation] (Santiago: February 1991). Similarly, in the Central American region, *see* Comisión de las Naciones Unidas para la Verdad en El Salvador, *De la Locura a la Esperanza. Informe de la Comisión de la Verdad de El Salvador*, [United Nations' Truth Commission for El Salvador, "From Madness to Hope: Report of the Truth Commission for El Salvador"] (New York: March 1993).

must prevent, investigate and punish any violation of the rights recognized by the Convention."[3] The Court also established that "The State has a legal duty to take reasonable steps to prevent human rights violations and to use the means at its disposal to carry out a serious investigation of violations committed within its jurisdiction [in order] to identify those responsible."[4]

The Inter-American Commission of Human Rights established the following: "Every society has the inalienable right to know the truth about past events, as well as the motives and circumstances in which aberrant crimes came to be committed, in order to prevent repetition of such acts in the future...Such access to the truth presupposes freedom of speech, which of course should be excercised responsibly; the establishment of investigating committees whose membership and authority must be determined in accordance with the internal legislation of each country, or the provision of the necessary resources so that the judiciary itself may undertake whatever investigations may be necessary."[5] This is reiterated in the Commission's Report Number 28-92 on Argentina, which established that victims and relatives have the right to a judicial investigation in a criminal court designed to individualize and sanction those responsible for the crimes.[6] The Commission took a similar position in its report number 29-92 on Uruguay. In that report, the Commission recommended that Uruguay "adopt the measures necessary to clarify the facts and identify those responsible for human rights violations that occured during the *de facto* period."[7]

---

[3] Inter-American Court of Human Rights, *Velázquez-Rodríguez Case*, Sentence of July 29, 1988. Series C, no. 4, paragraph 166.

[4] *Ibid.*, paragraph 174.

[5] Annual Report of the Inter-American Commission on Human Rights, 1985-1986, Washington, D.C., p 193.

[6] Cases 10,147, 10,181, 10,240, 10,262, 10,309 and 10,311 *reported in* Inter-American Commission on Human Rights, *Annual Report 1992-1993* (Washington, D.C. 1993), p. 41.

[7] Cases 10,029, 10,036, 10,145, 10,305, 10,372, 10,373, 10,374 and 10,375 *reported in* Inter-American Commission on Human Rights, *Annual Report 1992-1993* (Washington, D.C. 1993), p. 165.

The relatives of the victims of human rights violations have the right
to be informed about what actually happened to their relatives. This right
includes, *inter alia*, all the circumstances of their arrest, detention, and
eventual extrajudicial execution. This right extends as well to others who
were affected by these violations, and who have the right to know what
happened to their fellow citizens and who was responsible.

In general, a series of collateral human rights violations accompany
disappearances. Among those rights typically violated when a person is
disappeared are the right to family life, and the economic and social rights of
the relatives of the disappeared. Those close to the victims and their depen-
dents not only lose all contact with a loved one, but they also suffer long
term psychological, social, economic, and legal effects, as well as uncertainty
regarding the situation of the disappeared person. In many of the cases
studied, the persons disappeared (and probably executed) were the sole means
of support for their families.

III. Why Were Disappearances Practiced?

The military doctrine adopted by high military commands and
followed by security forces in this period considered it necessary to organize
clandestine groups and procedures to effectively combat persons considered
dangerous. These security forces considered the legal procedures that required the detention and judgment of individuals by courts guaranteeing fundamental rights to be slow, inefficient, and unnecessary for their objectives.
Thus, they chose to avoid democratic legal controls and substitute their
efforts for those of the police and the courts. These groups, acting in a
clandestine manner, granted themselves the power to decide on the freedom,
physical integrity, and life of Hondurans.

In determining the responsibility of these presumed "military enemies," these detention groups confused union-based or political protests with
criminal acts. Though necessary to combat guerilla groups militarily, these
clandestine groups proved unable to separate ideological from military
opposition. Nor did they distinguish between those merely suspected and
those guilty of illegal acts; all were kidnapped or executed alike. Even more
extreme, the combination of power without any meaningful civil and democratic control, led some units of the Armed Forces to use lethal force not
only to eliminate those determined to be enemies of the state, but also those

whose elimination personally benefitted the kidnappers.

In exceptional cases, after long periods of illegal detention and the eventual subjection to torture, the victims were set free. These cases, it appears, constitute an exception that it is confirmed by the rule. According to the testimonies analyzed, in the majority of cases, the disappeared were executed. The clandestine and illegal nature of the process made it dangerous to free the disappeared, who, by virtue of having experienced this condition, became witnesses to its existence.

Among the reasons for these actions, one finds the lack of respect for democratic legality, the rule of law, and the separation of powers. We can also identify intolerance and the errant conviction that one who thinks differently and engages in union activity is an enemy. The absence of transparent civil, democratic control—in sum, the lack of citizen control of the actions of security forces—permitted these actions to be ordered, known, and tolerated by individuals with important civilian and military positions in the country. Nonetheless, the Armed Forces were never responsible institutionally, insofar as institutions, as such, cannot commit crimes. It was always individuals, mistaken people, wayward members of the Armed Forces who were responsible for tolerating, ordering, or carrying out these actions.[8]

IV. Who Practiced Disappearances?

The protagonists of disappearances varied: while some acted enthusiastically, convinced of the military doctrine that permitted the disappearance of individuals without trial, others acted believing that it was their duty to follow orders. There were even those who participated for fear that they would be considered enemies or dissidents if they refused to carry out their illegal orders. However, common to all was their action in the name of official units of the Armed Forces or with official protection (as in the case of the contras).

Those who participated included specialized units within the Armed Forces (usually the DNI) and specialized intelligence units of the Armed Forces and of each military body (G-2), in particular, the Battalion 3-16. These units received specialized training in counterinsurgency, intelligence, and counter-intelligence. Their training and the status they enjoyed by virtue

---

[8] *Editor's Note:* We understand the National Commissioner's conclusion in this regard to be an assessment of responsibility under domestic criminal law rather than a declaration of institutional liability in international human rights law.

of membership in these specialized units gave them the security and conviction that they had the authority to detain, torture and execute citizens. As we have already mentioned, the mission of the Intelligence Battalion was to carry out intelligence operations against Hondurans and other citizens involved in subversive activities. Because citizens considered subversives—the target of Battalion 3-16's efforts—were the principal victims of disappearance, the accusations against Battalion 3-16 which have been compiled appear credible.

The contras also practiced disappearances of citizens that were abducted from Nicaraguan territory. These victims were taken from the zones of armed conflict and then disappeared on Honduran soil while Honduran authorities—despite their jurisdiction—failed to prevent it. The Nicaraguan armed opposition groups enjoyed total impunity and a lack of control over their actions due to their acceptance by Honduran authorities.

Because of its dimension, and the units involved in its realization, the practice of disappearance was known to some of the high command of the Armed Forces. Despite this, these individuals did not seek to prevent these acts, and, it appears, participated in the actions of these special units. Without omitting the responsibility of others (which should be determined by judicial investigation), it is clear that General Gustavo Alvarez Martínez was involved in this practice.

The responsibility of certain of the high command of the Armed Forces of Honduras, in particular the responsibility of some of the general commanders in each of the years in which these disappearances were produced, follows from the fact that all the security forces were under the jurisdiction of the Armed Forces. The FUSEP, as well as its investigation division, the DNI, are units of the Armed Forces. The specialized intelligence units, like the G-2 unit, later transformed for the most part into Battalion 3-16 and then absorbed by G-2, were all under the command of the Armed Forces General Staff (*Estado Mayor*) and thus under the jurisdiction of the Armed Forces. Some officers knew of, planned, and even took part in these disappearances. These acts were known or at least not investigated and stopped by some of those who occupied high positions in the Armed Forces during the period under study.

One of the reasons why these investigations/intelligence units were able to achieve this level of autonomy and commit the crimes they committed was the lack of citizen control of their activities. In Honduras, in contrast to other democratic countries, all intelligence gathering, as well as criminal investigation, fell to the Armed Forces, who would administer the information that should have gone to civil authorities. The work of investigating crimes, like intelligence gathering, also took on a level of autonomy from democratic authorities, thus permitting the numerous violations that Hondurans suffered during this period. Further, the secret atmosphere peculiar to these activities encouraged those who sought to exclude democratic authorities from information and operations.

The State of Honduras bears an obvious responsibility. In accordance with international law, whenever a governmental official acts in an official capacity and commits an act or acts that violate an international treaty, the state is responsible for that violation.

V. When Did the Disappearances Occur?

Disappearances occurred throughout the period analyzed. They began in 1980, and continued beyond the 1980s. The vast majority occurred between 1980 and 1984, during the administrations of Presidents Policarpo Paz García and Roberto Suazo Córdoba. The number of disappearances increased dramatically between January 1982 and March 1984, while General Alvarez was Commander-in-Chief of the Armed Forces. In this period, there existed within the Armed Forces a deliberate policy of kidnapping and forcibly disappearing persons suspected of having ties to the Nicaraguan government, the Salvadoran guerrillas, and people simply considered political or union leaders, or peasant activists.[9]

It was particularly tragic and ironic that the pattern of abuses in Honduras increased notoriously with the advent of democracy and civilian rule. In 1981, Honduras began a process of transition with the election of Roberto Suazo Córdoba. When Suazo Córdoba took power, General Gustavo Alvarez Martínez took command of the Armed Forces.

VI. Who helped to organize this practice of disappearances?

As explained in more detail in the chapter on international context, the practice of disappearances in Honduras in a systematic, secret, and organized fashion began at the end of 1979-1980 in the midst of growing armed conflicts in three neighboring nations: Nicaragua, El Salvador, and Guatemala. It has been established that after the overthrow of General Somoza in July 1979, specialized anti-subversive troops from Argentina's

---

[9] Amnesty International, *Honduras, Autoridad Civil-Poder Militar. Violaciones de los derechos humanos en le década de 1980,* (London: January 1988), p. 47.

military regime arrived in Honduras. These troops played the dual role of advising the Honduran Armed Forces and assisting in the organization of the anti-Sandinista movement composed of former members of the Nicaraguan National Guard established in Honduras. This second aspect was part of a secret plan of the government of the United States of America, executed by the Central Intelligence Agency (CIA) and approved by President Reagan.[10]

The American military and political presence during the years studied was quite important. Americans worked very closely with the Honduran security forces and Nicaraguan contras. Numerous testimonies and reports indicate that these American officials, stationed or operating in Honduras, were in charge of supporting counter-subversive actions and encouraging the actions of the contras. Further, these officials were aware of—and at least tolerated—the disappearance of Honduran citizens as well as those of Salvadorans, Nicaraguans, and nationals of other countries that occurred in Honduran territory.

The majority of the Argentine officers operating in Honduras came from Intelligence Battalion 601 of the First Army Corps, based in Campo de Mayo, Buenos Aires, whose commander, General Guillermo Suárez Mason, was tried and convicted for human rights violations, including the forced disappearance of persons. The "Argentine method" of anti-subversive warfare that was brought to Honduras was premised on the existence of an ideological war shaped by the East-West conflict. In this war, subversion had succeeded in imposing itself in some countries by using non-conventional methods of warfare that were impossible to combat with traditional counterinsurgent methodology. In the words of Argentine General Ramón J. Camps:

> France and the United States were the great disseminators of
> anti-subversive warfare. They organized centers, particu-
> larly the United States, to teach the principles of battle
> against subversion. They sent advisors, instructors. They
> disseminated an extraordinary quantity of literature. Unfor-

---

[10] On March 9, 1981, President Reagan took the first step in launching a covert war against the government of Nicaragua by issuing an official finding that the trafficking of arms by the Sandinista government to the guerrillas in El Salvador constituted a threat to the national security of the United States. On November 16, 1981, President Reagan authorized the expenditure of $19.5 million, instructing the CIA to carry out this secret war using primarily "non-Americans." Jonathan Marshall, Peter Dale Scott and Jane Hunter, *The Iran Contra Connection* (South End Press, 1987) p. 10.

tunately, all this was based on defeats (Vietnam and Alge-
ria), and thus it was only possible to analyze why it lost and
not simply take the doctrines and teachings and apply them.
All this until the time arrived in which we reached the age
of majority and applied our own doctrine that definitely
allowed us to achieve victory in Argentina against armed
subversion.[11]

This doctrine had as a central element the disappearance of people
considered enemies or subversives. In Argentina the military government
kidnapped and disappeared between 20,000 and 30,000 persons; the Sábato
Commission alone documented more than 8,000 cases of disappearances.

One of the fundamental characteristics of the organizational structure
of the kidnappings and disappearances in Argentina was the introduction of
"work groups." These groups were constituted within military structures and
compartmentalized tasks among their members in areas such as intelligence,
interrogation, kidnapping, and executions.

The similarity between this technique, as implemented in Argentina,
and the evidence and testimonies of this practice as developed in Honduras by
Battalion 3-16 is striking. In his testimony before the Inter-American Court of
Human Rights, former Battalion 3-16 member Florencio Caballero explained
that the Battalion was directly subordinate to the Second Intelligence Command (G-2) of the General Staff (*Estado Mayor*) and had four sections:

The first section was in charge of personnel. . . . The head of the
section was Lieutenant Hueso. Second Section, Intelligence and
Counter-intelligence commanded by Lieutenant Reyes. . . . The
Surveillance Section was also part of that section. After they obtai-
ned information it was taken to the Third Section, the Section of
Operations and Analysis that was under the command of Captain
Ciro Velázquez, . . . alias Urquía. The fourth section, the Supply
Section was under the command of Lieutenant Gravis. . . . Opera-
tions and Analysis handled the processing of information which was
passed along to the kidnapping group, under the command of Lieute-
nant Flores Murillo, that was subordinate to the Operations Section.
. . . There were four men from 3-16 that were the executioners of

---

[11] *La Prensa,* Buenos Aires, April 1, 1981.

the kidnapped. They were only responsible for executions, under the command of Mr. Juan Ramón Peña Paz, alias *"Mata"* ("kill").[12]

Some ex-Argentine officers have accepted, *a posteriori,* their participation in the dirty war in Honduras. Sánchez Reisse, an Argentine intelligence officer from Battalion 601, revealed that specialized units with experience in limitless warfare with supposed subversives participated directly in Central America. This included personnel from federal security, from the 601 Battalion, and from the Navy Mechanics' School. Sánchez Reisse indicated that what brought these men to Honduras was the "theory of ideological borders." When asked why they acted in Honduras, he responded "the idea is that borders did not end within the individual geography of each country but rather western politics had to be defended, if necessary. That is, according to this theory, if subversion fought internationally, you had to defend yourself internationally. It was supposed then that it was necessary to act against what could be a second Cuba, and work with the United States directly and indirectly. In Nicaragua, against the Sandinistas."[13]

VII. How did the judiciary react?

In democratic societies the judiciary is the guarantor of legality and human rights and is the arbiter of societal conflicts. The judicial branch must employ adequate and neutral criteria in the resolution of conflicts to assure that the law is applied to all and that institutions and citizens respect fundamental rights. In this way, the judicial branch serves to stabilize society, provide legal security, and affirm the rule of law. Judges themselves, by their conduct, assure their prestige in society.

The cases analyzed present the common characteristic of the judiciary's failure to fulfill its duty to protect citizens.[14] Petitions seeking writs

---

[12] IACHR Testimony of Florencio Caballero, pp. 165-167.

[13] *Somos,* February 25, 1987, Buenos Aires, pp. 20-22.

[14] In Honduras, the right to life, to individual security and personal freedom are duly guaranteed in articles 61, 65, 68, 69, 71, and 84 of the Constitution of the Republic, in force since January 20, 1982. In the previous political charter, the Constitution of 1965, these rights were guaranteed in articles 51, 52, 56, 57, 58, 62, 63, and 72. Article 58 regulated *habeas corpus,* as does its counterpart in the present Constitution. The security

of *habeas corpus* were not processed with the celerity required by the Constitution, and invariably produced no results. One study of 51 cases of *habeas corpus* undertaken in 1987 showed that the petitions in those cases uniformly failed to clarify the fate of the persons disappeared. Moreover, in more than one case, criminal actions were initiated against military and police authorities believed to be responsible, yet they were neither processed diligently nor subjected to any investigative process that might have clarified the facts.[15]

Judges, among other civilian authorities, abdicated their democratic authority and their constitutional control of legality (*See* Article 321 of the Constitution of the Republic). In general, judges did not undertake investigations at the scene of the crime, and ignored accusations and indicia that clearly identified those who were likely responsible. Judges inappropriately limited themselves, either because they believed that they lacked real control over the actions carried out by these repressive bodies, because they feared them, or because they were simply indifferent when faced with these repeated violations. Whatever their reasons, the failure of the judicial branch to fulfill its primary mission is unjustifiable.

Despite the fact that the actions described above constituted violations of international principles as well as Honduran constitutional norms and criminal law, the judges in the courts petitioned did not take action against the material and intellectual authors. This inaction not only characterized judicial response to disappearance, but also its response to other violations of fundamental rights like extrajudicial executions or torture. The certainty of the impunity of those responsible, given the absence of judicial investigation or sanction, clearly contributed to the continued commission of these crimes.

As one of the forms of expression of popular sovereignty, the judicial branch must guarantee to all citizens the exercise of their rights and

---

bodies of Honduras have the power to detain persons only with a judicial order issued by an appropriate judge or in the case of a crime *in flagrante delicto*. The detained must be brought before the appropriate judge within 24 hours. The Penal Code of 1906, in force until March 12, 1985, codified illegal detention as a crime in article 478. The present Penal Code also proscribes illegal detention, in article 333.

[15] José Miguel Vivanco, "El recurso de Exhibición Personal en Honduras. 1980-1987," Americas Watch [now Human Rights Watch/Americas], (Washington, D.C.: February 1987).

must act as social arbitrator and guarantor of those rights.[16] The Honduran Constitution classifies the right to life and the right to freedom as fundamental rights, and in the section that corresponds to individual rights in the very first article indicates that the State of Honduras is constituted to assure to its inhabitants the enjoyment of justice, liberty, culture, and economic and social well-being.[17] Judicial indifference and ineffectiveness regarding disappearances thus undermined the very basis of the rule of law.

When civil institutions do not fulfill their roles, by tolerating actions that clearly violate the law, a form of institutional complicity arises. Such was the case in Honduras. The best guarantee that these acts do not repeat themselves is the subjection of all citizens and institutions, both the judiciary and the organs of security, to the dictates of the law. This process is nothing more than the rule of law in a democratic society.

The judicial branch must investigate its own conduct. This review must consider the petitions for writs of *habeas corpus* that courts failed to process, delayed, or denied without adequate basis, as well as the reasons why those presumed to be responsible for these crimes were not tried or convicted. Where necessary, meaningful remedial measures should be proposed. Most importantly, though, the judiciary must explain to Honduran society why it was unable to investigate and sanction actions that violated the most important element of the legal state: the individual rights of citizens.

---

[16] Art. 303: The authority to render justice emanates from the people and is adminstered without charge in the name of the State, by independent magistrates and judges..." Constitution of the Republic of Honduras.

[17] Art. 1: Honduras is a sovereign, legal state, constituted as a free, democratic, and independent republic to assure its inhabitants the enjoyment of justice, liberty, culture,and economic and social well-being." Constitution of the Republic of Honduras.

VII

RECOMMENDATIONS

I. Introduction

The recommendations that we present are the result of a preliminary investigation of disappearances in Honduras. The National Commissioner for the Protection of Human Rights commits himself to each and every one of these recommendations, and will work to encourage their implementation. The recommendations constitute suggestions regarding human rights in the country that we hope all Hondurans will support.

a. Honduran Democratic Authorities Are Able to Arrive at the Truth

The Commissioner has complete confidence in the ability of the democratic authorities to carry out this investigation by judicial and administrative means. In this way, exact criminal responsibility may be established and thus, the nation may be informed of the entire truth about the disappeared. It is precisely due to this confidence in the nation's democratic institutions that the formation of a Truth Commission like those established in other countries after this sort of detailed evaluation is considered unnecessary. Fortunately, the Honduran government need not establish its own legitimacy, as was the case in those countries which had to resort to this type of commission.

The inauguration of a new government, and President-elect Carlos Roberto Reina's clear commitment to human rights, inspires great hope that we Hondurans will be able to resolve our past problems through our own democratic institutions. The confidence of our people in the ability of the executive, legislative, and judicial branches to fully respect fundamental rights is indispensable.

b. This Report Seeks an Authentic Reconciliation of the Honduran Family, Beginning with the Truth

The recommendations of this report are oriented by the principle that society must know the full truth and effectuate justice in order to achieve the necessary reconciliation of all Hondurans. We believe that the moral well-

231

being of the country requires that we find out what really happened with the disappeared.

After discovering the truth, which may only be fully established by the appropriate judicial investigations, the next step will be to render justice. This will require that responsibility be determined, and that those responsible be identified and subjected to trial. Only after the truth is known and justice is rendered are pardon and reconciliation possible. Those who do not repent cannot be pardoned, much less those who remain unknown. Although it is true that all human action is pardonable, achieving reconciliation is only possible through the full discovery of the truth and the establishment of justice.

c. The Report Seeks to Encourage Citizen Confidence in the Democratic Institutions of the Honduran State

This long and possibly painful process of investigation and search for the truth must seek to reestablish citizens' confidence in the institutions of the state. The best means of achieving this is by demonstrating to the Honduran public the state's ability to investigate itself. It is this ability to undertake a complete review of its own actions that characterizes a nation under the rule of law. The recuperation of the faith of all Hondurans in our institutions, in particular the judiciary, will lead towards the consolidation of democracy, an indispensable prerequisite to development.

d. The Commissioner Does Not Have Jurisdictional Powers

All the recommendations made in this report are the product of testimonies, interviews, reports, documents, and review of news provided by the daily press. The assertions contained in this report are not judicial sentences. Thus, they are not absolute nor do they claim to be. The Commissioner, mindful of the Constitution and the laws of the nation, cannot, nor does he seek to supplant the judiciary, which alone has the right and the duty to render justice. It is thus clear that this investigation has not sought to be, nor is it, a judicial function. Criminal conviction presupposes the right to defense in a court of law and the respect for the totality of rights which together constitute the right to due process. Only judges can guarantee the full enjoyment of these rights.

e. The Crimes Committed by Those Who Practiced Disappearances Have Not Been Amnestied

All crimes involved in the commission of disappearances may still be prosecuted by Honduran courts.[1] The Honduran amnesty laws do not expressly prohibit the trial and punishment of military or security personnel implicated in disappearances. The most recent amnesty decree in Honduras explicitly recognizes the state's international obligations to support and protect international human rights. This amnesty must be interpreted in a fashion that is consistent with these international obligations. The Honduran government, in full recognition of it obligations under the American Convention on Human Rights and the International Covenant on Civil and Political Rights, must apply its amnesty law so as to permit the trial and punishment of state officials implicated in cases of disappearance and other fundamental human rights violations. If the state by decree prohibits the prosecution of those who committed human rights abuses, it would, in effect, be prohibiting the punishment of these violations. In that case, the state would be in violation of its obligations under Article 1 of the American Convention which requires the state to ensure and respect the full and free exercise of the rights which the Convention establishes. So too would the state be in violation of Articles 9.1 and 25.1 of the Convention, which guarantee to all persons the right to a fair trial and to judicial protection.[2]

f. The Establishment of a Deadline for Judicial and Administrative Investigations as well as for Recommendations is Critical

It is very important that the people of Honduras be assured that there will be no further delays by state entities on this subject. Thus, the Commissioner suggests that the recommendations contained in this report be implemented within a reasonable time, but not exceeding twelve months from the

---

[1] On the responsibility of the state and its agents, *see* article 325 which states in relevant part: "There is no statute of limitations in cases of acts or omissions committed with the requisite mens and performed for political motives that cause the death of one or more persons."

[2] In this regard, *see* Cases 10,029, 10,036, 10,145, 10,305, 10,372, 10,373, 10,374 and 10,375 *reported in* Inter-American Commission on Human Rights, *Annual Report 1992-1993* (Washington, D.C. 1993)(report on the Uruguayan Amnesty Laws).

date of its publication.

II. Recommendation Regarding the Payment of Compensation to Victims and their Families

The existence of disappearances is an undeniable reality. The relatives of the disappeared have suffered one of the most terrible dramas of our society. The pain of not knowing what has happened to a loved one is terrible. Death, at least, puts an end to the questions regarding the fate of the loved one. By contrast, the loved one's disappearance allows both the hope of return, and the pain of absence to continue. Disappearance also violates the right to bury one's dead. Disappearance is all the more serious when it is performed and hidden by the state, whose function—to protect individuals—is exactly the opposite.

On this point, we recommend:

1. The Honduran state must recognize the harm caused and provide compensation. If the persons charged with the protection of the citizenry and the law were those who practiced disappearances, the state has the obligation to recognize the harm done, to seek forgiveness from the victims, and to compensate the damage.

2. A special commission should establish the specific means of compensating the harm caused to each of the families that lost loved ones. That compensation has been partially paid only in the cases judged by the Inter-American Court of Human Rights is patently unfair. All cases of disappearance must be compensated economically. The methods of compensation and rehabilitation must be discussed directly with the victims or the relatives.

3. The state of Honduras must recognize the unnecessary and unjust nature of the disappearances. In order that future generations not forget what happened and to assure that this history not repeat itself, the Commissioner recommends that a monument bearing the name of each disappeared person be built. Such a monument would also demonstrate that the state of Honduras wants to recover its legitimacy before the

families of the disappeared and the international community.

III. Recommendation Regarding Institutional and Legal Reforms to Prevent the Recurrence of Disappearances

Legal reforms that permit greater citizen protection, and those that restructure the legal gaps whose existence the practice of disappearance revealed, must be considered. Although the decision to carry out these disappearances necessarily involved violation of domestic and international law, the creation of greater legal protections will be necessary to prevent disappearances from happening again.

On this point, we recommend:

1.   A central registry of detained persons should be established, under the authority of the new Public Ministry. Public access to this registry must be guaranteed. All authorities with the power to arrest persons should inform the public registry of the arrest within 12 hours.

2.   A special law regarding detention should be passed. This legislation should state all the rights and obligations of detained persons. Arrests should be made only by those police agents authorized to arrest and then only according to law. Those empowered to make arrests should identify themselves to the arrestee and to any witness who so requests. The arrested person should be informed of the reason for his detention and should be permitted to contact his attorney and/or relatives by the most appropriate means. The arrestee's attorney and relatives should be given immediate access to him.

3.   All necessary information regarding detainees and releases from custody should be made available. Relatives, lawyers, and courts of law must receive all information about the arrest of persons and the site of their detention. Similarly, they must be made aware of any transfer or release. The release of detainees, as well as their physical condition at that time, must be verifiable.

4. A complete evaluation of the *habeas corpus* petition process must be performed with a view towards creating a rapid, simple, and effective remedy to counter arbitrary detention.

5. Judicial authorities and the recently created Public Ministry must make sure that all complaints of forced disappearances are investigated promptly, impartially, and effectively. The results of these investigations should be made available to the public.

6. The legislature should incorporate the crime of forced disappearance into the Penal Code.

7. National and international human rights organizations, both public and private, should be permitted to visit any detention center to verify that authorities respect the rights of those detained.

8. The State of Honduras should participate actively in the process of approving the American Convention on the Forced Disappearance of Persons, as well as ratifying the Convention promptly.

9. In order to fully protect all Honduran citizens, the State of Honduras should ratify, as rapidly as possible, the International Covenant on Economic, Social and Cultural Rights; the International Covenant on Civil and Political Rights; the Optional Protocol to the Covenant on Civil and Political Rights; the Convention against Torture and Other Cruel, Inhuman or Degrading Treatment or Punishment.

10. The State of Honduras should also formally condemn the practice of disappearance and make known to both the public and the Armed Forces and it will not tolerate forced disappearances under any circumstances.

IV. Recommendation on Accountability

The state has the duty and the right to use force against those who violate its laws. The legitimate use of force, however, flows from respect for the Constitution and laws of the nation. The state's coercive power must always be exercised within the framework of the law and the respect for human rights which it requires.

If civil authorities knew what was happening, then they committed the crimes of obstruction of justice and complicity (*encubrimento y colaoración*) codified in the Penal Code. If they ignored what they knew, then they failed to implement the necessary democratic control over domestic institutions. In the latter case, it is not tenable to argue that there are areas to which democratic authority does not extend.

If disappearances occurred it was because there were persons willing to carry them out. The State of Honduras has the duty to effectuate the relevant judicial and administrative investigations to establish these responsibilities with absolute precision. The officers and officials who ordered or permitted that agents under their command commit disappearances must be held criminally responsible. Because of its obligations to its citizens, as well as its international obligations, the state of Honduras must assure that those responsible for disappearances be made to answer in court. In this regard, it should not matter where these persons are currently located, where the crime was committed, what the nationality of the victimizers or the victims was, or the amount of time that has passed since the disappearance.

In this regard, we recommend:

1. The courts should initiate a process of investigation that clarifies exact responsibilities of the persons mentioned in this report, as material or intellectual authors of the disappearances, in the respective cases, and according to the information from complaints and witnesses.

2. The courts should exhaustively investigate the possible criminal responsibility of civil authorities during the period in which disappearances occurred. In particular, the courts should investigate whether or not these authorities knew what was happening.

3. Considering the information that various sources have provided regarding the functions of the specialized intelligence units and the allegations of their participation, the courts must investigate and clarify the precise responsibility of

those who occupied the following positions from 1980 through 1990:

    a.   Officers and/or those in charge of intelligence units, in particular the intelligence division of the General Staff, G-2. Special attention should be paid to those individuals responsible for the fight against subversion from 1980 to the present.

    b.   Officers and commanders of the Battalion 3-16.[3]

    c.   Directors of the National Investigations Directorate (DNI), previously the National Investigation Department (Departamento de Investigación Nacional).

    d.   Other officers and persons in charge of operations of investigation, pursuit, detention, and interrogation, such as the "Special Operations Team" of Battalion 3-16 or its predecessor the Special Investigations Detachment. Destacamento de Investigaciones).

4.   The court should begin an investigation of every magistrate or judge who denied petitions for writs of *habeas corpus* filed by relatives of persons disappeared from 1980 through 1990. This investigation should also consider the reasons why investigations and procedures contemplated in the Code of Criminal Procedure were not pursued. These investigations should propose changes in the judiciary that help assure that these incidents never occur again.

5.   The government of Honduras should solicit all information

---

[3] The names of all those officers pertaining to the 3-16 Intelligence Battalion from 1984 until 1988 appear in the appendix. This list was obtained from the records in the *Velásquez-Rodríguez* case before the Inter-American Court of Human Rights. According to this list, the commanders of this Battalion, at least during the period 1984-1988 were: Luis Discua Elvir (1984); Inocente Borjas Santos (1985-86); Luis Alonso Villatoro Villeda (1987-88).

which the governments of the United States and Argentina possess regarding the full identity of those who may have assisted in the forced disappearance of persons, as well as their activities in Honduras.

6. The government of Honduras should locate, and if necessary seek the extradition of those members of the Nicaraguan contras mentioned in this report, as well as the commanders of those individuals, in order to try these persons for the crimes committed during their presence in Honduras, which are described in this report. The government of Honduras should solicit information and support from the Nicaraguan government to determine the identity and residence of those persons mentioned above.

7. The government of Honduras should locate, and if necessary, seek the extradition of citizens of other nations who committed, ordered, financed, or concealed the crimes described in this report.

8. The Honduran government should create a special commission charged with localizing the clandestine cemeteries described in this report. It should also publicly solicit any person having information regarding other clandestine burial sites to come forward anonymously. The government should also guarantee—through the techniques of forensic anthropology—the exhumation and identification of the human remains that eventually are found at such sites.

9. The government of Honduras should form an investigative commission to fully clarify all actions undertaken in Honduran territory by the contras, their advisers, financial supporters, and trainers. This commission should propose political and legislative measures that prevent Honduran territory from being used as a base of illegal military operations.

10. The Armed Forces should open their files regarding the methods employed, the persons in charge, and the actions carried out in the context of the fight against subversion

during the years 1980 - 1990.

V. Recommendations to Assure Democratic and Citizen Control of all Public Security Actions

One of the pillars of democracy is the effective control and transparency of all acts performed by public officials. In this vein, we feel it is important to affirm citizen control over certain areas of state activity.

In this regard, we recommend the following:

1.   Criminal investigation must not be monopolized by the Armed Forces. The investigation of crimes committed by civilians must be under the direct supervision of civilian authorities. The Honduran government should study the possibility of specializing and differentiating between tasks that are related to the national defense and those labors which concern the investigation, pursuit, and prevention of crimes. Police functions should not be militarized, and instead should constitute an area that is specialized and distinct from military activities.

2.   All intelligence activities, in particular those directed at civilians should be subject to the effective control of the Executive, and if possible, the President. These activities should be subject to some form of legislative control as well. As in other countries, the National Congress should establish a specialized committee with oversight responsibility for intelligence activities.

VI. Recommendations Regarding Affirmation of a Culture of Life and Peace in Honduras

During the period of disappearances, an authoritarian culture which did not consider all persons to hold human rights dominated Honduras. One of the most important tasks to prevent the recurrence of disappearances is to promote a culture of life that affirms that all persons have inviolable rights, the most sacred of which is the right to exist. The government of Honduras, in keeping with its democratic tradition, should promote the dissemination and study of human rights as the base of all lasting efforts to achieve peace.

1. The teaching of specific courses on human rights ought to be mandatory in all levels of instruction in the Armed Forces and in public security.

2. The teaching of specific courses on human rights ought to be mandatory in universities and in the nation's centers of education.

3. Judges and magistrates should receive special, specific training in the application of international human rights norms.

4. All levels of the state should report on their efforts toward promoting, educating, and disseminating human rights throughout the nation's territory.

5. Every Honduran should be provided with a copy of the Constitution and the Universal Declaration of Human Rights.

APPENDICES[1]

I. List of Questions on Topics About Which Information
Is Requested from the United States Government[2]

The Government of the United States of America, in particular, agencies and departments such as the State Department, the Department of Defense, the CIA, and the FBI is hereby requested to provide all information that it may have on the following topics:

I. General Topics

1. Existing information about the "Group of Fourteen" and the "Group of Ten," comprised of members of the intelligence and other units of the Armed Forces of Honduras in the period from the end of the 1970s to the early 1980s.

2. Information on the origins, structure, members, and functions of the military unit known as Battalion 3-16 and the Directorate of Special Investigations (Dirección de Investigaciones Especiales—DIES).

3. What type of assistance, collaboration, advising and/or training, both in Honduran and American territory, did the United States authorize for the Battalion 3-6 [sic] as well as any other intelligence unit of the Honduran Army between 1979 and 1988.

4. Between 1979 and 1986, what information did the U.S. Embassy in Honduras have (including its representatives of civilian and military agencies) about human rights violations, in particular the specific cases of disappearances, a list of which is attached. Whether information existed about the practice of kidnapping, torture and summary executions. Information about the existence, within the

---

[1] *Editor's Note:* This chapter includes a selection of the documents included in the appendix to the Honduran version of this report.

[2] *Editor's Note:* This list of questions was appended to a letter from Leo Valladares to U.S. Ambassador William T. Pryce, dated December 21, 1993. The letter is included in the Honduran version, but is omitted here.

structure of the Armed Forces of Honduras, of special units dedicated to the kidnapping, interrogation and execution, and about the use of installations of the Armed Forces and Security Forces, as well as private buildings to carry out these practices.

5.   An article in the *New York Times* on February 14, 1986 indicates that "there may have been a secret United States Government investigation of abuses by the Honduran security forces."Similarly, an article in the *Washington Post* on the same date reported that "the Defense Department, alarmed by reports of such abuses in the press, ordered an investigation a year ago that turned up evidence that U.S.-trained units were guilty of some of the charges (torture and murder)."

    5.1   The Government of the United States is requested to provide the specific information that would have been obtained in these alleged investigations.

6.   What information exists—ties, relations etc.—between members of the so-called "contras" and the Battalion 3-16; with the unit known as the Directorate of Special Investigations (Dirección de Investigaciones Especiales); with the G-2 Section of the Armed Forces General Staff or with any intelligence or other unit of the Armed Forces of Honduras.

    6.1   What were the terms of relation among the contra forces, the Armed Forces of Honduras and the Government or agencies of the United States in Honduras beginning in 1979.

7.   What information exists regarding the capture of Nicaraguan citizens by the so-called "contras" and their involuntary transport to Honduras and whether these facts were known to the Armed Forces and Government of Honduras.

    7.1   Who, within the organization of the Nicaraguan groups termed "contras," were responsible for intelligence, counter-intelligence and any type of covert operation realized in Honduras against Honduran and/or Nicaraguan citizens.

9.   What information exists regarding the capture and subsequent disap-
        pearance of refugees and citizens of El Salvador, Nicargua, and
        Guatemala in Honduras between the years 1980 and 1985, in particu-
        lar, those who appear in the list attached to this questionnaire.

10.   What information [does the Government have] regarding the presen-
        ce of Argentine military advisers in Honduras between the years
        1979 and 1984, in particular, those whose names appear in the list
        that follows.

        10.1   What functions did these Argentines perform, what relations
                existed between them and agencies and departments of the
                Government of the United States and what information
                exists about their imparting training and the participation of
                these Argentine citizens in operations of capture, interroga-
                tion and/or execution of citizens of Honduras, Nicaragua or
                of other nations in Honduran territory.

        10.2   What type of relationship did these Argentine advisors have
                with the Government of Honduras, its Armed Forces or any
                other state or private entity. What relationship did these
                individuals have with the Nicaraguan opposition forces
                known as the "contras."

        10.3   List of Argentines:

                General Alberto Alfredo Valin or Mario Balin
                Colonel Osvaldo Ribeiro o Riveiro, alias "Balita"
                José Hoyas or Oyas, alias Santiago Villegas
                Héctor Francés or Héctor Fernando García or Estanislao
                Valdés
                Jorge O'Higggins (mentioned as the military attache in
                Teguicagalpa).
                Jorge de la Vega
                Emilio Jason
                Mario Davico
                Camilio Grande or Carmelo Gigante (MH 17 ABR 83 "CIA
                calls shots against Nicaragua says "Coronel Gigante was
                decorated by the Honduran Army in February 1983"

Carlos Alberto Durich
Juan Carlos Galasso or Galeso
Juan Martín Ciga or Ciga Correa, alias Mariano Santamaría
César Carro
Leandro Angel Sánchez Reisse
Roberto Alfieri González, alias Francisco Díaz, Carlos
Chacón and Dr. Murcia

II. Questions Regarding Specific Cases

1. What information does the Government of the United States have
    regarding the information that was obtained—in particular those
    aspects that were not made public—by the Special Commission to
    Investigate Complaints of Disappearances in Honduran Territory,
    created by the Commander-in-Chief of the Armed Forces in Hondu-
    ras, General Walter López Reyes, by means of Accord Number MD
    No.232 of June 14, 1984.

2. With reference to the proceeding point, two cables of agencies of the
    Government of the U.S. (TOR:050222Z MAR: 85 and TOR:032255Z
    APR 85) copies of which are attached, indicate: "...from conversa-
    tions with the member of the official commission of human rights
    investigation commission() that the commission was advised by LTC
    Eric Sánchez () that Lau had been involved in the disappearance of
    two Honduran leftists in 1981."

    2.1 The Government of the United States is requested to provide
         additional details on the identity of the said disappeared
         Honduran citizens and all additional information about the
         participation in these acts by the Nicaraguan citizen Ricardo
         Lau, known as "Chino" Lau ("Chinese" Lau) and in what
         conditions and under what authority he participated in these
         acts.

3. What information does the United States have regarding the deaths of
    José Isaías Vilorio in January 1987 and of Miguel Angel Pavón,
    Alternate Member of the Honduran Congress, Vice President of
    CODEH, and witness before the Inter-American Court of Human
    Rights, murdered with his colleague Moisés Landaverde in San

Pedro Sula on January 14, 1988.

4.   What knowledge do the following American officials (who performed duties in both Honduras and Washington) have about the practice of kidnapping, torture, disappearances and executions of Honduran and Nicaraguan citizens by the 3-16 Battalion, as well as by members of the contras. (Articles from the *Washington Post* entitled, "US Trained Squads Executed Suspects" dated February 14, 1986 and "Honduran Death Squad Alleged" dated May 2, 1987; from the *New York Times*, entitled "CIA accused [sic] of tolerating killings in Honduras," dated February 14, 1986; from the publication *The Progressive*, "A Contra's Story," dated August, 1986; and an article from the *Wall Street Journal* entitled, "Why the Covert War in Nicaragua Evolved and Hasn't Succeeded," dated March 5, 1985 are attached).

4.1   List of American public officials and citizens:

Thomas Enders, State Department;
Elliot Abrams, State Department;
Duane "Dewey" Clarridge (identified by the AP, WP and WSJ as the Director of the Latin American Division of the CIA);
Mr. Tom Clines;
General Paul Gorman, Commander of the Southern Command of the United States;
Lt. Col. Oliver North, National Security Council;
John D. Negroponte, Ambassador to Honduras;
John Ferch, Ambassador to Honduras;
Everett Briggs, Ambassador to Honduras;
Crescencio Arcos, public official and later Ambasador in Honduras;
Michael O'Brien, Spokesman of the Embassy of the United States in Honduras;
John Perman;
"Tony Feldman" (identified as the supervisor of the CIA's task force on Central America in the WSJ, March 5, 1985);
Commander Padron (MILGRP);
Major Freedman;

Mr. Armatt;

Mr. Jaramillo, public official with the Embassy in Tegucigalpa;

Mr. Rondon, public official with the Embassy in Tegucigalpa;

Mr. Binns, public official with the Embassy in Tegucigalpa;

Mr. Pastorino, public official with the Embassy in Tegucigalpa;

Nat Hamrick (American citizen from Rutherfordton, North Carolina, according to Dickey ("With the Contras"), p. 299, and the article in *WP* "Argentine Defector Tells of Multinational Plot for Sandinistas' Ouster," December 2).

And those known in Honduras as:

"Mister Mike" (supposedly the Chief of the CIA station in Tegucigalpa);

"Colonel Raymond" or "Papi" (mentioned by "Miguel" in the article by Linda Drucker in *The Progressive,* August 1986 and by Edgar Chamorro in a March 5, 1985 article in the *WSJ*; mentioned by Ex-Maj. Gen. Roberto Amador Narvaes and others);

"Major West";

"Mark";

"Major Alex";

"Kimberly";

"Jeffrey";

John Kirkpatrick (who wrote the training manual for the contras).

5.   What information exists about the circumstances and investigation of the death of Maj. Ricardo Zúniga in Honduras in 1985.

ARMED FORCES OF HONDURAS
JOINT CHIEFS OF STAFF

Comayaguela, M.D.C., November 26, 1993

REGISTRY: EMC(C-2)993

LETTER: No. 712

Dr. Leo Valladares
National Commissioner for
 the Protection of Human Rights
Office of the National Commissioner

Mr. Commissioner:

By means of this letter, I respond to your letter No. 451-DC/93, of November 15 of this year.

The information that you requested of this office, has been requested of the Commander-in-Chief of the Armed Forces, because this office—a subordinate body of the Commander-in-Chief—only responds to its superior in those matters that our Charter provides. In this regard, the required information will be channeled directly by the Command of the Armed Forces by the channels that it may determine.

Without more for the moment, it is my pleasure to express my regard and esteem.

Artillery Colonel D.E.M.
/s Herbert Munguia Morales
Director of Intelligence (C-2)
        EHO 0617

Discipline is the Basic Ingredient of Our Unity
Unity is the Basis of Success,
and Success is the Ultimate End of the Armed Forces

Armed Forces of Honduras
Offices of the Commander-in-Chief

Comayaguela, M.D.C.
December 23, 1993

Armed Forces Commander-in-Chief
Letter No. 1835

Mr. Leo Valladares, Esq.
National Commissioner for the
 Protection of Human Rights
Office of the National Commissioner

Mr. Commissioner:

1.   It is my pleasure to write to you, extending cordial greetings and
        best wishes for a Merry Christmas and a Happy New Year.

2.   The purpose of this letter is to respond to your request for informa-
        tion on the topic of disappearances which you sent recently sent me.
        In this regard, I am forwarding to you a photocopy of the only
        report that the Armed Forces of Honduras possesses.

3.   Without more for the moment, I extend my highest regards.

Division General
[official seal]

/s Luis Alonso Discua Elvir
Commander-in-Chief of the
 Armed Forces of Honduras
LADE/lade

                Discipline is the Basic Ingredient of Our Unity
                    Unity is the Basis of Success,
            and Success is the Ultimate End of the Armed Forces

Information Office
of the
MINISTRY OF THE PRESIDENCY
Tegucigalpa, D.C., Honduras, C.A

COMMUNIQUE

In the session of this date of the SECURITY COUNCIL, by initiative of the Constitutional President of the Republic, Dr. ROBERTO SUAZO CORDOVA, this body agreed to publish the March 1985 REPORT on alleged disappearances written by the Special Commission created by the ARMED FORCES in 1984 for this purpose. This report was submitted to the President of the Republic by the Commander-in-Chief of the Armed Forces, General Wálter López Reyes. It was also agreed to submit the report to the National Congress and the Commission on Constitutional Guarantees of the legislature.

The said REPORT states textually:

Comayaguela, D.C., March 27, 1985.

MATTER: REPORT
TO: COMMANDER-IN-CHIEF OF THE ARMED FORCES
BRIGADIER GENERAL
WALTER LOPEZ REYES
OFFICE OF THE COMMANDER-IN-CHIEF

With our customary respect, the members of the Special Commission to investigate complaints published in various media regarding the alleged disappearance of persons in Honduran territory; the Commission, which was constituted by order of that body, by means of Accord MD. No. 232 of June 14 of last year, by this letter we bring to your attention the Final Report of the activities and measures taken, the respective conclusions and recommendations:

1.   On December 28, 1984, this Commission had the honor of presenting to you a partial report of the activities undertaken to that date, in which the following recommendations were made:

a)   That it be made public that having undertaken investiga-
     tions, the location of the other alleged disappeared has not
     been determined;

b)   The legal actions of the interested parties before the appro-
     priate tribunals remain available so that those persons whom
     these interested parties consider responsible for disappearan-
     ces in Honduras, whether public officials or private citizens,
     may be accused by legal means.

c)   That the facilities of the tribunals and other organizations of
     the state be offered for the investigation and determination
     of responsibilities for abuse of authority.

d)   That the cooperation of organizations dedicated to the defen-
     se of human rights be requested to maintain the citizenry
     free from abuses of authority.

e)   That this Commission continue its investigations for ninety
     more days.

2.   Pursuant to these recommendations, we were ordered to continue our
     efforts for the requested period, which is the period that the present
     report covers.

3.   In accord with instructions received from the Commander-in-Chief,
     it was decided that the persons whom the media and human rights
     organizations have indicated to be those allegedly responsible for
     disappearances, including personnel currently carrying out missions
     outside the country, be called to render statements; thus, the state-
     ment of each of those interviewed, in the place and date indicated
     below was obtained.

4.   In this regard, the Commission prepared a procedure for questioning
     to be used with the personnel interviewed:

a)   In the Offices of the Auditor General of the Armed Forces
     on February 5 of this year, Police Majors Alexánder Her-
     nández and Juan Blas Salazar Meza were interviewed.

b)   In the Offices of the Auditor General on February 28 of this
     year, Infantry Col. D.E.M. Juan E. López Grijalva was
     interviewed.

c)   In the same offices on March 5, Lt. Col. (Infantry) D.E.M.

Luis Alonso Discua Elvir, Infantry Maj. Oscar René Barahona Valladares and Police Cpt. Rafael Canales Nuñez were interviewed.

d)   In the same offices, on March 6 of this year, Infantry Captain Oscar Ramón Hernández Chávez and Police 2d Sgt. José Blas Peña Paz were interviewed.

5   Additionally, two meetings were held in the Offices of the General Auditor with the Human Rights Commission of the Bar Association of Honduras, on the following dates and attended by the following persons:

a)   On January 29 of this year, the first meeting was held. Attending on behalf of the Commission of the Bar Association were the following persons:

1.   Dr. Carlos Roberto Reina
2.   Manuel Acosta Bonilla, Esq.
3.   Irma Violeta Suazo de Rosa, Esq.
4.   German Leitzelar, Esq.
5.   Mauricio Villeda Bermúdez, Esq.
6.   Miguel Angel Rivera Portillo, Esq.

b)   The second meeting was held on March 19 of this year. Attending for the Commission of the Bar Association were the following persons:

1.   Dr. Carlos Roberto Reina
2.   Manuel Acosta Bonilla, Esq.
3.   Mauricio Villeda Bermúdez, Esq.
4.   Irma Violeta Suazo de Rosa, Esq.
5.   Gustavo Acosta Mejía, Esq.

Both meetings were very cordial and provided the opportunity to exchange impressions regarding the different cases raised; nonetheless, in response to our request we be provided with information in their possession or of which they had knowledge and which would lead to the clarification of the facts investigated, the response was negative. This was due to the fact that the data on which they rely is very vague, confused and based on unreliable sources of information, and, in the two or three cases in which they agreed to provide some information, it was irrelevant to the Commission, since it was already known to it.

6.   Another comparison of the list of those allegedly disappeared with new information that was received from the General Directorate of Population and Migratory Policy and from security authorities, was made, without positive results from the said comparison.

7.   By means of the appropriate authorities, another attempt was made to find and locate the vehicles allegedly used in the alleged detentions of persons indicated as disappeared. However, due to the limited identifying data, this was not possible.

Conclusions

1.   It was not possible to determine with certainty that military elements participated in cases of disappearance.

2.   In no military or security unit have persons allegedly disappeared been found, nor is any such person presently detained (in these units).

3.   The information received by this Commission is vague, obscure and in many cases contradictory, which prevents the discovery of true facts.

4.   The authorities, such as the DNI (National Investigations Directorate), Immigration, etc., do not have these persons in detention and registries of these entities do not reliably establish that these persons were ever detained or that those foreign nationals included in the list ever legally entered the country.

Recommendations

1.   Adequately publicize the reports of the Commission.

2.   Emphasize the expedition of legal actions of individuals before the courts of law to determine the responsibility of those military person-

nel considered to have some type of participation in cases of disappearances.

3. Reiterate the firm position of the Armed Forces to undertake all efforts in their power to assure that acts such as those denounced not happen in the country.

4. Declare terminated the functions of this Commission.
    With the conviction of duty fulfilled, we extend to you our expression of respect and subordination.

L O Y A L T Y   H O N O R   S A C R I F I C E

Infantry Col. D.E.M.
Manuel Enrique Suárez Benavidez
President

Infantry Col. D.E.M.   Aviation Col. D.E.M.
Guillermo Thuman Cordón   Francisco Zepeda Andino

Infantry Col. D.E.M.   Infantry Col. D.E.M.
Diego Arturo Landa Celano   Humberto Regalado Hernández
Member   Member

Infantry Col. D.E.M.
Roberto Martínez Avila

Aux. Sub. Lt. of Military Justice
Mario Enrique Boquín Hernández
Secretary

Tegucigalpa, D.C., October 17, 1985

Office of Information
of the
Ministry of the Presidency

Embassy of the
United States of
America

Tegucigalpa,
D.C.
December 8,
1993

Mr. Leo Valladares, Esq.
Commissioner for the Protection
 of Human Rights
Office of the Commissioner

Dear Mr. Valladares:

Thank you for your letter of November 15, by which you informed me of your intention to present, at year's end, a preliminary report about the political disappearances in Honduras.

In reference to your specific request for information on this subject that might be available in the archives of the United States, I have sent a message to the Department of State recommending that all possible efforts to provide you the information requested be made.

Now that this has been clarified, I must tell you that time is short and, in light of that fact, it might not be possible to finish the pertinent investigations in the archives by the date that you have established as a goal for the release of your preliminary report. If you could provide us the names of the victims in the cases you anticipate including in your report, it would greatly facilitate our ability to provide you with whatever relevant information might be found in the archives of the Government of the United States.

In the hopes that we will be able to contribute to the success of your project, I send my regards.

Sincerely,

William T. Pryce
Ambassador

ANNEX TO THE ENGLISH LANGUAGE VERSION[1]

United States Assistance to Honduras
and Human Rights in the Most Critical Years

(amounts in millions of dollars)

Source: Department of State

1980

ECONOMIC AID:	53.1
MILITARY AID:	3.9
TOTAL:	57.0

1980 DEPARTMENT OF STATE REPORT ON HUMAN RIGHTS IN HONDURAS:

c. Disappearances

There are no abductions, secret arrests or clandestine detentions in Honduras.

1981

ECONOMIC AID:	6.4
MILITARY AID:	8.9
TOTAL:	45.3

---

[1] *Editor's Note:* The documents reprinted below appeared in the text of the chapter entitled "International Context" in the original spanish version of this report. In this edition, a brief summary of the content of these excerpts of those documents is presented in that chapter, and the excerpts themselves are reproduced here.

1981 DEPARTMENT OF STATE REPORT ON
HUMAN RIGHTS IN HONDURAS:

c. Disappearances

There have been reports of as many as 60 mysterious disappearances during 1981. Disappearances have previously occurred only rarely in Honduras. The government has denied allegations of security service involvement in these reported disappearances.

1982

ECONOMIC AID:	80.6
MILITARY AID:	31.3
TOTAL:	111.9

1982 DEPARTMENT OF STATE REPORT ON HUMAN
RIGHTS IN HONDURAS:

b. Disappearances

One local human rights organization alleges that twenty-two Hondurans have mysteriously disappeared in Honduras in 1982. The organization attributes the majority of disappearances to the police or the police investigative branch. . . . The Government has consistently denied any involvement by security services in these cases. However, there have been occasions in which persons, whom the Government denied detaining, have been later released.

1983

ECONOMIC AID:	106.0
MILITARY AID:	48.3
TOTAL:	154.3

1983 DEPARTMENT OF STATE REPORT ON
HUMAN RIGHTS IN HONDURAS:

b. Disappearances

The nongovernmental Committee for the Defense of Human Rights and the Committee of the Families of Disappeared Persons alleged that, as of October, some 10 persons seized in public during 1983 had not been released, turned over to the courts, acknowledged to be in custody, or found dead. In addition, the Human Rights Committee still has on its list of disappeared persons over 40 such cases from previous years. The records of these private groups indicated that the number of new unresolved disappearance cases was less in 1983 than in 1982 (24). Government officials often claimed that many of these "disappeared" persons were either involved in guerrilla training in Nicaragua or Cuba or vanished for personal reasons.

1984

ECONOMIC AID: 95.0

MILITARY AID: 77.4

TOTAL: 172.4

1984 DEPARTMENT OF STATE REPORT ON
HUMAN RIGHTS IN HONDURAS:

b. Disappearances

According to the Committee for the Defense of Human Rights, a total of 112 unexplained disappearances have occurred in Honduras during 1981-1984. Five new cases were claimed in 1984, compared to ten cases in 1983. These five cases date to the period January-March 1984, and there have been no substantiated incidents since then. The most dramatic of the disappearances were those in March of Rolando Vindel . . . and Gustavo Morales . . . Government officials continue to claim that many of those who "disappeared" are in fact exiles who left Honduras to receive guerrilla training in Nicaragua or Cuba. Several others, although their names appear on the "disappeared" list, have been found living normal lives.

In some instances during the year, in cases that involved alleged subversion of terrorism, the Government security forces denied knowledge of the whereabouts of disappeared persons but later arraigned those same individuals or released them after questioning. One such case involved the detention, in March, 1983 and release in July, 1984 of accused subversive Ines Murillo. . . . A military commission, appointed by the Chief of the Armed Forces . . . to investigate the problem of disappearances, submitted an interim report to President Suazo Cordova on December 29 . . . This report, short on specific information, was sharply criticized by a number of Honduran groups concerned with human rights issues as being vague, inconsistent and contradictory. It is not clear whether a final, more complete account of the commission's findings will be published.

1985

ECONOMIC AID: 224.0

MILITARY AID: 67.4

TOTAL: 291.4

1985 DEPARTMENT OF STATE REPORT ON HUMAN RIGHTS IN HONDURAS:

b. Disappearances

No disappearances were documented in 1985, although human rights organizations continue to assert that 118 disappearances between 1974 and 1984 remain unexplained. An Armed Forces investigation of alleged disappearances reportedly included interviews with human rights activists and with those members of the Armed Forces mentioned by name as having been involved in disappearance cases. The final report concludes that no evidence exists to determine that any military officials were involved in any disappearances, that no reportedly "disappeared" persons are held in military or public security facilities, and that the information provided to the investigation by the human rights activists was vague and at times contradictory. The inconclusive preliminary and final reports were heavily criticized by human rights spokesmen. The report recommends that any further accusations of involvement by members of the Armed Forces be taken to the proper judicial court. On December 12, a criminal court case against six officers accused of involvement in disappearances was dismissed.

The Iran-Contra Scandal:
Excerpts from the Prosecution
Lt. Col. Oliver North

March 10, 1989
In the court records of United States v. Oliver North, the following charges are presented[2]:

1. In late March 1984, Reagan's National Security Advisor, Robert C. McFarlane, was informed by the Director of the CIA, William Casey, that an official with a foreign government had indicated that he might be able to supply equipment and training to the Nicaraguan Resistance through Honduras. (Point 2 of the document, p.2-3)

2. In April 1984, McFarlane directed Howard Teicher, of the National Security Council (NSC) staff, to discuss assistance to the Nicaraguan Resistance with David Kimche of the Israeli government. McFarlane instructed Teicher to tell Kimche that Israeli aid to the Nicaraguan resistance should be arranged through Honduras. (Point 3, p. 3).

3. On June 25, 1985, the National Security Planing Group (NSPG)—- included President Reagan, Vice President Bush, Secretary of State Shultz, Secretary of Defense Weinberger, Director of Central Intelligence Casey, U.N. Ambassador Kirkpatrick, Chief of Staff Vessey, Admiral Moreau, Counselor to the President Edwin Meese, McFarlane and Admiral Poindexter—discussed third country funding to the Resistance. Director Casey noted that the CIA considered El Salvador, Guatemala, Honduras, and one South American country as possible sources of support for the Resistance. Casey suggested that the government of the United States provide Honduras and Costa Rica with increased economic aid as an incentive for them to assist the Resistance. (Point 5, p. 3-4)

---

[2] Stipulated Facts in *United States of America v. Oliver North*, Criminal No. 88-0080 - 02 - GAG (United States District Court for the District of Columbia). [NSA 3157]

4. In early May 1986, Lt. Col. Oliver North, of the NSC, notified his superior, Admiral Poindexter, that a representative of the Israeli Minister of Defense Rabin had offered on behalf of Israel to provide Spanish-speaking military trainers and advisors to the Resistance. These advisors would be placed in Honduras in connection with an Israeli plan to sell the Kfir fighter plane to the Hondurans. (Point 29, p. 11-12)

5. In May 1986, U.S. intelligence reports reflected that a South American nation was aware that the Reagan administration had asked Israel, Taiwan and South Korea and an organization headed by a U.S. resident to contribute to the purchase of weapons for the Resistance. The South American country was aware that the People's Republic of China had already given anti-aircraft missiles to the Contras, and that Honduras expected that Israel would provide extensive aid, including military assistance. (Point 31, p. 12)

6. In mid-September 1986, Lt. Col. North reported to Admiral Poindexter that Israeli Defense Minister Rabin was pleased with the reaction of Poindexter and Secretary Shultz to his plans to introduce the Kfir fighters into Honduras and in the process provide advisors to the Resistance. (Point 40, p. 15)

7. [from the section entitled "Central American Countries"] In early July 1984, a CIA officer reported to headquarters that Honduras was taking the position that it would continue to support the Resistance following the cut-off of U.S. aid, but that Resistance operations would have to be covert to avoid political embarrassment to Honduras. (Point 42. p. 16)

8. In mid-November 1984, a CIA officer reported to CIA headquarters about assistance provided to the Resistance by Guatemala and Honduras. Honduras had permitted the Resistance to operate from within its borders, had repaired Resistance aircraft at no cost, had allowed government aircraft to bring in aircraft parts, had permitted the Resistance to borrow ammunition when Resistance stocks were low, and had provided the Resistance with false end-user certificates for the purchase of weapons. (Point 44, p. 16)

9. In mid-November 1984, DCI Casey requested that Lt. Col. North be provided with a CIA analysis about the recent performance and near-term prospects for the Resistance. (Copies of this analysis also went to Vice President Bush and McFarlane). According to the analysis, Honduras had

facilitated the purchase of ammunition and hand grenades and had donated 10,000 pounds of military equipment and two C-47 aircraft. (Point 45, p. 16-17)

10. In December 1984, a CIA assessment concluded that the future of the FDN without United States government support depended on the FDN's capacity to obtain continued private funding and continued support from Honduras. The leader of the Honduran government had threatened to cease support for the FDN unless it received a signal of U.S. government support. Lt. Col. North urged McFarlane to visit Central America and deliver a signal of U.S. resolve. (Point 46, pp. 17-18)

11. In mid-January 1985, Lt. Col. North arranged a visit to Central America for McFarlane with stops in Panama, Costa Rica, El Salvador, Honduras, and Guatemala. At McFarlane's request, North arranged a secret meeting between McFarlane and Calero during the visit to Honduras. North, Vice Admiral Moreau and General Gorman, the Commander-in-Chief of U.S. Southern Command, accompanied McFarlane during this visit. (Point 48, p. 19)

12. On February 2, 1985, the CIA reported to the National Security Agency (NSA), the Department of State, the Defense Intelligence Agency (DIA), the FBI, the White House, NSC staff and U.S. SOUTHCOM, that Honduran military officers were assisting the Resistance in transporting materiel (including ammunition) bought on the international arms market through Guatemala to Resistance camps in Honduras. (Point 50, p. 20)

13. At a February 7, 1985, meeting of the Crisis Pre-Planing Group, attended by Admiral Poindexter, Don Fortier (NSC), Ray Burghardt (NSC), Michael Armacost (NSC), Fred Ikle (Defense), Nestor Sanchez (Defense), Clair George (CIA), Alan Fiers (CIA), Moreau (JCS) and North, it was agreed that a Presidential letter should be sent to President Suazo of Honduras and to provide several enticements Honduras in exchange for its continued support of the Nicaraguan Resistance. These enticements included expedited delivery of military supplies ordered by Honduras, the a phased release of withheld economic assistance (ESF) funds, and other support. (Point 51, p. 20)

14. In late February 1985, President Reagan sent the agreed-upon message to President Suazo through the U.S. Ambassador in Honduras. The letter urged

that Honduras do all in its power to support "those who struggle for freedom and democracy." Shortly thereafter, McFarlane sent a memorandum to Shultz, Weinberger, Casey, and Vessey informing them that President Reagan's letter had been sent and requesting that the Department of Defense commence the expedited delivery of military items, as previously planned and personally authorized by President Reagan, and requesting the necessary documentation to enhance other support programs in Honduras. (Point 54, p. 22)

15. In early March 1985, Vice Admiral Moreau was advised that Honduran military leaders had offered assurances that the Resistance could continue to deliver supplies through Honduras, and that Honduras would continue to supply end-user certificates for arms purchases by the Resistance. A significant shipment of arms was scheduled for the middle or end of March. North recommended that Honduran military officials be told that the United States government would soon discuss enhancing other support programs. (Point 55, p. 22)

16. In early March 1985, Secretary Weinberger informed McFarlane that the Department of Defense had commenced expedited procurement and delivery of military aid and other items to Honduras. (Point 57, p.23)

17. In March, when Vice President Bush met with President Suazo, Bush told Suazo that President Reagan had directed expedited delivery of U.S. military items to Honduras. Vice President Bush also informed Suazo that President Reagan had directed that currently withheld economic assistance for Honduras should be released; and that the United States would provide from its own stocks critical security assistance items that had been ordered by the Honduran armed forces. (Point 58, p. 23)

18. In late March 1985, the CIA reported to the NSC, the Department of Defense, the Department of State, the White House, U.S. SOUTHCOM, and U.S. ambassadors in Honduras, Panama, Nicaragua and Costa Rica, that a ship was scheduled to arrive in Honduras in mid-April 1985, carrying munitions worth almost $2 million that the Resistance had bought on the international arms market. The CIA reported that a Honduran military official had agreed to arrange the transportation of the weapons from the port of arrival to Resistance units. (Point 60, p. 24-25)

19. In late March 1985, North advised McFarlane that the initial deliveries of U.S. arms from the Department of Defense to Honduras had gone well and that the Honduran government had expressed its gratitude to those that were helping the Resistance. (Point 61, p. 25)

20. On April 25, 1985, McFarlane informed President Reagan that military support for the Resistance from Honduras was in jeopardy as a consequence of the House vote refusing to provide new funds to the Resistance. The Honduran military had stopped a shipment of ammunition from an Asian country on route to the Resistance after it had arrived in Honduras. McFarlane recommended that President Reagan call Suazo and to make clear that the Executive Branch was determined to maintain pressure on the Sandinistas. During the call between the two presidents, Suazo urged that the U.S. government continue to oppose communism. President Reagan's personal notes of his telephone call reflect that President Suazo told him that the Honduran military commander would be ordered to deliver the ammunition to the Resistance. President Suazo also raised the subject of U.S. government aid for his country and the fact that he hoped Secretary Shultz and Secretary Weinberger would meet with a high-level group of Honduran officials in Washington. (Point 62, p. 25-26)

21. On April 26, 1985, U.S. Ambassador Negroponte notified McFarlane that President Suazo had called Negroponte immediately after Suazo's telephone conversation with President Reagan to say that he was satisfied with the U.S. government commitment to continue support for the Resistance. President Suazo told Ambassador Negroponte that he (Suazo) had assured President Reagan of his full support and had promised to check into the interdicted munitions shipment, which he did immediately after the conversation with President Reagan by calling a senior Honduran military official. Suazo told Negroponte that Honduras supported the Resistance fully, and Suazo asked that Negroponte convey his strongest assurances to President Reagan that Honduras would not let down the Resistance. Ambassador Negroponte recommended that under these circumstances the Honduran delegation should be received by Vice President Bush in President Reagan's absence. (Point 63, p. 26)

22. In May 1985, President Reagan personally approved increased U.S. special support to Honduras and Guatemala for joint programs with those countries. (Point 64, p. 26)

23. During the period when the Boland Amendments were in effect, individuals within the State Department, the DIA, the NSA, the White House, and the NSC, among others, were informed that Honduras had agreed to provide the Resistance with end-user certificates for hand grenades and grenade-launchers, which the Resistance wanted to purchase from South Korea, and that a Honduran military official in charge of providing support to the Resistance had agreed to provide the Resistance end-user certificates for the purchase of automatic rifles. (Point 65, p. 27)

24. In October 1985, Honduras seized a shipment of NHAO (Nicaraguan Humanitarian Assistance Office) humanitarian goods in response to reports that Honduras was facilitating such deliveries. The U.S. ambassador requested that Lt. Col. North travel immediately to Honduras to brief senior Honduran military leaders on NHAO plans and procedures. (Point 68, p. 28)

25. In October 1985, following meetings with Honduran military officials, Colonel Comee, of U.S. SOUTHCOM informed General Galvin (Commander in Chief of the Southern Command), that Honduras was wavering in its support for the Resistance because U.S. aid had not been fully implemented; Hondurans officials were thinking of signing the Contadora Agreement in light of their conclusion that the Resistance could not prevail without more U.S. government assistance. The Honduran officials were particularly angry that the U.S. Embassy in Tegucigalpa had recently denied any connection with the Resistance, referring inquiries to representatives of Honduras. In Comee's view, the U.S. government had to respond to the concerns of the Hondurans or lose its support for the Resistance. (Point 69, pp. 28-29)

26. In December 1985, individuals within the Department of State, the CIA, the DIA, the White House, the NSC and U.S. SOUTHCOM were informed about the refusal of Honduras to permit NHAO flights into Honduras. The refusal stemmed from the failure of the U.S. government and Honduran officials to keep a senior Honduran military official informed of Resistance activities. The senior military official was concerned, among other things, because there was no local point of contact for coordination between Honduran government officials, the Resistance, and the U.S. government. (Point 70, p. 29)

27. In December 1985, the CIA reported to headquarters that Lt. Col. North would arrive in Tegucigalpa for a meeting with a senior Honduran military official, and that U.S. Ambassador Ferch wanted North to know that the

military official was anxious for the meeting. The most significant operational problem arising from Honduras's refusal to permit use of its airfields was not the restrictions on NHAO flights into Honduras, but the restriction re-supply flights into Nicaragua, which threatened to force 5,000 Resistance troops in Nicaragua to withdraw to Honduras. (Point 71, p. 29)

28. In mid-December 1985, Lt. Col. North and Admiral Poindexter visited Costa Rica, El Salvador, Guatemala, Panama, and Honduras to urge the continued support for the Resistance. Admiral Poindexter made clear to a senior Honduran military official that his country's assistance—particularly logistical support—was essential. (Point 72, p. 30)

29. In late December 1985, Deputy Assistant Secretary of State William Walker and Chris Arcos of the NHAO met in Honduras with one of its senior military officials as a follow-up to the Poindexter trip in mid-December. (Point 76, p. 30)

30. In January 1986, the American embassy in Honduras furnished Secretary of State Shultz and Assistant Secretary Abrams with a statement of U.S. objectives in Honduras for 1986. The embassy noted that Honduras had collaborated on a wide range of security issues—including support for the Resistance—during 1985. According to the embassy, Honduras regarded support for the Resistance primarily as a U.S. government program. The responsibility for ensuring Honduran support for the Resistance was assigned to the Ambassador, other officers from other government agencies assigned to the embassy, and the U.S. Military Group. (Point 77, pp. 30-31)

31. In mid-January 1986, Lt. Col. North recommended that Vice President Bush and Admiral Poindexter tell President Azcona of the need for Honduras to work with the U.S. government on increasing regional involvement with and support for the Resistance. (Point 78, p. 31)

32. In mid-January 1986, the State Department prepared a memorandum for Donald Gregg (the Vice President's national security advisor) for Vice President Bush's meeting with President Azcona. The meeting was to encourage continued Honduran support for the Resistance. The memorandum alerted Gregg that Azcona would insist on receiving clear economic and social benefits from his cooperation with the United States. (Point 79, p. 32)

33. In late January 1986, a U.S. official told the Department of State, CIA headquarters, the DIA, and U.S. SOUTHCOM, among others, that he believed Azcona would permit a temporary resumption of the NHAO flights based on an agreement by the United States to open negotiations on increased aid to Honduras. (Point 80, p. 32)

34. In late January 1986, the same U.S. official was instructed that, in seeking President Azcona's permission to flights and truck deliveries in support of the Resistance into and through Honduras, the categories of supplies should not be specified because Resistance flights from Ilopango airfield in El Salvador and Aguacate airfield in Honduras would have (lethal and non-lethal) loads. (Point 81, pp. 32-33)

35. On January 30, 1986, U.S. Ambassador Ferch met with President Azcona to request Honduran assistance in supplying the Resistance. (Point 83, p. 33)

36. At the end of February 1986, a CIA officer reported to headquarters on the conditions imposed by Honduras for the resumption of direct resupply flights to the Resistance into and out of the country. A key condition was that for the trial run there could be no leaks or publicity. (Point 86, p. 34)

37. In March 1986, a CIA official notified CIA headquarters that Honduras had approved a private shipment of lethal aid to the Resistance to arrive at a certain date. In addition, Honduras had approved shuttle flights to move lethal materiel from the Resistance from one Honduran military airfield to another. (Point 87, p. 34)

38. On March 20, 1986, the White House Situation Room was advised that senior Honduran military officers planned to ask for U.S. permission to control lethal aid sent through the country to the Resistance in Nicaragua, and that they wanted to receive some sophisticated weapons given to the Resistance that were not already in Honduras's inventory. (Point 89, p. 35)

39. In late March 1986, Elliott Abrams offered Honduran President Azcona immediate additional security assistance. Lt. Col. North prepared a memorandum from Admiral Poindexter to President Reagan describing the results of the Abrams's discussions with Azcona. The details of the enhanced security assistance to Honduras were worked out between Col. Royer (chief of the

Latin America division of the Department of Defense's DSAA) and various Honduran military officials. The Honduran army and navy specifically requested a sophisticated ground-to-air missile on the grounds that the U.S. had already supplied such weapons to the Resistance. The total cost of the items ultimately agreed upon came to approximately $20 million. (Point 91, p. 36)

40. In early May 1986, President Reagan wrote to Presidents Azcona and Duarte thanking them for their support for the Resistance and announcing that the U.S. was disbursing the economic support funds (ESF) that Honduras sought. (Point 92, p. 36-37)

41. In May 1986, Nestor Sanchez, Department of Defense Deputy Assistant Secretary, provided the Secretary of Defense a translation of a memorandum to President Reagan from President Azcona. The memorandum called for substantial increases in military aid for the next five years and increasing coordination between and among the U.S., the Honduran armed forces, and the leadership of the Resistance regarding UNO/FDN military operations. (Point 94, p. 38)

42. In May 1986, President Azcona indicated to President Reagan that Honduras's continued support for the Resistance depended upon significant increases in U.S. military aid to the Honduran armed forces and the Resistance. President Azcona noted that his armed forces wanted weapons and ammunition for use by the Resistance to be transferred to the Honduran armed forces to assure the military success of the Resistance. President Azcona stated that in past months these matters had been discussed with William Taft of the Department of Defense, Abrams, Admiral Poindexter and General Galvin. (Point 95, p. 38)

43. In early September 1986, General Galvin of SouthCom and an official of the U.S. Military Group met in Tegucigalpa to discuss Honduran support for the Resistance with a senior Honduran military official. General Galvin advised the senior Honduran official that a U.S. military official would go to Honduras to work with the Resistance. The senior Honduran military officer expressed concern about leaks to the media concerning arrangements between the U.S. Embassy, the Honduran military, and President Azcona in supporting the Resistance. General Galvin and the senior Honduran military official also discussed U.S. cooperation with Honduras on various military and

intelligence areas. (Point 100, p. 40)

44. In mid-September 1986, Lt. Col. North advised Admiral Poindexter that former U.S. Ambassador Negroponte, General Gorman, senior CIA official Duane Clarridge, and Lt. Col. North had worked out arrangements for support of the Resistance with the Honduran General Bueso Rosa, a former Honduran military officer who had recently been convicted of offenses in the United States. North suggested that efforts be made on Bueso Rosa's behalf to deter him from disclosing details of these covert activities. (Point 102, p. 40)[3]

---

[3] With regard to this issue, we transcribe below several declassified United States government documents. They are a series of notes from Lt. Col. North on the Bueso Rosa case.

Note: the brackets [ ], correspond to information that was rendered illegible in the declassified documents because it continues to be designated by the executive branch of the United States government as classified and confidential. Where there is text inserted between the brackets, it is information that is obvious or interpretations that we made based on other sources. We have maintained North's abbreviations exactly as they appear in the original.

September 17, 1986

MEMORANDUM FROM NORTH TO POINDEXTER

Subject: President Azcona

A Presidential call memo has been prepared, and after much wrangling w/ Ray, I have concurred. The problem w/ the [Bueso] case is that [Bueso] was the man with whom Negroponte, Gorman, Clarridge and I worked out arrangements. [ ] Only Gorman, Clarridge and I were fully aware of all that [Bueso] was doing on our behalf. Subsequent to the Alvarez ouster, Bueso was assigned as MilAttache in Chile and at one point last year was invited to meet w/ a group of disgruntled Hondurans who it turns out were plotting the assassination of Pres. Suazo. When the FBI broke the case Bueso was indicted for conspiracy. His legal advice was apparently to keep his mouth shut and everything would be worked out. Although subpoenas were prepared for Gorman, Clarridge, Negroponte and North, they were never issued because Bueso pleaded guilty (on advice of counsel). Several months ago Azcona wrote to the President, and was never answered. He now is going to call the President to ask if Bueso can be pardoned. Bueso is due to report to Tallahase [sic, prison?] to start serving sentence on Sep 25. He apparently still believed up until yesterday that he would be going to the minimum security facility at Eglin for a short period (days or weeks) and then walk free. Bueso's wife has implored Azcona to do something and he now wants an answer to his letter. I do not know if there has been action on the letter, but we (USG) should have answered same some time ago. Our major concerns—Gorman, North, Clarridge—is that when [Bueso] finds out what is really happening to him, he will break his longstanding silence about the Nic Resistance and other sensitive operations. Gorman, Clarridge, Revell, Trott and Abrams will cabal quietly in the morning to look at options: pardon, clemency, deportation, reduced sentence. Objective is to keep Bueso from feeling like he was lied to in the legal process and start spilling the beans. Will advise.

September 18, 1986

NOTE FROM: OLIVER NORTH
Subject: President Azcona

Done. Good mtg this morning w/ all concerned, including Gorman who flew up from Charlottesville. Bottom line: [ ] Four of the others involved in the conspiracy have already been convicted and as soon as the last is tried, convicted and sentenced, Justice, FBI, and others as necessary will have the defense attny. request that the judge review the sentence, and in camera have Gorman, et al explain to the judge our equities in this matter. Revell/Trott both believe that this will result in approval of the petition for probationary release and deportation to Honduras. Discretely briefing Bueso and his attorney on this whole process shd ameliorate concerns (both with us and Azcona) that Bueso will start singing songs nobody wants to hear. Justice is justifiably upset that none of this info was made available to them prior to indictment or before/during the trial, but there is much blame to go around on that score. Clarridge was totally unaware that the CIA has responded to a Justice query on the case with the terse comment that they "had no interest in the case." Elliott was also somewhat chagrined to learn that some at State had been urging rigorous prosecution and sentencing. Bottom line: all now seems headed in the right direction. New Subject: R's nephew is on the ground at Dulles. All seems o.k. He, Sam, Dick, Abe and I will meet here tomorrow from 1130 until necessary. Will take care of clearing them in such a way that Dick can drive them directly into the south court of OEOB [Old Executive Office Building] and leave his car inside during the meeting. This procedure should suffice for ensuring that he knows he is really meeting with the USG and not someone else. We will walk him over to the Hay Adams for lunch and then back in through the front gate so that we can get some good polaroid photos for him to take back home (he asked Dick for some way to bring these back with him so that he would not have to worry about getting the film developed back at home.)
We will also wire my office appropriately for recording tomorrow's conversations. Questions: Would you or Al want to meet with the nephew at some point during his time here? Do you think that it wd be good to introduce him at some point during his brief

In this example, as with many others presented in this chapter, we found that the Honduran authorities confused the national interests of Honduras with those of the United States administration of that time. This attitude led to an unnecessary tolerance that permitted the presence and illegal activities of the so-called Nicaraguan resistance, or contras. For Honduras, these years were the worst in terms of registered disappearances and violations of human rights.

---

stay here (he will probably depart Saturday afternoon), to RCM in that RCM is likely to be heading the next delegation back in his homeland?

September 18, 1986

NOTE FROM: OLIVER NORTH
SUBJECT: Bueso Rosa

According to what I have been able to put together, our best option appears to be to have Justice go back to the U.S. Attorney and the Judge after the other defendants have been tried, convicted and sentenced and quietly discuss a petition from the Defense attorney that the sentence be further reduced and that he be remanded to custodial probation for the remainder of his sentence to a responsible authority in Honduras. He wd then be deported back to Honduras. None of this can take place until after the remaining trial has been held (the other four have been tried, convicted and sentenced w/ the American, Lechinian, receiving 30 yrs). [ ] While there are other options (parole, pardon, clemency) they all have varying degrees of political risk attached in that the first wd require briefing the entire parole commission and the latter two wd involve the President in the matter. Justice has said that they will be back to us with definitive recommendations based on the remaining trial and discussions with the U.S. Attorney. This shd also be useful as input to the Azcona letter—though it might be best to have JMP, Meese or even Elliott answer the April letter, rather than the President. Bottom line, the talking points appear to be about right. We just need to make sure that at the right time the right people go to talk to the Judge and U.S. Attorney. Gorman has volunteered to fill this role—and that may be just about right since he's no longer in the government.